ROGER VOSS'

GUIDE TO

THE WINES OF
THE LOIRE, ALSACE,
THE RHONE

AND OTHER FRENCH REGIONAL WINES

GW00750570

ROGER VOSS'

GUIDE TO

THE WINES OF THE LOIRE, ALSACE, THE RHONE

AND OTHER FRENCH REGIONAL WINES

Mitchell Beazley

Edited and designed by
Mitchell Beazley Publishers
part of Reed International Books Ltd
Michelin House
81 Fulham Road
London SW3 6RB

First published 1987 as *The Mitchell Beazley Pocket Guide to French Regional Wines*.
This edition, revised, updated and expanded, published 1992.

A CIP catalogue record for this book
is available from the British Library.

ISBN 1 85732 912 0

Executive Editor: Anne Ryland
Art Director: Tim Foster

Art Editor: Paul Tilby
Index: Ann Barrett
Production: Sarah Schuman

Illustrations: Linda Smith
Maps: Sue Sharples

Typeset in Bembo by
Servis Filmsetting Ltd
Manchester, England
Produced by Mandarin Offset, Hong Kong
Printed and bound in Hong Kong
Colour Reproduction by Scantrans Pte Ltd, Singapore

Contents

Introduction

I drank my first glass of wine in France. I was eight. I was staying with a family in a small, rather dilapidated château somewhere in the depths of Poitou. It was my hostess' birthday and a glass of something white (and watered) was thrust into my hand at the end of the meal. It was sweet, and I rather liked it: I asked for more. Perhaps luckily for my reputation as a guest, my request was received with a severe frown and a firm refusal.

I have no idea what that wine was – could it have been a Sauternes? But French wine has been a starting point – I almost wrote reference point – for most of my wine researches over the years. I am sure I am no different from most wine drinkers in that respect. We are still conditioned to start from the belief that French wine offers, if not always the finest quality, certainly the greatest variety of any wine-producing country.

This book is designed to set out that variety. From the cool of the Loire and Alsace to the heat of Provence and Corsica, France's vineyards straddle the divide between cool-climate wines and those from hot, dry areas. With one style (Muscadet) influenced directly by the Atlantic, and others (from Provence, the Midi and Corsica) influenced by the benign Mediterranean, France can truly say that it offers a wine to suit all palates.

It was not so long ago, however, that for those outside the country, France stopped at Bordeaux, Burgundy and Champagne. These were – and still are – the classic areas of winemaking. That France also makes wines in other parts was known but little talked about, except among a few specialists and travellers. Gradually, the realization dawned that France has more to offer than these few wine styles, great though they are.

One excellent reason for the discovery of France's other regions was the escalating price of wines from the classic areas. But I like to think that it was also because here was a wide and exciting range of tastes. I am sure it was also no coincidence that the gradual arrival of new technology in winemaking helped launch wines that other-wise would have languished in their corners of France, dismissed as 'a little wine that won't travel'.

Some of these wines have gone on to achieve fame and fortune overseas. Take the classic pair from the Loire made from the Sauvignon Blanc grape: Sancerre and Pouilly Fumé. Their style has been the role model for wines from vineyards as far apart as Washington State and New Zealand. The red wines of the northern Rhône have become the model for a new generation of wine producers in California – known as the Rhône Rangers. Wines modelled on the Gewurztraminer of Alsace have turned up in Australia and New Zealand . . . the list could go on.

There is one vital element in these French regional wines which – in French eyes at least – the New World wines lack. That is the carefully observed relationship between grape variety, climate and soil, built up by empirical experimentation over centuries. Traditionally, the French would no more think of planting Pinot Noir in Bordeaux than Cabernet Sauvignon in Burgundy, although more recently, certainly in the south of France, growers are prepared to put together more unorthodox combinations.

Typically of the French, this experimentation has had to be codified and legalized before it could be recognized, which is why a new category, called Vin de Pays, has been created to recognize not only traditions in areas not considered quite good enough for Appellation Contrôlée status, but also to allow space for 'foreign' grape varieties to infiltrate the wines.

This experimentation has begun not a moment too soon. France's wines may have a great tradition and a great reputation, but they are in the process of losing their pre-eminence in the wine world (not helped, it must be said, by a small harvest in 1991). The New World and other European countries, Italy especially, are overtaking France in the quality stakes, as their growers experiment, absorb new ideas and move onwards – even if onwards also means a rediscovery of old traditions long forgotten.

France has been slow to catch on to the viticultural and vinicultural revolution, content to rely on its hitherto superior reputation and tradition. The experimentation in the Midi, the introduction of *vins de pays* as vehicles for this experimentation is all new. The arrival of a new generation of growers and producers who have travelled the world, who have maybe even studied in California or Australia, has brought the philosophy of tradition and the relationship of wine to its *terroir* into conjunction with the freer approach of the New World.

France may never regain its total dominance of wine – nor should it. What will keep it in the forefront of any wine drinker's mind is the range of what it produces. I hope this book offers a glimpse of that variety.

France's Appellation System

Legally speaking, there are four categories of wine in France.

The top category in quality and reputation is Appellation d'Origine Contrôlée, abbreviated to AOC or AC. Nearly 30 percent of all French wine comes into this category. It is a guarantee not only of origin, but also increasingly of minimum standards in the vineyard and the cellar. An AC wine must come from a particular area, and from suitable vineyard sites in that area. It can be made only from a list of recommended grape varieties, planted to a certain density per hectare, and yielding a specified amount (which is allowed to vary from harvest to harvest). The wine has to be vinified and matured in a certain way, and can only be commercialized after a certain time. The finished wine must have a minimum alcohol level, and must pass a tasting test. The grower has to declare his production and his stock each year on August 31.

The second category is Vins Delimités de Qualité Supérieure, or VDQS. This is found generally in smaller, out-of-the-way areas or in areas that are only just establishing their reputations. It is seen very much as a stepping stone to full AC status, and seems to be gradually disappearing. Only 1·3 percent of French wine falls into this category, whose requirements are the same as for AC.

The third category is relatively new. *Vin de pays* was created in 1973, and the late 1970s and 1980s saw a mushrooming of *vin de pays* regions. The idea was to give areas producing basic table wine a chance to improve standards, quality, price and market. As with AC and VDQS wines, geographical area, grape varieties, yields and vineyard and winemaking requirements are specified, although they are less restrictive than for AC and VDQS. In addition, some *vins de pays* allow the use of non-local grape varieties – for example Cabernet Sauvignon or Chardonnay in the south of France – and it is these that often produce the most interesting examples. There are three categories of *vin de pays*.

1   Regional *vins de pays*, covering huge areas of the country, certainly more than one department of France;

2   Departmental *vins de pays*, covering the whole of one department;

3   Zonal *vins de pays*, covering smaller areas within a department. Often these can overlap with an AC or VDQS zone, but have different regulations, especially about permitted grape varieties.

Since, under European Community rules, the *vin de pays* is still only basic table wine, any *vin de pays* label will also carry the legend 'Vin de Table de France'.

The fourth category is table wine (*vin ordinaire*, *vin de table*). This includes wine for distilling into brandy. It is sold by alcohol degree, and the rules say its origins cannot appear on any label, although it is likely that most comes from the Midi.

How to Use this Book

This book is a region-by-region guide to over 600 wine producers of Appellation Contrôlée (AC) wines, Vins Delimités de Qualité Supérieure (VDQS) and *vins de pays* in all the wine-growing regions of France apart from Bordeaux, Burgundy and Champagne (which are dealt with in separate Mitchell Beazley wine guides).

Each region is treated in the same way. There is an introduction, setting out the general styles and character of the wines that come from that region and giving some indication of the character of the countryside. This general introduction is followed by detailed notes on each of the AC, VDQS and *vin de pays* areas within the main region. These notes contain information on the colours of the wines made (red, rosé and white), whether sparkling wine is made, and the grape varieties permitted.

Producer entries follow. These are arranged alphabetically by producer within AC or VDQS areas. The AC and VDQS order is the same as in the introduction to each section. Where a producer or *négociant* makes more than one AC or VDQS wine, he or she will be listed under the area in which their cellars are situated or where their principal vineyard holding is.

Information contained in the producer entry is standardized as much as possible. The name of the producer is given first, followed by his or her address, including the Cedex code (essential to use when writing to France). Details of the vineyards owned follow. This is followed by the production given in terms of 75 centilitre bottles. This figure refers only to wine bottled by the producer – any sold in bulk is not included. In addition, producers are codified by the type of business they operate.

At the end of the entry, there are details of when the producer's tasting room is open. Often, the entry will indicate that an appointment is required or preferred, but even when this is not stated, it is courteous to write to smaller producers in advance. Larger firms and cooperatives normally have tasting rooms that are open to the public.

Abbreviations

ha   hectares

VP-R   a *vigneron proprietaire-récoltant*, a producer who only makes wine from his or her own land and does not buy in grapes or wine.

N   *négociant*, or wine merchant, who buys in grapes or wine which is then sold under the firm's own name. A *négociant* may also own land, in which case the code will read VP-R and N.

Coop   cooperative of producers. This code is followed by the number of members in the cooperative.

The Grape Varieties

Each region of France has a range of mainstream grape varieties which make up the bulk of the wine they produce. But each region also has some unknowns or has attracted some foreign grape varieties. This list, arranged alphabetically by grape variety, shows in which AC and VDQS each grape variety is permitted.

Red

Abourieu
Southwest: Côtes du Marmandais

Alicante
Provence: Coteaux Varois

Aramon
Midi: Coteaux du Languedoc-Coteaux de Vérargues
Provence: Coteaux Varois

Braquet
Provence: Bellet

Cabernet Franc
Loire: Bourgueil, Chinon, Coteaux du Loir, St-Nicolas de Bourgueil, Touraine, Touraine Villages, Touraine-Mesland, Coteaux du Vendômois, Anjou, Saumur, Saumur-Champigny, Vin du Thouarsais, Coteaux d'Ancenis, Fiefs Vendéens
Midi: Côtes de la Malepère
Southwest: Béarn, Bergerac, Buzet, Côtes de Bergerac, Côtes de Duras, Côtes du Frontonnais, Côtes du Marmandais, Gaillac, Irouléguy, Madiran, Marcillac, Pécharmant, Côtes du Brulhois, Côtes de Saint-Mont, Tursan, Vin d'Entraygues et du Fel, Vin d'Estaing

Cabernet Sauvignon
Loire: Bourgueil, Chinon, Touraine, Anjou, Saumur, Vin du

Haut-Poitou, Vin du Thouarsais, Fiefs Vendéens
Midi: Cabardès, Côtes de la Malepère
Provence: Coteaux d'Aix en Provence, Coteaux des Baux en
Provence, Côtes de Provence, Coteaux Varois
Southwest: Béarn, Bergerac, Buzet, Côtes de Bergerac, Côtes de
Duras, Côtes du Frontonnais, Côtes du Marmandais, Gaillac,
Irouléguy, Madiran, Marcillac, Pécharmant, Côtes du Brulhois,
Côtes de Saint-Mont, Tursan, Vin d'Entraygues et du Fel, Vin
d'Estaing

Calitor
Provence: Bandol
Rhône: Lirac

Camarèse
Rhône: Côtes du Rhône, Côtes du Ventoux

Carignan
Midi: Costières de Nîmes, Coteaux du Languedoc, Coteaux du
Languedoc-Cabrières, Coteaux du Languedoc-La Clape,
Coteaux du Languedoc-La Méjanelle, Coteaux du Languedoc-
Coteaux de St-Christol, Coteaux du Languedoc-Coteaux de
Vérargues, Coteaux du Languedoc-Montpeyroux, Coteaux du
Languedoc-Pic-St-Loup, Coteaux du Languedoc-Quatourze,
Coteaux du Languedoc-St-Drézéry, Coteaux du Languedoc-St-
Georges d'Orques, Coteaux du Languedoc-St-Saturnin,
Faugères, Minervois, St-Chinian, Corbières, Fitou, Cabardès,
Collioure, Côtes du Roussillon, Côtes du Roussillon-Villages
Provence: Bandol, Cassis, Coteaux d'Aix en Provence, Coteaux
des Baux en Provence, Côtes de Provence, Coteaux de
Pierrevert, Coteaux Varois
Rhône: Côtes du Rhône, Côtes du Rhône-Villages, Coteaux du
Tricastin

Cinsault
Midi: Costières de Nîmes, Coteaux du Languedoc, Coteaux du
Languedoc-Cabrières, Coteaux du Languedoc-La Clape,
Coteaux du Languedoc-La Méjanelle, Coteaux du Languedoc-
Coteaux de St-Christol, Coteaux du Languedoc-Montpeyroux,

Coteaux du Languedoc-Pic-St-Loup, Coteaux du Languedoc-Quatourze, Coteaux du Languedoc-St-Drézéry, Coteaux du Languedoc-St Saturnin, Faugères, Minervois, Corbières, Fitou, Cabardès, Côtes de la Malepère, Collioure, Côtes du Roussillon, Côtes du Roussillon-Villages
Provence: Bandol, Bellet, Cassis, Coteaux d'Aix en Provence, Coteaux des Baux en Provence, Côtes de Provence, Palette, Coteaux de Pierrevert, Coteaux Varois
Rhône: Côtes du Rhône, Côtes du Rhône-Villages, Châteauneuf-du-Pape, Coteaux du Tricastin, Côtes du Lubéron, Gigondas, Lirac, Tavel
Southwest: Côtes du Frontonnais

Counoise
Midi: Costières de Nîmes, Coteaux du Languedoc
Provence: Coteaux d'Aix en Provence, Coteaux des Baux en Provence
Rhône: Côtes du Rhône, Châteauneuf-du-Pape, Côtes du Ventoux

Courbu Noir
Southwest: Béarn

Duras
Southwest: Gaillac

Fer
Midi: Cabardès
Southwest: Béarn, Bergerac, Côtes de Bergerac, Côtes du Marmandais, Gaillac, Irouléguy, Madiran, Marcillac, Tursan, Vin d'Entraygues et du Fel, Vin d'Estaing, Vin de Lavilledieu

Folle Noire
Provence: Bellet

Gamay
Loire: Châteaumeillant, Côtes d'Auvergne, Côtes du Forez, Côtes de Gien, Côte Roannaise, Saint-Pourçain, Coteaux du Loir, Touraine, Touraine Villages, Touraine-Mesland,

Cheverny, Coteaux du Vendômois, Valençay, Anjou, Anjou
Gamay, Saumur Mousseux, Vin du Haut-Poitou, Coteaux
d'Ancenis, Fiefs Vendéens
Lorraine: Côtes de Toul, Vin de Moselle
Rhône: Coteaux du Lyonnais, Châtillon-en-Diois, Côtes du
Lubéron, Côtes du Vivarais
Savoie: Vin de Savoie, Vin de Bugey
Southwest: Côtes du Frontonnais, Côtes du Marmandais, Gaillac,
Marcillac, Vin d'Entraygues et du Fel, Vin d'Estaing, Vin de
Lavilledieu

Grenache Noir
Midi: Costières de Nîmes, Coteaux du Languedoc, Coteaux du
Languedoc-Cabrières, Coteaux du Languedoc-La Clape,
Coteaux du Languedoc-Coteaux de St-Christol, Coteaux du
Languedoc-Coteaux de Vérargues, Coteaux du Languedoc-La
Méjanelle, Coteaux du Languedoc-Montpeyroux, Coteaux du
Languedoc-Pic-St-Loup, Coteaux du Languedoc-Quatourze,
Coteaux du Languedoc-St-Drézéry, Coteaux du Languedoc-St-
Saturnin, Faugères, Minervois, St-Chinian, Frontignan VDN,
Corbières, Fitou, Cabardès, Côtes de la Malepère, Collioure,
Côtes du Roussillon, Côtes du Roussillon-Villages, Banyuls
VDN, Maury VDN, Rivesaltes VDN
Provence: Bandol, Bellet, Cassis, Coteaux d'Aix en Provence,
Coteaux des Baux en Provence, Côtes de Provence, Palette,
Coteaux de Pierrevert, Coteaux Varois
Rhône: Côtes du Rhône, Côtes du Rhône-Villages, Châteauneuf-
du-Pape, Coteaux du Tricastin, Côtes du Lubéron, Côtes du
Ventoux, Gigondas, Lirac, Tavel, Rasteau VDN

Grolleau (Groslot)
Loire: Coteaux du Loir, Rosé de Loire, Touraine, Touraine-
Amboise, Touraine-Azay-le-Rideau, Anjou, Saumur Mousseux,
Vin du Haut-Poitou

Jurançon Noir
Southwest: Cahors, Gaillac, Marcillac, Vin d'Entraygues et du
Fel, Vin d'Estaing, Vin de Lavilledieu

Ladoner Pelut
Midi: Côtes du Roussillon, Côtes du Roussillon-Villages

Malbec (Cot or Auxerrois)
Loire: Coteaux du Loir, Touraine, Touraine Villages, Touraine-Mesland, Anjou, Saumur Mousseux
Midi: Cabardès, Côtes de la Malepère
Southwest: Bergerac, Buzet, Cahors, Côtes de Bergerac, Côtes de Duras, Côtes du Frontonnais, Côtes du Marmandais, Pécharmant, Côtes du Brulhois

Manseng Noir
Southwest: Béarn

Merlot
Midi: Cabardès, Côtes de la Malepère
Southwest: Bergerac, Buzet, Cahors, Côtes de Bergerac, Côtes de Duras, Côtes du Frontonnais, Côtes du Marmandais, Gaillac, Marcillac, Pécharmant, Côtes du Brulhois, Côtes de Saint-Mont, Vin d'Entraygues et du Fel, Vin d'Estaing

Mondeuse
Savoie: Vin de Savoie, Vin de Bugey

Mourvèdre
Midi: Costières de Nîmes, Coteaux du Languedoc, Coteaux du Languedoc-St-Saturnin, Minervois, Corbières, Cabardès, Collioure, Côtes du Roussillon, Côtes du Roussillon-Villages
Provence: Bandol, Cassis, Coteaux d'Aix en Provence, Coteaux des Baux en Provence, Côtes de Provence, Palette, Coteaux Varois
Rhône: Côtes du Rhône, Côtes du Rhône-Villages, Châteauneuf-du-Pape, Coteaux du Tricastin, Côtes du Lubéron, Côtes du Ventoux, Gigondas, Lirac, Tavel

Muscardin
Rhône: Côtes du Rhône, Châteauneuf-du-Pape, Côtes du Ventoux

Négrette
Southwest: Côtes du Frontonnais, Gaillac, Vin d'Entraygues et du
Fel, Vin d'Estaing, Vin de Lavilledieu

Pineau d'Aunis
Loire: Coteaux du Loir, Touraine, Coteaux du Vendômois,
Anjou, Saumur, Saumur Mousseux, Fiefs Vendéens

Pinenc
Southwest: Béarn

Pinot Meunier
Loire: Vins de l'Orléanais, Touraine
Lorraine: Côtes de Toul

Pinot Noir
Alsace: Alsace, Crémant d'Alsace
Jura: Arbois, Arbois Pupillin, Côtes du Jura
Loire: Ménétou-Salon, Reuilly, Sancerre, Côtes de Gien, Saint-
Pourçain, Touraine, Coteaux du Vendômois, Saumur Mousseux,
Vin du Haut-Poitou, Fiefs Vendéens
Lorraine: Côtes de Toul, Vin de Moselle
Rhône: Châtillon-en-Diois
Savoie: Vin de Savoie, Vin de Bugey
Southwest: Vin d'Entraygues et du Fel, Vin de l'Estaing

Portugais Bleu
Southwest: Gaillac

Poulsard (Plousard)
Bugey: Vin de Bugey
Jura: Arbois, Arbois Pupillin, Côtes du Jura, L'Etoile

Syrah
Midi: Costières de Nîmes, Coteaux du Languedoc-
Montpeyroux, Coteaux du Languedoc-St-Saturnin, Minervois,
Corbières, Cabardès, Côtes de la Malepère, Collioure
Provence: Bandol, Coteaux d'Aix en Provence, Coteaux des
Baux en Provence, Côtes de Provence, Coteaux Varois

Rhône: Côtes du Rhône, Côtes du Rhône-Villages, Cornas, Côte-Rôtie, Coteaux du Lyonnais, Crozes-Hermitage, Hermitage, Saint-Joseph, Châteauneuf-du-Pape, Châtillon-en-Diois, Coteaux du Tricastin, Côtes du Lubéron, Côtes du Ventoux, Gigondas, Lirac

Tannat
Southwest: Béarn, Cahors, Irouléguy, Madiran, Côtes du Brulhois, Côtes de Saint-Mont, Tursan

Terret Noir
Midi: Costières de Nîmes, Coteaux du Languedoc, Coteaux du Languedoc-La Clape, Corbières
Rhône: Côtes du Rhône, Châteauneuf-du-Pape, Côtes du Ventoux

Tibouren
Provence: Bandol, Côtes de Provence

Trousseau
Jura: Arbois, Arbois Pupillin, Côtes du Jura

Vaccarèse
Rhône: Côtes du Rhône, Châteauneuf-du-Pape, Côtes du Ventoux

White

Aligoté
Savoie: Vin de Savoie, Vin de Bugey

Altesse (Roussette)
Savoie: Roussette de Savoie, Seyssel, Seyssel Mousseux, Vin de Savoie, Vin de Savoie Ayse Mousseux, Vin de Savoie Mousseux, Vin de Bugey, Vin de Bugey Mousseux

Baroque
Southwest: Béarn, Irouléguy, Tursan

Bourboulenc

Midi: Costières de Nîmes, Coteaux du Languedoc, Coteaux du Languedoc-La Méjanelle, Coteaux du Languedoc-Pic-St-Loup, Coteaux du Languedoc-Quatourze, Corbières
Provence: Bandol, Bellet
Rhône: Côtes du Rhône, Côtes du Rhône-Villages, Châteauneuf-du-Pape, Coteaux du Tricastin, Côtes du Lubéron, Côtes du Ventoux, Lirac, Tavel, Côtes du Vivarais

Chardonnay

Alsace: Crémant d'Alsace
Jura: Côtes du Jura, Côtes du Jura Mousseux, L'Etoile
Loire: Saint-Pourçain, Touraine, Cheverny, Coteaux du Vendômois, Valençay, Anjou, Saumur, Saumur Mousseux, Vin du Haut-Poitou, Fiefs Vendéens
Midi: Blanquette de Limoux
Provence: Bellet
Rhône: Coteaux du Lyonnais, Châtillon-en-Diois, Côtes du Lubéron
Savoie: Roussette de Savoie, Vin de Savoie, Vin de Bugey, Vin de Bugey Mousseux

Chasselas

Alsace: Alsace
Loire: Pouilly-sur-Loire
Savoie: Crépy, Seyssel Mousseux, Vin de Savoie

Chenin Blanc (Pineau de la Loire)

Loire: Coteaux du Loir, Jasnières, Montlouis, Touraine, Touraine Villages, Touraine-Azay-le-Rideau, Touraine-Mesland, Vouvray, Cheverny, Coteaux du Vendômois, Anjou, Anjou Coteaux de la Loire, Anjou Mousseux, Bonnezeaux, Coteaux de l'Aubance, Coteaux du Layon, Coteaux du Layon Villages, Coteaux du Saumur, Quarts-de-Chaume, Saumur, Saumur Mousseux, Savennières, Vin du Haut-Poitou, Vin du Thouarsais, Coteaux d'Ancenis, Fiefs Vendéens
Southwest: Bergerac Sec, Montravel, Saussignac, Vin d'Entraygues et du Fel, Vin d'Estaing

Clairette
Midi: Clairette de Bellegarde, Costières de Nîmes, Clairette du Languedoc, Coteaux du Languedoc, Coteaux du Languedoc-La Clape, Coteaux du Languedoc-La Méjanelle, Coteaux du Languedoc-Picpoul de Pinet, Coteaux du Languedoc-Pic-St-Loup, Coteaux du Languedoc-Quatourze, Faugères, Blanquette de Limoux, Corbières
Provence: Bandol, Bellet, Cassis, Coteaux d'Aix en Provence, Coteaux des Baux en Provence, Côtes de Provence, Palette, Coteaux de Pierrevert, Coteaux Varois
Rhône: Côtes du Rhône, Côtes du Rhône-Villages, Châteauneuf-du-Pape, Clairette de Die, Clairette de Die Mousseux, Côtes du Lubéron, Côtes du Ventoux, Lirac, Tavel, Côtes du Vivarais

Courbu Blanc
Southwest: Béarn, Irouléguy, Jurançon, Jurançon Sec, Pacherenc du Vic-Bilh

Grenache Blanc
Midi: Costières de Nîmes, Banyuls VDN
Provence: Cassis, Coteaux d'Aix en Provence, Coteaux des Baux en Provence, Palette, Coteaux Varois
Rhône: Côtes du Rhône, Châteauneuf-du-Pape, Côtes du Lubéron, Côtes du Ventoux, Côtes du Vivarais

Grenache Gris
Midi: Banyuls VDN

Gros Plant (Folle Blanche)
Loire: Gros Plant du Pays Nantais, Fiefs Vendéens

Gewurztraminer
Alsace: Alsace, Alsace Grand Cru

Jacquère
Savoie: Vin de Savoie, Vin de Bugey, Vin de Bugey Mousseux

Jurançon Blanc
Southwest: Côtes de Saint-Mont

Lauzat
Southwest: Béarn, Irouléguy

Loin de l'Oeil
Southwest: Gaillac, Gaillac Doux, Gaillac Mousseux, Gaillac Premières Côtes

Maccabeo
Midi: Banyuls VDN, Rivesaltes VDN
Rhône: Lirac

Malvoisie (Pinot Beurot)
Loire: Coteaux d'Ancenis
Midi: Coteaux du Languedoc, Côtes du Roussillon, Banyuls VDN, Rivesaltes VDN
Provence: Coteaux Varois

Manseng, Gros
Southwest: Béarn, Irouléguy, Jurançon, Jurançon Sec, Pacherenc du Vic-Bilh

Manseng, Petit
Southwest: Béarn, Irouléguy, Jurançon, Jurançon Sec, Pacherenc du Vic-Bilh

Marsanne
Provence: Cassis, Coteaux de Pierrevert
Rhône: Côtes du Rhône, Crozes-Hermitage, Hermitage, Saint-Péray, Saint-Péray Mousseux, Coteaux du Tricastin, Côtes du Lubéron, Côtes du Ventoux, Côtes du Vivarais

Mauzac Blanc
Midi: Blanquette de Limoux
Southwest: Côtes de Duras, Gaillac, Gaillac Doux, Gaillac Mousseux, Gaillac Premières Côtes, Vin d'Entraygues et du Fel, Vin d'Estaing, Vin de Lavilledieu

Melon de Bourgogne (Muscadet)
Loire: Muscadet des Coteaux de la Loire, Muscadet de Sèvre et Maine

Meslier
Southwest: Côtes de Saint-Mont

Mondeuse Blanche
Savoie: Roussette de Savoie, Vin de Bugey, Vin de Bugey Mousseux

Muscadelle
Southwest: Bergerac Sec, Buzet, Côtes de Bergerac Moelleux, Côtes de Duras, Côtes de Montravel, Gaillac, Gaillac Doux, Gaillac Mousseux, Gaillac Premières Côtes, Haut Montravel, Monbazillac, Montravel, Rosette, Saussignac

Muscat Blanc à Petits Grains
Alsace: Alsace, Alsace Grand Cru
Midi: Muscat de Frontignan VDN, Muscat de Lunel VDN, Muscat de Mireval VDN, Muscat de St-Jean-de-Minervois VDN, Banyuls VDN, Muscat de Rivesaltes VDN
Rhône: Clairette de Die Mousseux, Muscat de Beaumes de Venise VDN

Muscat Ottonel
Alsace: Alsace, Alsace Grand Cru

Ondenc
Southwest: Bergerac Sec, Côtes de Duras, Gaillac, Gaillac Doux, Gaillac Mousseux, Gaillac Premières Côtes, Montravel, Saussignac

Picardan
Rhône: Châteauneuf-du-Pape

Picpoul
Midi: Coteaux du Languedoc, Coteaux du Languedoc-La Méjanelle, Coteaux du Languedoc-Picpoul de Pinet, Coteaux du

Languedoc-Pic-St-Loup, Coteaux du Languedoc-Quatourze,
Corbières
Rhône: Châteauneuf-du-Pape, Lirac, Tavel
Southwest: Côtes de Saint-Mont, Vin de Lavilledieu

Pineau Menu (Arbois)
Loire: Touraine, Cheverny, Valençay

Pinot Auxerrois
Alsace: Alsace, Crémant d'Alsace

Pinot Blanc (Klevner)
Alsace: Alsace, Crémant d'Alsace
Jura: Côtes du Jura, Côtes du Jura Mousseux
Lorraine: Vin de Moselle

Pinot Gris (Tokay Pinot Gris)
Alsace: Alsace, Alsace Grand Cru
Loire: Reuilly, Touraine
Lorraine: Vin de Moselle
Savoie: Vin de Bugey

Riesling
Alsace: Alsace, Alsace Grand Cru

Rolle
Provence: Bellet, Côtes de Provence

Romorantin
Loire: Cheverny, Valençay

Roussanne
Provence: Bellet, Coteaux de Pierrevert
Rhône: Côtes du Rhône, Côtes du Rhône-Villages, Crozes-
Hermitage, Hermitage, Saint-Péray, Saint-Péray Mousseux,
Châteauneuf-du-Pape, Côtes du Ventoux, Côtes du Vivarais

Ruffiac
Southwest: Pacherenc du Vic-Bilh

Sauvignon
Loire: Ménétou-Salon, Pouilly-Fumé, Quincy, Reuilly, Sancerre,
Côtes de Gien, Touraine, Cheverny, Valençay, Anjou, Saumur,
Saumur Mousseux, Vin du Haut-Poitou, Fiefs Vendéens
Provence: Bandol, Cassis, Coteaux d'Aix en Provence, Coteaux
des Baux en Provence
Southwest: Béarn, Bergerac Sec, Buzet, Côtes de Bergerac, Côtes
de Bergerac Moelleux, Côtes de Duras, Côtes du Marmandais,
Côtes de Montravel, Gaillac, Gaillac Mousseux, Gaillac
Premières Côtes, Haut Montravel, Irouléguy, Monbazillac,
Montravel, Pacherenc du Vic-Bilh, Rosette, Saussignac, Côtes de
Saint-Mont

Savagnin (Gringet)
Jura: Arbois, Arbois Mousseux, Arbois Pupillin, Château-
Chalon, Côtes du Jura, L'Etoile
Savoie: Vin de Savoie Ayse Mousseux, Vin de Savoie Mousseux

Sémillon
Provence: Coteaux d'Aix en Provence, Coteaux des Baux en
Provence, Côtes de Provence
Southwest: Béarn, Bergerac Sec, Buzet, Côtes de Bergerac
Moelleux, Côtes de Duras, Côtes du Marmandais, Côtes de
Montravel, Gaillac, Gaillac Doux, Gaillac Mousseux, Gaillac
Premières Côtes, Haut Montravel, Irouléguy, Monbazillac,
Montravel, Pacherenc du Vic-Bilh, Rosette, Saussignac

Sylvaner
Alsace: Alsace
Lorraine: Vin de Moselle

Terret Blanc
Midi: Coteaux du Languedoc-Picpoul de Pinet

Tressalier
Loire: Saint-Pourçain

Ugni Blanc
Midi: Costières de Nîmes

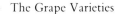

Provence: Bandol, Cassis, Coteaux d'Aix en Provence, Coteaux des Baux en Provence, Côtes de Provence, Palette, Coteaux Varois
Rhône: Côtes du Rhône, Côtes du Lubéron, Côtes du Vivarais
Southwest: Côtes de Duras, Côtes du Marmandais, Montravel

Viognier
Rhône: Château Grillet, Condrieu, Côte-Rôtie

Half-timbered houses and sheltered vineyards in Alsace

Alsace

Alsace wines are often said to be Germanic wines made in a French way. But that, I feel, is to play up the German element of the equation and to play down the French. Because there is no doubt that, despite differences in history and philosophy, Alsace produces wines that could only be French.

It is true that if you listened to an Alsace grower talking to a colleague from the next village, you could be forgiven for thinking you were on the east bank of the Rhine and not the west. Between themselves, Alsatians often speak a curious dialect which is much more German than French. As one grower put it 'we think we're talking a dialect, but really we're talking German'.

But that is hardly surprising. Alsace became part of modern France only in 1648 at the end of the 30 Years' War. Before that, it had either been part of the Holy Roman Empire or part of the Frankish kingdom of the Merovingians. Its history has not been without troubles. Twice reoccupied by Germany (from 1870 to 1919 and from 1940 to 1945), it has been fought over as a prized borderland for centuries. Now, it is French but European as well – the European Parliament meets in Strasbourg, the capital of Alsace.

Alsace is well to the north in terms of French vineyards and to the south in terms of German vineyards – level with south Baden and the Kaiserstuhl. But geography is kinder to Alsace than history has been: the sheltering Vosges mountains run from north to south for virtually the whole length of Alsace parallel to the Rhine.

The vineyards lie in the eastern lee of the mountains, in a narrow strip that is never more than two miles wide. The Vosges protect the vines from rain – in Colmar in the central vineyards of Alsace the rainfall is the lowest in France, apart from Perpignan in the deep south. The result is that for weeks on end in the summer, the skies of Alsace can be clear and blue, while a few miles away in the uplands of the Vosges it will be raining hard.

Alsace is picturesque wine country. The ribbon of vineyards is broken by small villages, full of tall, overhanging half-timbered houses, decorated in the summer with brightly planted window boxes. Curious mediaeval signs indicate the cellars of wine producers, who often invite visitors to taste their wines. Everyone seems to be connected in some way with wine.

The most northerly Alsace vineyards virtually touch the German border near the southern end of the Rheinpfalz. The vineyards of Rott and Cleebourg, dominated by their cooperative, have only recently been expanded and now have 120 hectares planted. Little of the wine, though, travels far beyond Strasbourg.

The main Alsace vineyard area begins 48 kilometres (30 miles) south, through the northern outcrops of the Vosges, where the village of Marlenheim marks the beginning of the Alsace wine road. From Marlenheim to Orschwiller, south of Sélestat, the vineyards are in the Bas-Rhin *département* (ie lower down the course of the Rhine). While they have never achieved the fame of the vineyards further south, they give a definite character of their own to the wines. Some would describe this northern Alsace wine as lighter and drier than the wine of the south. The rainfall here is certainly higher, because the Vosges are lower, and the grapes tend not to ripen so quickly or so completely. Many of the grapes for the sparkling Crémant d'Alsace (*see below*) come from the Bas-Rhin vineyards. Famous wine villages in the Bas-Rhin include: Wangen, Barr, Goxwiller, Mittelbergheim, Itterswiller, Dambach-la-Ville, Kintzheim and Orschwiller.

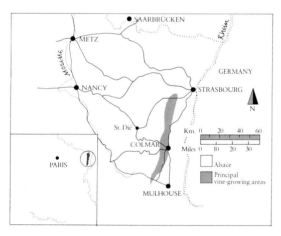

At St-Hippolyte the Haut-Rhin *département* begins. The vineyards run the full length of this *département*, passing the famous villages of Bergheim, Ribeauvillé, Riquewihr, Kaysersberg, Ammerschwihr, Eguisheim, Husseren-les-Châteaux, Rouffach, Guebwiller and Soultz and ending with the small vineyard concentration around Thann, just west of Mulhouse and the Swiss border. Here the Vosges are higher, the rainfall lower and the grapes ripen over a long growing period running into warm, dry autumns.

Négociants (merchants) dominate the Alsace wine trade, just as they did – until recently – in Burgundy. Many have been in the business for centuries. The reason is the same as it was in Burgundy – the vineyards are owned by many growers with small holdings, who could not afford or did not wish to bottle and sell their own wine. Even now, there are 9,000 growers farming the 12,000 hectares of vineyard.

Cooperatives also account for much of the produce – about 25 percent. Growers are beginning to bottle their own wine as they realize they can obtain high prices which cover their costs, so that now nearly 30 percent of the wine is bottled by growers, leaving 45 percent in the hands of the *négociants*, the balance going to cooperatives.

Inevitably with such northerly vineyards, it is white wines that dominate the viticulture. White and sparkling white wine make up 95 percent of production, and although Alsace growers like to show their red wines at a tasting, when it comes to the meal it is bottles of Bordeaux that will be drunk.

Although vines have been grown in Alsace probably since the Romans and certainly since the Merovingians in the eighth and ninth centuries, the development of the Alsace vineyard as we know it today is relatively new – dating from after the First World War. The Appellation Contrôlée system reached Alsace in 1962.

When they were introduced, the new AC laws recognized a system of labelling which was unique in France – and certainly not one inherited from Germany. Until very recently (*see below* under Grand Cru) the whole Alsace vineyard – from the north by the border with Germany down to the Swiss border near Basle – was covered by only one *appellation*. Everything was AC Alsace.

On the labels, a system operates which will be familiar to Californian and Australian wine drinkers but which is still rare in the rest of France: the wines are labelled with the name of the grape variety. The grape named has to make up 100 percent of the contents of the bottle. This applies to the bulk of wines exported from Alsace. At home, Alsatians drink blended wines quite happily – sometimes calling them Edelzwicker, sometimes using a brand name.

Another revolution was adopted at the same time – revolutionary when compared with the rest of France. The AC rules stipulate that all Alsace AC wines have to be bottled in Alsace – not even elsewhere in France, let alone abroad. This, more than anything else, has given Alsace its reputation for reliability. As a consequence of this regulation, it is almost unknown to find a bad bottle of Alsace wine – bad, that is, in the sense of faulty.

Alsace Grape Varieties

The permitted grape varieties, with characteristics of the wine they produce, are as follows:

Chasselas This used to be a widely planted grape, but is now down to about 3·5 percent of the vineyard. It is also grown in Savoie and Switzerland. In Alsace it only appears as part of an Edelzwicker blend. When tasted by itself, it has a smoky, herby taste with soft, low-acid fruit.

Gewurztraminer The grape that has brought more fame to Alsace than any other. It has a distinctive, spicy, full, oily taste, high alcohol, and sometimes a bitter finish and dryness in even the sweetest examples. It is the grape most frequently used in the late-picked *Vendange Tardive* and *Sélection des Grains Nobles* (*see* page 35) wines. Not a wine to drink in vast quantities, it is excellent with some of the rich Alsace cooking such as *choucroute* (pickled cabbage) and spicy sausages.

Pinot Blanc This produces some of the most readily drinkable wines in Alsace. It is no surprise that it has been such a success in London wine bars: it is very quaffable on its own as it is relatively low in alcohol, fresh-tasting, soft with a pleasing touch of acidity and not too pronounced a character. There are two forms of the Pinot Blanc in Alsace – the Pinot Blanc itself and the Pinot Auxerrois. The latter is generally regarded as producing the better-quality wine, but the two are normally blended and sold under the name Pinot Blanc – or further blended with other grapes and sold as Edelzwicker or a branded wine.

Muscat The grape that in the south of France produces the sweet sparkling Clairette de Die and the Vins Doux Naturels such as Beaumes de Venise, in Alsace makes a wine that is a perfect combination of sweetness and lightness, dry yet with a honeyed tone, absolutely delicious as an aperitif wine. The trouble is that there is very little of it in Alsace: it is a difficult vine to grow so far north, and growers are reluctant to devote much of their vineyard space to a vine which only yields well in good years. As with the Pinot Blanc, there are two types of Muscat: the Muscat Blanc à Petits Grains (or Muscat d'Alsace) and the Muscat Ottonel. While the latter causes fewer growing problems, the former produces the finer wine.

Riesling By general assent the Riesling makes the finest wine in Alsace and epitomizes the difference between Alsatian and German winemaking. In Alsace, the Riesling produces a wine that has medium alcohol, is bone dry with a flinty, steely taste, very fresh and often acidic when young, softening with maturity to give a superb wine with a petrolly taste. In very fine vintages, it is allowed to make sweeter wines which still retain a dryness and firmness no German wine is ever intended to achieve.

Sylvaner A widely planted grape which produces a neutral, reliable wine, attractive for quaffing and often used as a component of Edelzwicker blends. Twenty percent of the Alsace vineyard is planted with this variety. It is especially popular in the northern Bas-Rhin vineyards where its early ripening and low acidity cope well with the cooler, wetter weather.

Tokay d'Alsace or Pinot Gris This bears no relation to the Tokay wine of Hungary (which is made with a different grape variety, the Furmint), but has links with eastern Austria and western Hungary, as well as parts of northern Italy. The name Tokay, while formally banned by the EC because of the confusion with the Hungarian wine, is still widely used – and in fact most producers now refer to the wine as Tokay Pinot Gris. Many Alsatians would call this their favourite style of wine: full, rich, soft, well balanced with much acidity, a touch of pepper, quite high in alcohol and with the ability to age over a long period. It is often drunk with foie gras, which it certainly complements perfectly. If I am given the choice of Alsace wines, I am generally torn between a good Tokay and a good Riesling.

The Appellations
Appellations Contrôlées

Virtually all the wine made in Alsace has AC status. Alsace produces 20 percent of all white AC wine in France – around 143 million bottles a year.

Alsace This is the general AC to cover all the vineyards of Alsace. Any of the permitted grape varieties (*see above*) grown in any village in any AC vineyard can qualify for the *appellation*.

Alsace Grand Cru A new AC, first introduced with the 1985 vintage. It covers certain specified vineyards for certain grape varieties. In other words, if Grand Cru vineyard X is designated as Grand Cru for Riesling, any Gewurztraminer in that vineyard will be simple AC Alsace. Grand Cru wines can be either 100 percent from one vineyard (which will be named on the label) or from a number of Grand Cru vineyards (when it will simply be called Alsace Grand Cru). All Alsace Grand Cru wines must be 100 percent from one grape variety, and only the four top Alsace grape varieties – Riesling, Gewurztraminer, Tokay and Muscat – can produce Grand Cru wines.

Like so many changes in AC laws anywhere in France, local politics has played an important role in the Grand Cru

designations. The *négociant* houses are not in favour of
Grand Cru status at all because it implies that single-
vineyard wines are better than wines blended from a
number of top vineyards. The growers, however, are all for
Grand Cru status (if they have Grand Cru land themselves)
because it will increase the price they can charge. There was
much argument about the size of each designated Grand
Cru and it took ten years for the first vineyards to be
organized; it will probably take the same again for the
second *tranche* of Grand Crus (*see* second list).

The current (February 1991) list of Grand Cru vineyards (with
their commune and the *département*), which takes in ten percent of
Alsace production, is as follows:

Altenberg de Bergbieten (Bergbieten, Bas-Rhin)
Altenberg de Bergheim (Bergheim, Haut-Rhin)
Brand (Turckheim, Haut-Rhin)
Eichberg (Eguisheim, Haut-Rhin)
Geisberg (Ribeauvillé, Haut-Rhin)
Gloeckelberg (Rodern and St-Hippolyte, Haut-Rhin)
Goldert (Gueberschwihr, Haut-Rhin)
Hatschbourg (Hattstatt and Voegtlinshoffen, Haut-Rhin)
Hengst (Wintzenheim, Haut-Rhin)
Kanzlerberg (Bergheim, Haut-Rhin)
Kastelberg (Andlau, Bas-Rhin)
Kessler (Guebwiller, Haut-Rhin)
Kirchberg de Barr (Barr, Bas-Rhin)
Kirchberg de Ribeauvillé (Ribeauvillé, Haut-Rhin)
Kitterlé (Guebwiller, Haut-Rhin)
Moenchberg (Andlau and Eichhoffen, Bas-Rhin)
Ollwiller (Wuenheim, Bas-Rhin)
Rangen (Thann and Vieux-Thann, Haut-Rhin)
Rosacker (Hunawihr, Haut-Rhin)
Saering (Guebwiller, Haut-Rhin)
Schlossberg (Kaysersberg and Kientzheim, Haut-Rhin)
Sommerberg (Niedermorschwihr and Katzenthal, Haut-Rhin)
Sonnenglanz (Beblenheim, Haut-Rhin)
Spiegel (Bergholtz and Guebwiller, Haut-Rhin)
Wiebelsberg (Andlau, Bas-Rhin)

There are currently another 25 vineyards that have been nominated by their villages for Grand Cru status. Producers are allowed to add the name Grand Cru to these vineyards even though the final decision has not been made. With these, Alsace Grand Cru will become 15 percent of total Alsace production.

Altenberg de Wolxheim (Wolxheim, Bas-Rhin)
Engelberg (Dahlenheim, Bas-Rhin)
Florimont (Ingersheim, Haut-Rhin)
Frankstein (Dambach-la-Ville, Bas-Rhin)
Froehn (Zellenberg, Haut-Rhin)
Furstentum (Kientzheim and Sigolsheim, Haut-Rhin)
Kaefferkopf (Ammerschwihr, Haut-Rhin)
Mambourg (Sigolsheim, Haut-Rhin)
Mandelberg (Mittelwihr, Haut-Rhin)
Markrain (Bennwihr, Haut-Rhin)
Muenchberg (Nothalten, Bas-Rhin)
Osterberg (Ribeauvillé, Haut-Rhin)
Pfersigberg (Eguisheim, Haut-Rhin)
Pfingstberg (Orschwiller, Haut-Rhin)
Praelatenberg (Orschwiller, Bas-Rhin)
Schoenenbourg (Riquewihr, Haut-Rhin)
Sporen (Riquewihr, Haut-Rhin)
Steinert (Pfaffenheim, Haut-Rhin)
Steingrubler (Wettolsheim, Haut-Rhin)
Steinklotz (Marlenheim, Bas-Rhin)
Vorbourg (Rouffach and Westhalten, Haut-Rhin)
Wineck-Schlossberg (Katzenthal, Haut-Rhin)
Winzenberg (Blienschwiller, Bas-Rhin)
Zinnkoepfle (Westhalten and Soultzmatt, Haut-Rhin)
Zotzenberg (Mittelbergheim, Bas-Rhin)

Crémant d'Alsace A *méthode champenoise* sparkling wine that can be made from grapes grown anywhere in the Alsace AC area. The *appellation* is fairly new and came in with the 1976 harvest. Permitted grape varieties for Crémant d'Alsace are: Pinot Blanc, Pinot Auxerrois, Pinot Noir, Pinot Gris, Riesling and Chardonnay. Most *crémant* is made from Pinot Blanc and Pinot Auxerrois.

Vendange Tardive and Sélection des Grains Nobles Sweeter
wines made either from bunches or selected berries that
have particularly high sugar levels and levels of potential
alcohol. To that extent they correspond to the German
categories of *Beerenauslese* and *Trockenbeerenauslese*. The taste
of noble rot (*pourriture noble*) is often found in these wines,
which do not have to consist totally of grapes which have
noble rot. While the terms have been around for some
time, it was only in 1984 (referring to the 1983 vintage) that
their use was regulated.

Lorraine VDQS

Côtes de Toul Red, rosé, *gris* and dry white wines from a small
vineyard area around the city of Toul in the Meurthe-et-
Moselle *département*. Most of the wine is *vin gris*, a pale rosé
made from Gamay grapes. Pinot Noir and Pinot Meunier
are also planted.

Vin de Moselle Red and dry white wines from the *département*
of Moselle. The red is made from Pinot Noir, Pinot Gris
and Gamay, the white from Pinot Blanc and Sylvaner.

Vins de Pays

Departmental Vins de Pays

Vin de Pays de Bas-Rhin Wines from an area covering the
whole of the Bas-Rhin *département*. A tiny amount of rosé
and white wine is produced from the Alsace grapes and also
the Chardonnay and Auxerrois.
Vin de Pays de Haut-Rhin A small quantity of wines, made
from Alsace grapes as well as Chardonnay and Auxerrois.
These wines may come from anywhere in the Haut-Rhin.
Vin de Pays de la Meuse An area covering the *département* of
the Meuse in Lorraine. Production is of mainly white
wines, coming from the Auxerrois, Chardonnay and a
range of Alsatian grape varieties.

Bas-Rhin Producers

E Boeckel
67140 Mittelbergheim. Vineyards owned: 20ha. 420,000 bottles. VP-R and N
Riesling wines are the speciality of this *négociant*, the biggest wine producer in Mittelbergheim. Their vineyard holdings include two in Grand Cru vineyards – the Zotzenberg and the Wiebelsberg – as well as in the Brandluft vineyard. Curiously, despite Zotzenberg's previous reputation for Sylvaner, Boeckel has always concentrated on Riesling and Gewurztraminer from this vineyard. Their wines, on the whole, should be drunk relatively young. *Open: By appointment only.*

Vignobles Raymond Engel et Fils
I Route du Vin, 67600 Orschwiller. Vineyards owned: Grand Cru Praelatenberg 6ha; Alsace AC 9ha. 150,000 bottles. VP-R
The Grand Cru Praelatenberg vineyard supplies all four varietals – Gewurztraminer, Riesling, Tokay and Muscat – using the name Domaine des Prélats, while M Engel's other vineyards also produce the complete range of wines. He makes a small amount of Crémant d'Alsace, and a Rouge d'Alsace. The wines are normally aged briefly in wood before bottling. The vineyards are in a fine situation at the foot of the Haut Koenigsbourg castle. *Open: Mon–Fri 8am–noon; 3–7pm.*

Louis Gisselbrecht
67650 Dambach-la-Ville. Vineyards owned: Alsace AC 12ha. 900,000 bottles. VP-R and N
This firm produces a full range of wines in a modern style, vinified in stainless steel, which are always attractively fresh and drinkable, but without great depth. They are proudest of their Riesling produced from their own vineyards in Dambach-la-Ville. *Open: Appointment preferred.*

Willy Gisselbrecht et Fils
3a Route du Vin, 67650 Dambach-la-Ville. Vineyards owned: Alsace AC 15ha. 1·8 million bottles. VP-R and N

A large *négociant* business, producing a range of good-quality wines. They use a mixture of wood, glass-lined tanks and stainless steel and follow traditional vinification methods. Their philosophy is to bottle the wines quickly to cut the use of sulphur down to a minimum. The range covers all the varietal styles, plus Edelzwicker and Crémant d'Alsace. They also make a small amount of Grand Cru Frankstein. Brand names used are Willy Gisselbrecht and Antoine Heinrich. *Open: Mon–Fri 9am–noon; 2–6pm.*

Domaine André et Rémy Gresser
2 Rue de l'Ecole, 67140 Andlau. Vineyards owned: Grand Cru Wiebelsberg 1ha; Grand Cru Moenchberg 0·4ha; Grand Cru Kastelberg 0·2ha; Alsace AC 8·5ha. 60,000 bottles. VP-R
This small family vineyard was established in 1667, but they have moved with the times. They now use stainless steel for vinification, but still age in wood. The largest production is of Sylvaner and Riesling, and their Grand Cru wines are all Riesling. Some of the Wiebelsberg wine is from 60-year-old vines. *Open: Mon–Fri 11am–7pm.*

Bernard Haegi
33 Rue de la Montagne, 67140 Mittelbergheim. Vineyards owned: Grand Cru Zotzenberg 0·5ha; Alsace AC 5·5ha. 50,000 bottles. VP-R
The leading wine at this small firm is of Riesling, both Alsace AC and Grand Cru Zotzenberg. The vinification is mainly in wood, with some of the Pinot Noir being treated in stainless steel to give extra colour. They also make a Crémant d'Alsace from Pinot Noir and Pinot Blanc. *Open: By appointment only.*

Jean Hauller et Fils
92 Rue du Mal-Foch, 67650 Dambach-la-Ville. VP-R and N
A medium-sized *négociant* firm that also owns some vineyards around Dambach-la-Ville, with Riesling from Schwerwiller and Gewurztraminer from Hahnenberg. However, they do not vinify their own grapes separately from fruit which they buy in. They make *Vendange Tardive* from Gewurztraminer under the name

Cuvée Saint-Sebastian. Quality is enjoyable rather than exciting. *Open: Mon–Sat 9–11:30am; 1:30–6pm.*

Hering et Fils
67140 Barr. Vineyards owned: Kirchberg Grand Cru and Alsace AC 8ha. 90,000 bottles. VP-R
Apart from a holding in the Kirchberg Grand Cru, Pierre Hering has vines in two other vineyards: Clos de la Folie Marco (for Sylvaner) and Gaensbroennel (for Gewurztraminer). His best wine is the Riesling from the Kirchberg vineyard, but he makes a full range of wines (apart from Tokay Pinot Gris). *Open: By appointment only.*

Domaine Klipfel
6 Avenue de la Gare, 67140 Barr. Vineyards owned: 39ha. N
The largest merchant house in Barr. It operates under two names: Louis Klipfel for estate wines and Eugène Klipfel for *négociant* wines. Unsurprisingly, the estate wines are better, and examples such as the Gewurztraminer Grand Cru Clos Zisser are well able to age. On their Freiberg estate, they make some deliciously spicy Tokay Pinot Gris. *Open: 10am–noon; 2–6pm.*

Michel Laugel
102 Rue Général de Gaulle, 67520 Marlenheim. Vineyards owned: Alsace AC 6ha. 6 million bottles. VP-R and N
A large *négociant* firm which dominates the northern end of the Alsace vineyards. They produce a wide range, of which the most interesting is the selection of village wines. These are varietals made from vineyards in villages that are particularly famous for that grape variety: Riesling de Wolxheim, Gewurztraminer de Wangen, Pinot Noir de Marlenheim (a rosé) and Pinot Rouge de Marlenheim. They also produce Crémant d'Alsace. *Open: By appointment only.*

Frédéric Mochel
56 Rue Principale, 67310 Traenheim. Vineyards owned: Grand Cru Altenberg de Bergbieten 4ha; Alsace AC 4ha. 80,000 bottles. VP-R

M Mochel produces Sylvaner, Pinot Blanc (locally called Klevner), Riesling, Muscat, Tokay Pinot Gris, Gewurztraminer and Pinot Noir from his vineyard in and around Traenheim. His methods are traditional. Riesling Grand Cru Altenberg is his finest wine, and some of it forms a Cuvée Henriette, made from 30-year-old vines. *Open: 8am–noon; 2–4pm.*

Mosbach
67520 Marlenheim. VP-R
There's no mistaking the cellars of the family of Mosbach on the main street of Marlenheim: the large pink bottles proclaim it all. As with other producers in the village, their speciality is wine from the Pinot Noir grape; they also make a rosé called Vorlauf. Their vineyards represent nearly one-third of the village's total production.

Cave Vinicole d'Obernai Divinal
30 Rue du Général Leclerc, 67210 Obernai. Vineyards owned: Alsace AC 800ha. 6 million bottles. Coop
A modern cooperative, founded in 1962, using stainless steel and producing a full range of Alsace wines. Brand names include Divinal and Fritz Kobus. They also make a Crémant d'Alsace. *Open: By appointment only.*

Cave Vinicole d'Orschwiller
67600 Orschwiller. Vineyards owned: Alsace AC 110ha. 1·2 million bottles. Coop (141 members)
This cooperative produces the full range of varietal wines from vineyards around Sélestat and Ribeauvillé. They have two labels, Moenchenbornes and the rather better Les Faîtières. Quality is good generally, and the wines are fresh, fruity and light in style. *Open: Appointment preferred.*

Domaine Ostertag
87 Rue Finkwiller, 67680 Epfig. Vineyards owned: Grand Cru Muenchberg 1·2ha; Alsace 3ha. 70,000 bottles. VP-R
A small firm producing high-quality wine, marred only by the head of a paschal lamb on their label (Ostertag means Easter Day). They make the full range of varietals, but their finest wine is the

Riesling Muenchberg which is well balanced, green, steely and full. A small amount of Gewurztraminer is made in good years, and they offer a Crémant d'Alsace. *Open: Appointment preferred.*

Alsace Seltz
21 Rue Principale, 67140 Mittelbergheim. Vineyards owned: Grand Cru Zotzenberg 3ha; Alsace AC 6ha. 130,000 bottles. VP-R and N
While the majority of this firm's production is from their own vineyards, they buy in some Sylvaner from the Zotzenberg vineyard (which cannot make Grand Cru wine), and produce one of the best Alsace Sylvaners I have tasted. They have a small amount of Riesling in the Brandluft vineyard, but their Grand Cru wine is all Gewurztraminer. Brand names are Alsace Seltz and Pierre Seltz. *Open: By appointment only.*

Louis Siffert Fils
16 Route du Vin, 67600 Orschwiller. Vineyards owned: Grand Cru Praelatenberg 2ha; Alsace AC 9ha. 100,000 bottles. VP-R
An old-established (1792) family vineyard holding, specializing in Gewurztraminer and Riesling wines. They make half the wine in wood, half in stainless steel and blend the two. They make Gewurztraminer *Vendange Tardive* in good years. *Open: Mon–Sat 8am–noon; 2–7pm.*

Alsace Willm
BP 13, 32 Rue du Docteur Sultzer, 67140 Barr. Vineyards owned: Grand Cru Kirchberg 3ha; Alsace AC 17ha. 500,000 bottles. VP-R and N
The top wines from this medium-sized *négociant* firm are vinified in wood, while the standard range goes through stainless steel and early bottling. Apart from the usual Alsace range, labelled Alsace Willm, they make a Riesling Kirchberg and a Gewurztraminer from the Clos Gaensbroennel. The *réserve* wines are called Cuvée Emile Willm. They also make a range of Crémant d'Alsace including Crémant Prestige from *réserve* wines. The cooperative of Eguisheim has bought an interest in the firm. *Open: Mon–Fri 8:30am–noon; 1:30–6pm.*

A Zimmermann Fils
3 Grand Rue, 67600 Orschwiller. Vineyards owned: Alsace
AC 12ha. 100,000 bottles. VP-R
The vineyard, on the slopes of the Haut Koenigsbourg château, has
been in the Zimmermann family since 1693. They make all the
varietal wines, with particular emphasis on Riesling, Gewurztraminer and Tokay Pinot Gris. Methods are traditional and wood is
used. *Open: By appointment only.*

Haut-Rhin Producers

Caves Jean-Baptiste Adam
5 Rue de l'Aigle, 68770 Ammerschwihr. Vineyards owned:
Grand Cru 4ha; Alsace AC 5·4ha. 1 million bottles. VP-R
and N
The large merchant house of Adam has been in existence since 1614,
and is now by far the largest producer in Ammerschwihr. Their
small vineyard holding includes some land in the Kaefferkopf
vineyard (the most famous in the village), from which they make
Riesling and Gewurztraminer, Cuvée Jean Baptiste, which is a
speciality of the house. Their Grand Cru holding is in the
Sommerberg vineyard. They mix modern and traditional techniques to produce a standard range of quite acceptable quality.
Open: Appointment preferred.

Lucien Albrecht
68500 Orschwihr
The biggest domaine in Orschwihr, in existence since 1770. The
wines, especially Riesling and Gewurztraminer, are often of high
quality. Grand Cru wines such as the Grand Cru Riesling
Pfingstberg can age gracefully for many years. Of the less expensive
wines, the Riesling Himmelreich has excellent zest. Gewurztra-
miners include the Cuvée Martine, named after one of the
daughters of the family.

Coopérative Vinicole de Beblenheim et Environs
Rue de Hoen, 68980 Beblenheim. Vineyards owned: Grand

Cru and Alsace AC 275ha. 4 million bottles. Coop (200 members)
Newly installed modern equipment at this large cooperative produces the usual range of varietal wines, including some Grand Crus from the Sonnenglanz vineyard. The standard is average, and their wines are drunk with pleasure but without too much seriousness. *Open: Mon–Sun 10am–noon; 2–6pm.*

J Becker
4 Route d'Ostheim, Zellenberg, 68340 Riquewihr.
Vineyards owned: Grand Cru 3·5ha; Alsace AC 8·6ha.
400,000 bottles. VP-R and N
One-third of the production at this firm is from its own vineyards, two-thirds is from bought-in grapes and wine. They tend to a dry style of wine and are keen to produce wines which age well – 15-year-old Rieslings from this firm are often more appealing than two-year-old wines. They vinify grapes from their own vineyards separately, and make quite a range of single-vineyard wines as well as the generic varietals. Their brand names are J Becker and Gaston Beck. *Open: (Summer) Mon–Sun 8am–noon; 2–6pm. (Winter) Mon–Fri and Sat morning.*

Les Caves de Bennwihr
Rue de Général de Gaulle, 68630 Bennwihr. Vineyards owned: Alsace AC 350ha. 3 million bottles. Coop (260 members)
Bennwihr's vineyards were devastated in the Second World War; the cooperative took over the replanting and now nearly every grower in the village is a member. They have modern equipment which allows them to make clean, simple wines which can be very pleasant to drink. Their brand names include Les Caves Klug, Victor Preiss and Cuvée Hansi (for the Crémant d'Alsace). *Open: Mon–Fri 9–11am; 2–5pm.*

Léon Beyer
BP 1, 68420 Eguisheim. Vineyards owned: Alsace AC 20ha. 700,000 bottles. VP-R and N
A most respected firm, whose origins date back to 1580, making it one of the oldest in Alsace. Their wines cover the usual range of

Alsace varietals, but they are particularly proud of their Riesling Cuvée des Ecaillers and Cuvée Particulière, as well as their Gewurztraminer, for which Eguisheim is noted. They also have a soft spot for their Rosé Pinot Noir – but I am less convinced about that.

The prized borderland of Alsace, combining the cultures of France and Germany

MM Paul Blanck et Fils (Domaine des Comtes de Lupfen) 32 Grand-Rue, Kientzheim, 68240 Kayserberg. Vineyards owned: 22ha. 192,000 bottles. VP-R and N

This firm operates both as *négociant* and as *viticulteur* for its own domaine, which takes its name from the castle of Kientzheim, built by the counts of Lupfen and now the home of the Confrérie de Saint-Etienne. It owns a portion of the Grand Cru Schlossberg from which it produces a Riesling; other parts of the production include Gewurztraminer from Furstentum and Riesling from Patergarten. They specialize in Tokay Pinot Gris (a Comte de Lupfen is reputed to have brought the vine from Hungary). The *négociant* side of their business goes under the name of Blanck Frères. *Open: By appointment only.*

Paul Buecher et Fils (Domaine Sainte Gertrude) 15 Rue Ste Gertrude, Wettolsheim, 68000 Colmar. Vineyards owned: Grand Cru and Alsace AC 20ha. 200,000 bottles. VP-R

This firm owns vineyards in eight communes which gives them, they believe, the possibility of producing blends which are very typical of Alsace. Their Grand Cru wine comes from the Hengst vineyard in Wintzenheim. Their best wines are vinified in wood, while the standard range goes through stainless steel. *Open: Mon–Sun 8am–noon; 2–6pm.*

Theo Cattin
68420 Voegtlinshoffen. VP-R and N
Their own vineyards provide half the grapes needed by this firm: the rest come from local growers. The family has been in Voegtlinshoffen since the 17th century. They make a speciality of the Muscat, which is widely appreciated in this village. Their top *cuvées* go under the name of Cuvée de l'Ours Noir. *Open: By appointment only.*

Dopff 'Au Moulin'
2 Avenue J-Preiss, 68340 Riquewihr. Vineyards owned: Grand Cru 12·3ha; Alsace AC 50ha. 2·5 million bottles. VP-R and N
Seventy-five percent of the firm's grapes are bought in from 600 growers. Production is on a large scale, covering the complete varietal range plus some Grand Cru wines from the Brand in Turckheim and the Sporen and Schoenenbourg in Riquewihr. Standards are maintained, though, and most Alsace wine drinkers will have enjoyed bottles from this firm. The 'Au Moulin' was added to their name to avoid confusion with Dopff et Irion (*qv*). The families in the two firms are related but there are no business connections. *Open: Mon–Sat 8am–noon; 2–6pm.*

Dopff et Irion (Château de Riquewihr)
68340 Riquewihr. Vineyards owned: Grand Cru and Alsace AC 27ha. 2·8 million bottles. VP-R and N
The largest producer in Riquewihr, whose old premises occupy one side of the courtyard behind the Hôtel de Ville. They have recently constructed immense warehouse and bottling facilities on the edge of the village. Most of their production is in stainless steel, after pressing with modern pneumatic presses rather than the Vaslin press which is seen more often in Alsace. Their wines are highly enjoyable considering the scale of the operations, and I particularly like the wines from their own estates – Riesling Les Murailles,

Gewurztraminer Les Sorcières, Muscat Les Amandiers and Tokay Pinot Gris Les Maquisards. Their style is light and fresh, but they also make some *Vendange Tardive* and *Sélection des Grains Nobles* wines. Dopff et Irion were pioneers of the concept of Crémant d'Alsace. *Open: Mon–Sun 8am–6pm. By appointment in winter.*

Cave Vinicole d'Eguisheim
6 Grand Rue, 68420 Eguisheim. Vineyards owned: Grand Cru and Alsace AC 967ha. 9 million bottles. Coop (750 members)
The largest cooperative in Alsace, drawing its grapes from nine communes surrounding Eguisheim. In addition, it bottles wine for the cooperatives at Dambach-la-Ville and Cave Vinicole du Vieil Armand. Under the brand name Wolfberger it makes a full range of wines, from standard quality to special *cuvées*. Grand Cru wines come from Hengst, Eichberg, Steingrubler, Hatschbourg, Oll-willer, Spiegel and Pfersigberg vineyards. *Open: Appointment preferred.*

Paul Ginglinger
8 Place Charles de Gaulle, 68420 Eguisheim. Vineyards owned: Grand Cru and Alsace AC 9ha. 80,000 bottles. VP-R
Dryness and lightness are the characteristics of the wines from this small firm, which dates back to 1636. They use wood for much of the vinification and for maturing. Their largest production is of Riesling, but they also make the usual range of varietal wines. Also produced are a Crémant d'Alsace and *Vendange Tardive* wines. Grand Cru wines come from the Eichberg and Pfersigberg vineyards in Eguisheim. *Open: Mon–Sat morning and afternoon.*

Hugel et Fils
3 Rue de la Première Armée, 68340 Riquewihr. Vineyards owned: Grand Cru 13·3ha; Alsace AC 2ha. 1·3 million bottles. VP-R and N
Certainly the most famous name in Alsace wine, the Hugel firm, founded in 1639, manages to live up to its reputation. Their style is for full, rich wines, but their standard range of varietals is always appealingly fresh and clean and of high quality. Their finest wines

are matured in wood, but they also use stainless steel, and they use as few chemicals as possible in their winemaking. Hugel pioneered the idea of late-harvest wines – the *Vendange Tardive* and *Sélection des Grains Nobles* – and their examples are always superb and never too cloyingly sweet. Recently they have been producing quite the best red Pinot Noir wine in Alsace. Their range consists of three levels – standard varietals, *Cuvée Tradition* and *Réserve Personelle* – topped up by the late-harvest wines. *Open: Mon–Thur 9am–noon; 2–5pm. Fri 9am–noon. Shop open Mon–Sun.*

Cave Coopérative d'Ingersheim
1 Rue Georges Clémenceau, Ingersheim, 68000 Colmar. Vineyards owned: Grand Cru and Alsace AC 260ha. 3 million bottles. Coop (210 members)
A long-established cooperative which dates from 1925. Today, it makes the full range of varietals in a simple, attractive, very drinkable style. They also make a few more serious wines, including Gewurztraminer from the Letzenberg and Florimont vineyards, Riesling from the Steinweg vineyard and Riesling Grand Cru Sommerberg. *Open: Mon–Fri by appointment only; Sat–Sun no appointment necessary.*

Cave Vinicole de Kientzheim-Kaysersberg
Kientzheim, 68240 Kaysersberg. Vineyards owned: Grand Cru and Alsace AC 140ha. 2 million bottles. Coop (150 members)
A 30-year-old cooperative making all the Alsace varietal wines, including some from the Grand Cru vineyards of Schlossberg, Kaefferkopf and Altenberg de Bergheim. They also produce a Crémant d'Alsace. *Open: Groups only, by appointment.*

Kuehn
3 Grande Rue, 68770 Ammerschwihr. Vineyards owned: Alsace AC 140ha. 500,000 bottles. VP-R and N
A famous house, dating back to 1675, which makes good-quality wines from its own vineyards in Ammerschwihr (including some in the Kaefferkopf vineyard) and from grapes brought in from local growers. They use wood for most of their vinification, to make quite full, rich wines in a fine, old-fashioned style. Brand names

include Charme d'Alsace (for an Edelzwicker), a Crémant d'Alsace called Baron de Schiele and a Gewurztraminer called Cuvée St-Hubert. A good way to try Kuehn wines is to visit the three-star Michelin restaurant Aux Armes de France which occupies the same building as Kuehn. *Open: Appointment preferred.*

Kuentz-Bas
14 Route du Vin, Husseren-les-Châteaux, 68420
Herrlisheim. Vineyards owned: Alsace AC 12ha. 300,000
bottles. VP-R and N
A medium-sized firm producing excellent wines at all quality levels. They produce two ranges: *Cuvée Tradition* which is made from bought-in grapes, and *Réserve Personelle* from their own vineyards. *Vendange Tardive* wines are called Cuvée Caroline. In the past ten years, they have increased the number of wines so as to make smaller quantities of each *cuvée*. I have particularly enjoyed their Muscat (blended from Muscat d'Alsace and Muscat Ottonel) and their Tokay Pinot Gris *Réserve Personnelle*, but all their wines are of high quality and are elegantly restrained. *Open: Mon–Fri 8am–noon; 2–6pm.*

Gustave Lorentz
35 Grand Rue, 68750 Bergheim. Vineyards owned: Grand
Cru 46ha; Alsace AC 105ha. 3 million bottles. VP-R and N
A large-scale firm which nevertheless manages to retain high quality in a wide range of wines, which includes *Vendange Tardive* and *Sélection des Grains Nobles*. They use some modern equipment in the cellars, with some temperature control of fermentation, and only use the natural yeast from the grapes because it 'gives a natural quality to the wine'. They have vineyards mainly in Bergheim, but also buy from growers in Ribeauvillé and Bergheim. Better wines are matured in wood, lesser ones in glass-lined tanks. Grand Cru wines come from the Altenberg de Bergheim and Kanzlerberg vineyards. *Open: Mon–Fri 8am–noon; 2–5pm.*

Jos Meyer et Fils
76 Rue Clémenceau, Wintzenheim, 68000 Colmar.
Vineyards Grand Cru and Alsace AC 14ha. 400,000 bottles.
VP-R and N

Vineyards in Turckheim and Wintzenheim (including some land in the Grand Cru Hengst) form the core of this grower-*négociant* business. While one of their specialities is Pinot Blanc, I have always been impressed by their Rieslings, especially Les Pierrets, and by the Gewurztraminer Les Archenets. The Hengst vineyard produces fine Riesling and Gewurztraminer including some *Vendange Tardive*. Their style is often dry and elegant, but some of their top wines have considerable fullness. *Open: Mon–Fri 10am–noon; 2–5pm.*

Muré (Clos St-Landelin)
68250 Rouffach. Vineyards owned: Grand Cru 16ha. 500,000 bottles. VP-R and N
The land in the Clos St-Landelin Grand Cru Vorbourg vineyard is treated without chemicals, and vinified traditionally in wood. This vineyard produces about 140,000 bottles a year. Grand Cru varietals are Riesling, Tokay Pinot Gris, Muscat and Gewurztraminer. Standard Alsace AC wines include the full range of varietals. Since 1982, they have also made a Crémant d'Alsace. All their wines tend to be full and soft, while the Grand Cru wines often age particularly well. *Open: Mon–Sat 8am–6pm.*

Cave Vinicole de Pfaffenheim
5 Rue du Chai, 68250 Pfaffenheim. Vineyards owned: Grand Cru Goldert and Alsace AC 200ha. 2·5 million bottles. Coop (200 members)
A well-run modern cooperative, using stainless steel, and making wines that are attractive to drink young. They make a full range, but the largest production is of Sylvaner, Pinot Blanc and Gewurztraminer. The Grand Cru Goldert wine is Gewurztraminer. Company names used are Hartenberger, J Hornstein and Ernest Wein, plus a whole range of different *cuvée* names. *Open: Mon–Sun 8am–noon; 1:30–6pm.*

Preiss-Henny
68630 Mittelwihr. Vineyards owned: Alsace AC 20ha. 250,000 bottles. VP-R and N
The Preiss family came to Mittelwihr in 1535 and the family firm is now the largest in the village. They supply over a half of their

requirements from their own vineyards. In the cellars, they use few chemicals and like to bottle their wines *sur lie* direct from the fermentation vats to give extra flavour and to avoid any contact with the air by racking. Quality is high, and I have enjoyed all their wines. Cuvée Marcel Preiss and Camille Preiss are two of their brand names.

Preiss-Zimmer
42 Rue du Général de Gaulle, 68340 Riquewihr. Vineyards owned: Alsace AC 8ha. 200,000 bottles. VP-R and N
A small *négociant* house, whose reputation is higher than its production. They operate very traditionally in cellars beneath the main street of Riquewihr. All the vinification is in wood. Their best wines are Gewurztraminer, but they also make a good, peppery Tokay Pinot Gris. They produce Grand Cru Schoenenberg. *Open: By appointment only.*

Cave Coopérative de Ribeauvillé et Environs
2 Route de Colmar, 68150 Ribeauvillé. Vineyards owned: Alsace AC 175ha. 2 million bottles. Coop (90 members)
Pinot Blanc, Riesling and Sylvaner are the biggest production from what is probably the oldest cooperative in France, founded in 1895. They have a range of modern equipment producing some very good middle-of-the-road wines. The small Clos de Zahnacker (planted with Riesling, Gewurztraminer and Tokay) produces their best wines. Brand names they use include Martin Zahn, Traber, Medaillon and Armoires. Their Crémant d'Alsace is called Giersberger. *Open: Mon–Sat 9am–noon; 2–5:30pm. Oct–Mar by appointment only.*

Rolly Gassmann
Rorschwihr, 68590 St-Hippolyte
Louis Gassmann and his wife Marie-Thérèse (née Rolly) have built up an enviable reputation for high-quality wines, including the Gewurztraminer Kappelweg, Riesling Silberberg, the Tokay Pinot Gris Réserve, and even a ripely aromatic Pinot Blanc. Louis Gassmann likes to vinify the grapes from his different vineyards separately in order to produce wines with strong individual characteristics.

Domaine Martin Schaetzel
68770 Ammerschwihr. Vineyards owned: Alsace AC 5·2ha. 50,000 bottles. VP-R
M Jean Schaetzel, who studied oenology in Dijon, uses small (30 hectolitre) barrels for vinifying his wines, partly because he is handling small quantities of wine and partly because he believes this gives him better temperature control. He makes his wines – especially his Gewurztraminer and Tokay Pinot Gris – for ageing (up to ten years, he says). His top Gewurztraminer is called Cuvée Isabelle. *Open: Mon–Sat 8am–7pm.*

Edgard Schaller et Fils
1 Rue du Château, 68630 Mittelwihr. Vineyards owned: Grand Cru 2ha. Alsace AC 5·5ha. 75,000 bottles. VP-R
One of the many ancient family firms, founded in 1609. Much of their production is of Crémant, but they also make the full range of varietals. *Open: Mon–Fri 8am–noon; 2–7pm.*

André Scherer
Husseren-les-Châteaux, 68420 Herrlisheim. Vineyards owned: Grand Cru and Alsace AC 8ha. 120,000 bottles. VP-R and N
A wide range is produced by this firm. Half the wines come from their own vineyards, half from grapes which are bought locally. They make the usual range of varietals, including Grand Cru wine from the Eichberg vineyard of Eguisheim. Brand names include Cuvée Jean–Baptiste and Cuvée Blanche. One of their best varietals is their Tokay Pinot Gris, and they are one of the rare Alsace producers whose red Pinot Noir is full-bodied and has good colour. *Open: By appointment only.*

Charles Schleret
68230 Turckheim
A grower who has established a modern cellar in Turckheim from which he produces a range of true-to-type varietal wines. He is best known for his Tokay Pinot Gris, his Gewurztraminer and his Pinot Noir, from which he gets more colour than usual by means of heated fermentation vats. *Open: By appointment only.*

Domaines Schlumberger
100 Rue Théodore Deck, 68500 Guebwiller. Vineyards owned: Grand Cru 60ha; Alsace AC 80ha. 1 million bottles. VP-R

Schlumberger dominates the village of Guebwiller, controlling much of the vineyard area. Being the largest private vineyard owners in Alsace, they are able to develop new techniques of large-scale planting in horizontal rows on the steep slopes above Guebwiller, which contrasts with the normal Alsace method of vines growing up single stakes. They make Grand Cru wines from Kitterlé, Kessler, Spiegel and Saering vineyards. Their wines can be variable, but their Riesling Kitterlé and the Gewurztraminer Cuvée Christine Schlumberger are both good wines. *Open: By appointment only.*

Domaine Sick-Dreyer
9 Route de Kientzheim, 68770 Ammerschwihr. Vineyards owned: Alsace AC 12ha. 90,000 bottles. VP-R

The finest wine from this small estate is its Gewurztraminer from their holding on the Kaefferkopf vineyard. They make the full range of varietals to a good quality level, using a mix of traditional and modern techniques and vinifying 90 percent of the wine in wood. While most of their vineyards are in Ammerschwihr, they also own land in Eguisheim, Katzenthal and Sigolsheim. *Open: Appointment preferred.*

Société Coopérative Vinicole de Sigolsheim et Environs
12 Rue Saint-Jacques, Sigolsheim, 68240 Kaysersberg. Vineyards owned: Grand Cru 31·5ha; Alsace AC 248ha. 3 million bottles. Coop (230 members)

One of the largest cooperatives in Alsace, with modern equipment producing a wide range of good-quality wines. They produce wines from the Grand Cru Mambourg vineyard and from the Vogelgarten vineyard, plus *Vendange Tardive* and *Sélection des Grains Nobles* – all from Gewurztraminer. The brand names of this company include Comte de Sigold for Crémant d'Alsace. *Open: Mon–Fri 8–10:30am; 2–4:30pm. Sundays in summer. Appointments preferred for groups.*

Louis Sipp
68150 Ribeauvillé. VP–R and N

A firm that has concentrated on producing commercial wines, both from its vineyard holdings and from grapes bought in from growers. They vinify grapes from their holding in the Grand Cru of Kirchberg de Ribeauvillé separately, but otherwise do not identify their estate wines.

Pierre Sparr et ses Fils
2 Rue de la Première Armée Française, 68240 Sigolsheim. Vineyards owned: Grand Cru 4·2ha; Alsace AC 23·8ha. 1·6 million bottles. VP–R and N

This firm of *négociants* buys in three-quarters of its requirements from other growers in the Sigolsheim and Kaysersberg area. Their own vineyards are in Sigolsheim (including Grand Cru Mambourg), Kientzheim and Turckheim (including Grand Cru Brand). Brand names they use include Edelzwicker Alsaflor, Edelzwicker Rayon d'Alsace, Diamant d'Alsace (for Pinot Blanc), Crustalsa and Sparr Prestige (for their best wines). They make *Vendange Tardive* from Tokay Pinot Gris and *Sélection des Grains Nobles* from Gewurztraminer. *Open: Sun–Fri 8am–noon.*

F E Trimbach
68150 Ribeauvillé. Vineyards owned: Alsace Grand Cru and Alsace 28ha. 750,000 bottles. VP–R and N

One of the oldest firms in Alsace (1626), with a long tradition of making fine wines both as a merchant house and vineyard owner. They make three quality levels: standard, *Réserve* and *Réserve Personnelle*. Their own vineyards include land in Ribeauvillé, Hunawihr (Clos Ste-Hune), Bergheim, Riquewihr and Mittelwihr. Top *cuvées* are of Clos Ste-Hune, Frédéric Emil and Seigneurs de Ribeaupierre.

Cave Coopérative de Turckheim
68230 Turckheim. Vineyards owned: Alsace Grand Cru and Alsace 200ha. Coop (260 members)

One of the most go-ahead cooperatives in Alsace, which has had great success with its well-priced wines, widely available in the export markets. Wines such as the Pinot Blanc and Gewurztraminer regularly win awards. The cellars of the cooperative are highly modern and rely on the latest computer technology, as well as rows of stainless steel tanks. *Open: Mon–Sat 8am–noon; 2–6pm.*

Domaine Weinbach
68240 Kaysersberg. Vineyards owned: Alsace AC 22ha. 180,000 bottles. VP-R
Mme Théo Faller and her children, who run the Domaine Weinbach estate (also known as the Clos des Capucins), have established an enviable reputation for top-quality Alsace wines. They have stayed faithful to traditional methods, vinifying in wood, avoiding the centrifuging which so many Alsace producers seem to insist on, and producing full-bodied yet perfectly characteristic wines. The grapes are harvested late to give the wines considerable ageing potential. Cuvée Théo is the best Riesling from this estate. *Open: By appointment only.*

Coopérative Vinicole de Westhalten
52 Rue de Soultzmatt, 68250 Westhalten. Vineyards owned: Grand Cru and Alsace AC 270ha. 3 million bottles. Coop (220 members)
This cooperative now controls the *négociant* firm of Alfred Heim, also based in Westhalten. They make a wide range of wines at different levels of quality, including Grand Cru wine from the Vorbourg and Zinnkoepfle vineyards. The quality of some of the more basic wines is disappointing, but in the top ranges they make some good wines, especially Muscat d'Alsace (Westhalten is in a sheltered side valley which is advantageous for the ripening of Muscat) and Gewurztraminer. The Heim wines are still sold under separate labels. *Open: Mon–Sat 8am–noon; 2–6pm.*

Widerhirn
68340 Riquewihr. Vineyards owned: Grand Cru and Alsace AC 5·3ha. 40,000 bottles. VP-R
High-quality, but small-scale producer who has a small holding in the Schoenenbourg and Sporen vineyards. His methods are traditional, with much wood in evidence in his small cellar. M Widerhirn's wines age well – especially his Riesling and Tokay Pinot Gris. He makes small quantities of Gewurztraminer *Vendange*

Tardive, but normally his style is dry. *Open: By appointment only.*

Domaine Zind-Humbrecht
34 Rue du Maréchal Joffre, Wintzenheim, 68000 Colmar.
Vineyards owned: Grand Cru and Alsace AC 30·5ha.
200,000 bottles. VP–R

For Alsace, this is a large vineyard holding. The majority of it consists of 30 percent Riesling and 34 percent Gewurztraminer, but they have the full range of varietals. They bottle their wines *sur lie* without filtration, which gives them extra body and considerable depth of flavour. Their Grand Cru wines come from Brand in Turckheim, Goldert in Gueberschwihr, Hengst in Wintzenheim and Rangen in Thann – the southernmost vineyard in Alsace, which Zind-Humbrecht has effectively resurrected in recent years. *Open: Mon–Fri 8am–noon; 2–6pm.*

Savoie

The Alpine vineyards of Savoie lie south of Lake Geneva. Most are set along the upper valley of the Rhône as it flows towards Lyon, in its tributary valley with the Lac du Bourget, and along the valley of the Isère as it flows southwest to Grenoble. Slopes above the lakes or the Rhône at around 300 metres are the favoured sites. Major towns in the area include Annecy and Aix-les-Bains as well as Chambéry, the home of France's best vermouths. It is almost as if the wines of Savoie were designed for the après-ski parties during which they are consumed in quantity. Both the reds and the whites are best drunk within a year of the harvest – light, refreshing and enjoyably unmemorable. The sparkling wines are the only ones that tend to leave the region. Because the vineyards of Savoie are so scattered, microclimates play an important part in the quality of the wines. The two lakes, of Geneva and of Bourget near Aix-les-Bains, influence and moderate the Alpine weather extremes, as do the fast-moving rivers.

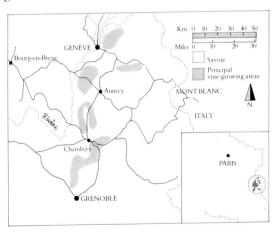

There is a hint of Switzerland in the wines made from the Chasselas grape on the southern shores of Lake Geneva at Crépy, and an influence from Beaujolais in the Gamay which is used to make light red wines. But there are also local grape varieties in the

1,500 hectares of vineyard. The Mondeuse makes a simple full-bodied red. The Jacquère is a widely planted white grape which makes crisp wines to be drunk young. The Altesse (or Roussette) makes soft wines, while the Bergeron (akin to the Roussanne of the southern Rhône) makes finer whites around Chambéry. The sparkling wines, made in the region of Seyssel, are a blend of Chasselas with Altesse and Molette.

Vintages: most Savoie wines need to be drunk young. Wines made from the Mondeuse grape occasionally repay keeping for a couple of years. '83, '85 and '86 were good recent vintages.

The Appellations
Appellations Contrôlées

The AC system is probably more complex than the styles of wine warrant – a product of the fragmented vineyards.

Crépy Dry, slightly sparkling whites from the southern shore of Lake Geneva. The grape is the Chasselas (Swiss Fendant). Some claim they age, but the chance to prove this is rare since most is drunk young and locally.

Roussette de Savoie Dry white wines made mainly around Frangy north of Lac du Bourget and around Cruet in the Isère valley. The wine is normally a blend of Roussette (or Altesse) and Chardonnay (called locally Petite Sainte-Marie) with Mondeuse.

Roussette de Savoie Crus Four communes have the right to add their name to the generic Roussette de Savoie AC – Frangy, Marestel, Monterminod and Monthoux.

Seyssel Dry white wines from the commune of Seyssel on the Rhône. Only the Roussette (or Altesse) is permitted.

Seyssel Mousseux Sparkling *méthode champenoise* wines made from the Altesse and Chasselas.

Vin de Savoie Widespread AC taking in reds, dry whites and rosés. Reds and rosés are more from Mondeuse, Gamay and Pinot Noir; whites from Jacquère and Altesse with smaller amounts of Chardonnay, Aligoté and Chasselas.

Vin de Savoie Crus The 17 communes allowed to add their name to generic Vin de Savoie are: Marignan, Maurin and Ripaille (on Lake Geneva); Ayse, Charpignat, Chautagne and Jongieux (on Lac du Bourget); les Abîmes, Apremont, Arbin, Chignin, Chignin-Bergeron, Cruet, Montmélian, St Jean-de-la-Porte and Ste Jeoire-Prieuré (south of Chambéry) and Ste Marie d'Alloix (towards Grenoble).

Vin de Savoie Ayse Mousseux Sparkling *méthode champenoise* wine made in the commune of Ayse.

Vin de Savoie Mousseux Mainly white (with a little rosé) sparkling *méthode champenoise* wine made in other Vin de Savoie Cru villages.

Vin de Savoie Pétillant Lightly sparkling, sometimes sweet wines are made in the Roussette de Savoie Cru villages of Frangy, Marestel and Monthoux.

Vins de Pays

Regional Vin de Pays

The regional *vin de pays* of Comtes Rhodaniens (*see also* the Rhône) covers the whole of the Savoie area. The wines come from a wide range of grape varieties: Cabernet Sauvignon, Cinsault, Syrah, Grenache and Merlot for reds; Chardonnay, Marsanne, Roussanne, Sauvignon Blanc, Viognier, Ugni Blanc, Clairette and Grenache Blanc for the whites. Of total production, 70 percent is of red wines. There are two subzones in Savoie: Vin de Pays des Coteaux du Grésivaudin and Vin de Pays des Balmes Dauphinoises.

Zonal Vin de Pays

Vin de Pays de l'Allobrogie Mainly white wines made from Jacquère, Chardonnay or Chasselas grapes, in a region to the west and south of Annecy. Some reds are also made, from Gamay, Pinot Noir and Mondeuse grapes.

Savoie Producers

Canelli-Suchet
Caves de la Tour de Marignan, 74140 Sciez. Vineyards owned: Vin de Savoie 5ha. 25,000 bottles. VP-R
M Canelli-Suchet's family has been in Savoie for more than three centuries and his name recalls that the area used to be part of an Italian kingdom. He makes wine traditionally, from Chasselas grapes. His range includes still wine aged in cask under the Marignan name and a small amount of *méthode champenoise* dry and medium-dry sparkling wine, called La Perle. *Open: By appointment only.*

Cave Coopérative de Chautagne
73310 Ruffieux. Vineyards owned: Chautagne 150ha. 400,000 bottles. Coop (200 members)
The grapes for this cooperative come from the area north of Lac du Bourget. Unusually for Savoie, over half the production here is of red and rosé wine, mainly from the Gamay, with some Pinot Noir and Mondeuse. Some reds are aged in wood after stainless steel vinification. The Pinot Noir wines age well for a couple of years. *Open: By appointment only.*

Cave Coopérative des Vins Fins Cruet
73800 Cruet. Vineyards owned: 83ha. 400,000 bottles. Coop
The best wine from this cooperative is the Vin de Savoie Arbin, made from Mondeuse, more sophisticated than the usual red from this grape. They also make a varietal Mondeuse and a white from Chignin. *Open: Mon–Sat 8am–noon; 2–6pm.*

Savoie – south of Lake Geneva

Caveau du Lac St-André (J-C Perret)
St André-les-Marches, 73800 Montmélian. Vineyards owned: 10ha (including some in the cru of Apremont). 100,000 bottles. VP-R

The main production in this modern winery is of an attractively perfumed white Vin de Savoie Apremont, made in stainless steel with a long cool fermentation to bring out the fruit. Red and rosé are made from Gamay using carbonic maceration. *Open: By appointment only.*

L Mercier et Fils
Grande Cave de Crépy, 74140 Douvaine. Vineyards owned: Crépy (Vin de Savoie AC) 30ha. 350,000 bottles. VP-R and N

The principal wine made by this large firm is a white, slightly sparkling Chasselas Vin de Savoie Goutte d'Or, which is vinified traditionally in wood. They also act as *négociants. Open: Mon–Fri 5–6pm. By appointment only.*

Michel Million Rousseau
Monthoux, 73170 St-Jean de Chevelu. Vineyards owned: Vin de Savoie 4ha; Roussette de Savoie Monthoux 1ha. 40,000 bottles. VP-R

The range of Vin de Savoie AC from this small family firm includes Gamay, Mondeuse, Pinot Noir and Jacquère, all of which are vinified and sold separately. M Million Rousseau also makes small quantities of an attractive fresh Roussette de Monthoux. The reds need around three to seven years, but the whites need to be drunk young. *Open: Mon–Sat 8am–noon; 2–7pm.*

Michel et Jean-Paul Neyroud
Les Aricoques, Designy, 74270 Frangy. Vineyards owned: Les Aricoques (Frangy) 3ha; Planaz (Designy) 3·5ha. 35,000 bottles. VP-R
While most of this firm's production is a nutty white Roussette de Savoie from Frangy, made in a modern style using stainless steel, there is also some more traditional red Vin de Savoie made from the Mondeuse grape, which can age well for two or three years. The other wine made is a Gamay, Vin de Savoie Rouge. *Open: During working hours. Appointments necessary for groups.*

J Perrier et Fils
St André-les-Marches, 73800 Montmélian. Vineyards owned: Apremont 8ha; Les Abîmes 2ha. 1,500,000 bottles. VP-R and N
Apart from their own vineyards at Apremont and Les Abîmes which produce 100 percent Jacquère Vin de Savoie AC wines, the firm also makes a large range of wines: a white Chignin and Roussette de Savoie, and Gamay de Savoie and Gamay de Chautagne. Pinot Noir is also bought in to make a Pinot de Savoie, while Mondeuse is bought from Arbin. Recent launches include a sparkling *méthode champenoise* and a *pétillant* wine. The quality from one of the largest firms in the area is generally good, if not particularly exciting. *Open: Mon–Fri 8am–noon; 2–6pm. By appointment only.*

André Quenard et Fils
Tormery, 73800 Chignin. Vineyards owned: Chignin and Chignin-Bergeron 14ha. 100,000 bottles. VP-R
All the wines made in this modern winery are 100 percent varietals. Chignin Blanc is Jacquère; Chignin-Bergeron is Roussanne; Vin de Savoie rouge is Mondeuse, with some ageing potential; Vin de Savoie rosé is Gamay. The brand name is Coteaux de Tormery. The top wine made is a rich, intense Chignin-Bergeron. *Open: By appointment only.*

Les Fils René Quenard
73800 Chignin. VP-R
Another branch of the Quenard family. They make Chignin and
Chignin-Bergeron. The Chignin Coteaux de la Maréchale is dry,
while the Chignin-Bergeron Coteaux de Mont-Ronjoux is
medium-sweet, made from Roussanne grapes.

Le Vigneron Savoyard
73190 Apremont. Vineyards owned: Apremont AC 25ha;
les Abîmes AC 8ha; Vin de Savoie AC 3ha. 40,000 bottles.
Coop (10 members)
White Vin de Savoie from the two *cru* villages of Apremont and les
Abîmes is the main production of this cooperative. Small quantities
of red Vin de Savoie are also made. Modern equipment produces
straightforward attractive clean wines. The cellars are in the farm of
the château at Apremont.

Marcel Tardy et Fils
La Plantée, Apremont 73190 Challes-les-Eaux. Vineyards
owned: 5ha. 40,000 bottles. VP-R
Small producer making a very attractive white Vin de Savoie
Apremont, adding a touch of Sauvignon to give it extra crispness
and freshness. *Open: By appointment only.*

Varichon et Clerc
Les Sechallets, 01420 Seyssel. Vineyards owned: Seyssel
100ha. 600,000 bottles. VP-R and N
Good-quality sparkling wines are the speciality of this firm. Some,
such as the Royal Seyssel, are made from local grapes, but their
Seyssel Mousseux is made from grapes bought in from other areas.
They also make a Pétillant de Savoie and still wines from the AC
Savoie. *Open: Appointments preferred.*

Bugey

Bugey lies immediately to the west of the Savoie vineyards. This
small VDQS area has recently returned to life after a long period

when it was almost moribund. In style the white wines are directly related to Savoie, while the reds (made principally from the Gamay) are closer to the Jura. The various *appellation* names are extraordinarily complex for such a minor area.

Bugey VDQS

Vin de Bugey Red, dry white and rosé from Gamay, Pinot Noir, Poulsard, Mondeuse (for red and rosé) and Altesse, Jacquère, Mondeuse Blanche, Chardonnay, Aligoté and Pinot Gris (for white).

Vin de Bugey Crus As above. Five communes can use their names: Cerdon, Machuraz, Manicle, Montagnieu, Vineu-le-Grand.

Roussette de Bugey A white made from Roussette (Altesse) and Chardonnay.

Roussette de Bugey Cru A 100 percent Roussette from six communes: Anglefort, Arbignieu, Chanay, Lagnieu, Montagnieu, Vineu-le-Grand.

Mousseux de Bugey/Pétillant de Bugey Sparkling *méthode champenoise* and naturally semi-sparkling white made with the white grapes used in Vin de Bugey. The commune of Cerdon can attach its name to the wine.

Bugey Producers

Le Caveau Bugiste
01350 Vognes. Coop
The main cooperative of the area produces a full range of wines to an acceptable standard, and a mouthwatering Gamay that reminds you that these vineyards are not too far from Beaujolais.

Eugène Monin
01350 Vognes. VP-R
The largest private producer in Bugey. M Monin makes a number of wines: a Chardonnay, which he regards as his best wine; a Roussette de Bugey, which has 75 percent Chardonnay and 25 percent Roussette (Altesse); a sparkling wine with Jacquère, Chardonnay, Aligoté and Molette; and, for reds, Pinot Noir and Gamay. Stainless steel is now used to make white.

Jura

The Jura vineyard is a shadow of its former self. As with so many out-of-the-way areas, phylloxera during the last century is to blame for the decline. But traditions have survived in this remote corner of France and at least two remarkable wines are still made here. And today new ideas are reviving old fortunes. The vineyard area of 1,450 hectares is on the eastern slopes of the Saône valley, facing across to the Burgundian Côte d'Or. The vines grow at heights of between 250 and 500 metres in wooded valleys and between half-timbered towns. The Burgundian influence is here in some of the grape varieties – Chardonnay and Pinot Noir – but there is also a flourishing set of local grape varieties which are still commonly planted.

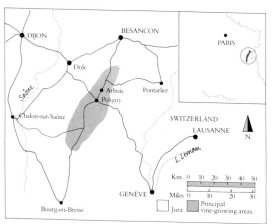

Red, white, rosé and sparkling wines are all made in the Jura. Some of the rosé is known as *vin gris*, on account of its pale pink colour achieved before fermentation. Little Jura wine – apart from *vin jaune* (*see below*) – is seen outside the area. Methods tend to be old-fashioned, although the main producer of the region (Henri Maire) has an ultra-modern plant. Traditionally, the wines are aged for considerable periods, which can make them over-oxidized for modern tastes. Sparkling wine is increasing in popularity.

Red grapes include the Poulsard (or Plousard), a light-coloured grape which is used to make rosé wines. Because of its paleness, the Poulsard can be left in contact with the must for several days, so Jura rosés tend to have great weight – akin to the Tavel of the southern Rhône. The Trousseau is used to give bite in red wines and is also used to make a sparkling *blanc de noirs*.

While Chardonnay is used to make many of the white Jura wines, it is the local grape, the Savagnin (a type of Traminer), which is used in the most unusual wines of the region. *Vin jaune* – yellow wine – is a sherry-type wine, made by ageing Savagnin in small barrels for a minimum of six years. A type of yeast – like the *flor* of Jerez – grows on the surface of the wine, producing a characteristic dry, oxidized taste. The barrels are not topped up, thus allowing the *flor* to develop in the air. It is bottled in the traditional *clavelin* of Jura, a bottle containing 64 centilitres (the amount left from a litre after evaporation), with a long neck and sloping shoulders.

The other rare wine of the region – rarer now than *vin jaune* – is called *vin de paille*. This is a sweet wine made from grapes dried on straw (*paille*) mats until they are like raisins. The nearest equivalent is the Italian Vin Santo.

Vintages: reds '82, '83, '85, '87, '88, '89. *Vin jaune*: '67, '71, '73, '76, '78, '82, '83. Whites and rosés should be drunk within two years.

The Appellations
Appellations Contrôlées

Arbois Red, dry white, rosé, *gris* and *vin jaune*.

Arbois Mousseux Sparkling wines fermented in the same bottle.

Arbois Pupillin Red, dry white and rosé from the commune of Pupillin. Slightly richer than straight Arbois.

Château-Chalon Tiny *appellation* making only 70,000 bottles a year, but producing the best *vin jaune*.

Côtes du Jura Catch-all AC, making red, dry white, rosé, *gris* and *vin jaune*.

Côtes du Jura Mousseux Sparkling wines.

L'Etoile White wines made from Chardonnay, Savagnin and Poulsard (vinified as white). Also *vin jaune* and *vin de paille*. Small production, but good quality.

L'Etoile Mousseux Sparkling version of above, blending Chardonnay and Savagnin.

Vins de Pays

Regional Vin de Pays

Vin de Pays de la Franche-Comté A *vin de pays* covering the *départements* of Jura and Haute-Saône, using the Chardonnay and Auxerrois for its white wines and Pinot Noir, Pinot Gris and Gamay for the reds.

Zonal Vin de Pays

Vin de Pays des Coteaux de Coiffy A tiny zone, in the southeast of the Haute-Marne *département*, producing 500 hectolitres of red and white wines each year.

Producers

Château d'Arlay
Arlay, 39140 Bletterans. Vineyards owned: Château d'Arlay (Arlay) 27ha. 60,000 bottles. VP–R and N
The English King William III was, among other things, Baron d'Arlay, a title still held by the Dutch Royal family. The estate has a history stretching back to the Middle Ages and vines cover the slopes beneath the mediaeval castle. A 19th-century château is home to the present owner, Comte de Laguiche.

Quality is important at the estate and only the free-run juice is used for the top Château d'Arlay range of red, rosé and white. Modern vinification is followed by wood-ageing (seven years for *vin jaune*). A small quantity of top-quality *vin jaune* is made, and in 1985, for the first time, some *vin de paille*. *Négociant* marques include Comte de Guichebourg, Baron de Proby and Cuvée de l'Epinette. *Open: Mon–Sat 9am–noon; 2–5:30pm.*

Caves Jean Bourdy
Arlay, 39140 Bletterans. Vineyards owned: Côtes du Jura 4·5ha; Château-Chalon 0·5ha. 20,000 bottles. VP–R and N
Vin jaune and Château-Chalon are the star wines from this old-established (1781) firm. They buy in finished wine as well as making Côtes du Jura white and red from their own vineyards. They also make a Marc de Franche-Comté. A highly reliable producer. *Open: Mon–Fri 9am–noon; 2–7pm. Appointments necessary for groups.*

Hubert Clavelin et Fils
Le Vernois, 39120 Voiteur. Vineyards owned: Côtes du Jura 24ha. 100,000 bottles. VP–R
The bulk of production here is of a good *méthode champenoise* made from Chardonnay, but M Clavelin also makes Côtes du Jura white and red and *vin jaune* (from Savagnin). Methods are traditional and vinification takes place in wood. *Open: By appointment only.*

Cave Coopérative de Château-Chalon et Côtes du Jura
39120 Voiteur. Vineyards owned: 66ha. 240,000 bottles. Coop (69 members)
The importance of this small cooperative is that it is one of the few sources for the *vin jaune* of Château-Chalon AC. But they also make Côtes du Jura white and rosé, and *vin jaune* from the Côtes du Jura AC. *Open: By appointment only.*

Grand Frères
39120 Voiteur. VP–R
Red and white Côtes du Jura are made by this small firm. Both wines offer considerable weight and richness, and the red especially repays some ageing.

Château Gréa
**Rotalier, 39190 Beaufort. Vineyards owned: Le Clos
(Rotalier) 3·3ha; Sur Laroche (Rotalier) 0·7ha; Le Chanet
(Rotalier) 1·5ha; En Cury (Rotalier) 1ha. 30,000 bottles.
VP-R**
A small domaine in the same family since 1679. The existing
château dates from the 1770s when the cellars were also built. The
vineyards are all in the Côtes du Jura general AC. Despite the
history, modern methods are used to make a clean rosé, and a
méthode champenoise brut from Chardonnay and Pinot Noir. A fine,
richer white, Le Chanet, is made from a blend of Chardonnay and
Savagnin which is given three years in wood. Around 2,000 bottles
of *vin jaune*, called En Cury, are made in good years. Fine eau-de-
vie wines are also made here. *Open: Mon–Fri 10am–12:30pm; 2–7pm.
Appointments preferred.*

Henri Maire (Château Montfort)
**39600 Arbois. Vineyards owned: 321ha. 4·8 million bottles.
VP-R and N**
Henri Maire dominates Jura in a way that few producers can ever
dominate larger wine-producing areas. The firm has revitalized the
region, and its offices at Château Montfort house a fine collection of
19th-century glasses as well as the largest stocks of *vin jaune*
anywhere. The estate is located mainly around Montfort, Grange
Grillard, Sorbief and La Croix d'Argis. All the Jura AC wines are
made, plus a number of brands (sparkling Vin Fou is the best
known). The company also produce small quantities of one of the
best *vins jaunes*. *Open: By appointment only.*

Désiré Petit
**Pupillin, 39600 Arbois. Vineyards owned: Pupillin 8ha;
Arbois 0·8ha; Côtes du Jura 3·3ha. 75,000 bottles. VP-R**
Modern vinification in stainless steel produces whites, rosés and reds
which need little ageing. A *vin jaune* is also made and this is aged in
wood. The firm is one of the major landowners in the Arbois
Pupillin AC. *Open: Mon–Sun.*

Rolet Frères
Montigny-lès-Arsures, 39600 Arbois. Vineyards owned:

50ha. VP-R

The second-biggest producer in the Jura, this is a family business run by father, two sons and a daughter. As befits their size they have modern production facilities, where they specialize in making single-variety wines, unusual in the area. Reds include a Trousseau and a Pinot Noir, while there is a rosé from Poulsard and a white from Chardonnay which matures in new wood.

André Tissot
Quartier Bernard, Montigny-lès-Arsures, 39600 Arbois.
Vineyards owned: Montigny-lès-Arsures (Arbois) 11ha.
80,000 bottles. VP-R

A relatively new firm (founded 1959) which produces traditional wines in the vineyards where Pasteur made his studies of vine disease. Red and rosé are made from a blend of Trousseau, Poulsard and Pinot Noir, giving the red considerable depth of colour for the region. The white is 100 percent Chardonnay. All these wines are aged in wood for at least 18 months and treatments are minimal. *Vin jaune* and *vin de paille* are also made. *Open: Mon–Sun.*

Fruitière Vinicole d'Arbois
39600 Arbois. Vineyards owned: Arbois 195ha. 700,000
bottles. Coop (152 members)

As the name suggests, this cooperative is also involved in other fruit crops and is certainly one of the oldest cooperatives in France (founded 1906). A new stainless steel vinification plant has been installed to produce two principal wines: a *méthode champenoise* sparkler and a dry white. Red and rosé are also made. *Open: Mon–Fri (summer) 9am–noon; 2–6pm. Appointments necessary for groups.*

Fruitière Vinicole de Pupillin
Pupillin, 39600 Arbois. Vineyards owned: Arbois Pupillin
40ha. 200,000 bottles. Coop (25 members)

The cooperative keeps this tiny village alive. The bulk of production is of rosé, made from Poulsard. Red is made from Pinot Noir, white from Chardonnay. *Méthode champenoise* sparkling *brut* and rosé are made under the brand name Papillette. There are also small quantities of *vin jaune. Open: Mon–Sun (May to Sept) 8am–noon; 2–6pm. By appointment only.*

Loire

In its unhurried 1,021-kilometre meander through France, the Loire passes through some of the most quintessentially French countryside. Leaving the mountainous Ardèche region behind, the river passes woods and open fields, great châteaux and historic towns, travelling its tree-lined route through gentle countryside mostly devoted to agriculture – much of it to the growth of vines.

For the first part of its course the river runs north, parallel to the Saône and the Burgundy vineyards, which are only a few miles west. Almost halfway along its journey, in a huge arc, it turns west towards the Atlantic.

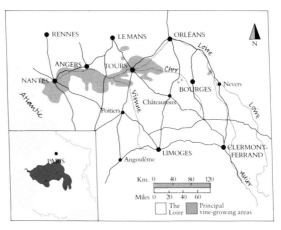

The largest Loire vineyards are almost entirely in the second half of the river's course. Well to the south, on a level with the Beaujolais, are the small VDQS areas of Côte Roannaise, Côtes du Forez and Côtes d'Auvergne and, a few miles north, Saint-Pourçain-sur-Sioule. But the first major wine areas appear just before the river turns to the west, at Sancerre and Pouilly-sur-Loire. Nearby but away from the river are the wine districts of Reuilly, Quincy and Ménétou-Salon. A little further north of Pouilly there is a small vineyard area at Gien.

At the top of the river's arc, to the west, the historic cathedral city of Orléans is the centre of a minor area of light red, white and rosé wine production. From here the river runs on westward, passing the châteaux of Touraine. At Blois, the vineyards of Cheverny produce white wines. This district is on the edge of the main Touraine wine-producing area, which has a number of smaller *appellations*: Vouvray and Montlouis, Chinon and Bourgueil, and towns like Amboise and Mesland that are *crus* within the general Touraine area.

Away to the north are the outlying vineyards of Vendôme, Coteaux du Loir and Jasnières, while to the south are the vineyards of Valençay and Haut-Poitou.

Touraine – centred around the cathedral city of Tours – is at the transitional point of the Loire vineyards. Here the Sauvignon Blanc of Sancerre and Pouilly-Fumé meets the Chenin Blanc of Anjou; the Pinot Noir and Gamay of Burgundy meet the Cabernets of Bordeaux. It is the Chenin Blanc and the Cabernets that take over in the neighbouring province of Anjou. The Chenin makes a whole range of whites, from piercingly acid and dry, still and sparkling, to lusciously sweet. The Cabernet Franc is joined by the Groslot to produce rosés: on its own it makes reds. Then, as the river continues westward, nearing its mouth, there is an abrupt change. The Chenin Blanc is replaced by the Melon de Bourgogne and the vineyards of Muscadet stretch out to the Atlantic horizon. Small pockets of Malvoisie produce a sweet white at Ancenis and the Gros Plant makes a white that can make lemon juice seem soft. While there is a great variety in the wines of the Loire, there is also a common thread. These are northern vineyards. The growing season is long and comparatively cool. This gives Loire wines their general character of intense fruit flavours and often piercing acidity. They are cool wines in climate and also in taste.

A few years ago, Loire wines were relatively unknown. Some have been discovered now but others are still waiting. The wines of Sancerre and Pouilly-Fumé and those of Muscadet are the classic discoveries and, suddenly fashionable, their price has shot up. Often the price rises have been unreasonable: these are, after all, still country wines, never reaching the peaks of Bordeaux and Burgundy.

While some wines have become fashionable, others – potentially greater – have languished. Anjou makes some of the world's great sweet wines in the small areas of Quarts de Chaume and Bonnezeaux, but few people bother to know more about them. They are the equals of Sauternes, German *Trockenbeerenauslese* or late-harvest wines and their prices are crazily cheap.

The reds of Chinon and Bourgueil also deserve more attention than they normally receive. While always suffering from their northerly situation, in good years these vineyards can produce smooth, rich wines, much more generous and rewarding than the tart reds of Sancerre that command such absurd prices.

And finally there are the tiny VDQS areas, hanging like forgotten fruit from the branches and tributaries of the Loire. Many were devastated by phylloxera and only a few dedicated growers keep them alive. Others – Haut-Poitou for example – have been discovered because they have learnt how to compete in the commercial wine world.

The Appellations

There are currently 60 names or permutations on the full list of Loire AC and VDQS areas. The list is arranged here as it is in the producers' directory that follows.

Upper Loire AC

Blanc Fumé de Pouilly *See* Pouilly-Fumé.

Ménétou-Salon White, red and rosé wines, made on 100 hectares of chalky soil to the west of Sancerre. Whites from Sauvignon, rosés and reds from Pinot Noir. The whites can match the average Sancerre in quality, reds and rosés can often be fuller.

Pouilly-sur-Loire White wine made in the same area as Pouilly-Fumé, but from the Chasselas grape.

Pouilly-Fumé White wines made from Sauvignon around the village of Pouilly-sur-Loire on 606 hectares of calciferous (*marne argileuse*) and flint (*silex*) soils. There are no reds or rosés produced under this *appellation*. The wines tend to be fuller, higher in alcohol, richer and longer-lasting than Sancerre, but sometimes lack the initial crisp fruit.

Quincy White wine from the Sauvignon grape. 108 hectares of gravelly soil along what was once the bed of the River Cher. The wine can be attractively soft and round while retaining the gooseberry acidity of the Sauvignon grape.

Reuilly White from Sauvignon and rosé from Pinot Gris and Pinot Noir. 60 hectares of chalk soil. The white wine is light and fresh, the rosé (especially from the Pinot Gris) is very attractive.

Sancerre White from Sauvignon, red and rosé from Pinot Noir. About 1,620 hectares. This is the most important *appellation* in terms of production in the upper Loire. The soil – a mixture of *caillottes* (calciferous and gravel), flint and the heavier *marne argileuse* – produces three distinct styles of wine. While many are blended, wines from Chavignol and Bué reflect the qualities of the *caillottes* soil, while those from Verdigny have more of the character of the heavier *marne argileuse*. Around the town of Sancerre, flint (*silex*) soil predominates. The whites have the classic Sauvignon taste of gooseberries and grapefruit and are immediately attractive. Some fine barrel-aged reds are made, but on the whole these and the rosés tend to be overrated.

Upper Loire VDQS

Châteaumeillant Red and rosé from Gamay, due south of Sancerre.

Côtes d'Auvergne Gamay red from near Clermont-Ferrand in the Puy de Dôme.

Côtes du Forez Gamay red from near St-Etienne, almost at the source of the Loire.

Côtes de Gien or Vin des Coteaux du Giennois Area centred around Cosne, north of Sancerre and Pouilly-sur-Loire. Red from Pinot Noir and Gamay, white from Sauvignon.

Côte Roannaise Attractive Gamay red, further down-river from Côtes du Forez. Due west of Beaujolais.

Saint-Pourçain On the Allier river, north of the Côtes d'Auvergne. Whites from Tressalier and Chardonnay, reds and rosés from Gamay and Pinot Noir.

Vin de l'Orléanais Vineyards around the city of Orléans make this the most northerly Loire vineyard. Red, white and rosé wines are made. Largest production is rosé from Pinot Meunier.

Touraine AC

Bourgueil Red and rosé wines made from the Cabernet Franc and Cabernet Sauvignon, in a district at the western end of Touraine on the north bank of the Loire. There are about 890 hectares under vine on three different soil types running in bands parallel to the Loire: gravelly soil near the Loire (the least important); a higher level called *la terrasse* made of sand and gravel soil (the most important); and *les coteaux* at a higher level. Bourgueil is one of the few Loire reds that needs time to develop. Five or six years is a minimum. Vintages: '82, '83, '85, '88, '89, '90.

Chinon This district lies due south of Bourgueil, between the Loire and Vienne rivers. There are nearly 1,212 hectares and like Bourgueil, there are three soil types moving away from the Vienne river: the gravel nearest to the river; clay and gravel on *les plateaux*; and clay and lime from *les coteaux* which produces the best wines. More immediately attractive than Bourgueil, Chinon wines tend to mature more quickly, although given careful ageing in old barrels, they can last for some years. Vintages: '83, '85, '88, '89, '90.

Coteaux du Loir Le Loir is a tributary of the main river La Loire, running northwest from Angers past Vendôme. The Coteaux du Loir vineyards are tiny – only 74 hectares – lying 40 kilometres north of Tours. Red wines are made from Cabernet Franc, Pineau d'Aunis, Gamay and Cot; rosés from Groslot; whites from Pineau de la Loire.

Crémant de Loire A general Loire-wide AC for white and rosé wines made in small quantities in Touraine and Anjou (including Saumur). A *crémant* has lower pressure than a normal *méthode champenoise* sparkler, but it is otherwise made with the same second fermentation in the bottle. This method can give good flavour and the wine ages well in bottle.

Jasnières White wine made from Pineau de la Loire in two communes: L'Homme and Ruille-sur-Loir in the Coteaux du Loir AC. 19 hectares make this rare dry wine.

Montlouis The twin vineyard of Vouvray (*qv*) on the southern bank of the Loire east of Tours on the tongue of land between the Loire and the Cher. The wines come from the three communes of Montlouis-sur-Loire, Lussault and St-Martin-le-Beau. Chalk underlies a sandy top-soil. Only white wines are produced from the Chenin Blanc. Most of the still wines are dry, less full-bodied but softer than Vouvray and more attractive when young. In very good years, *demi-sec* and *moelleux* (sweet) wines can be made. Vineyard area is around 300 hectares.

Montlouis Pétillant and Mousseux Slightly sparkling (*pétillant*) and *méthode champenoise* sparkling wines (*mousseux*) are made from the same vineyards as still Montlouis. Generally made in cooler years.

Rosé de Loire Dry rosé which can be made in Touraine, Anjou
and Saumur, but comes mainly from Touraine. Groslot and
the two Cabernets (minimum of 30 percent Cabernet –
higher than for Rosé d'Anjou).

Saint-Nicolas-de-Bourgueil A commune just west of the
main Bourgueil vineyard makes a lighter red from
Cabernet Franc that ages more quickly. Some regard the
wine as nearer to a Chinon than a Bourgueil in style. 498
hectares. Vintages: '88, '89, '90.

Touraine A catch-all AC for the whole Touraine region. It
covers 2,990 hectares – about one-third of the vineyard area
in the province (the other two-thirds are in smaller, more
precise ACs). Red, rosé and white, still and sparkling wines
are made from a variety of grapes. The reds are made from
Cabernet Franc, Cabernet Sauvignon, Gamay and Malbec,
or from Pinot Gris, Pinot Meunier and Pinot Noir. Rosés
from the red grapes or from Groslot or Pineau d'Aunis.
Whites from Chardonnay, Chenin Blanc, Pineau Menu and
Sauvignon. Gamay and Sauvignon are the most widely
planted grapes.

Touraine Villages Three smaller districts have the right to add
their name to the general Touraine AC. Touraine-Amboise
is on the Loire due east of Tours and makes reds from
Gamay, Malbec and both Cabernets; rosé from Gamay and
Cabernet Franc and a little dry white from Chenin Blanc
(149 hectares). Touraine Azay-le-Rideau, to the southwest
of Blois, makes dry and semi-sweet white from the Chenin
Blanc and rosé from Groslot and red grapes (98 hectares).
Touraine-Mesland produces red from Gamay, the
Cabernets and Cot (Malbec), smaller amounts of white
from Chenin Blanc (250 hectares). On the whole, the reds
are better than the whites in Mesland and Amboise:
Mesland especially makes some fine long-lasting wines from
Cabernet Franc. Azay-le-Rideau is better at whites
(especially the sweeter wines) than rosés.

Touraine Pétillant and Mousseux Slightly sparkling (*pétillant*) and *méthode champenoise* sparkling (*mousseux*) wines made all over the Touraine AC area. Little *mousseux* under this AC is made, most produced, confusingly, as Crémant de Touraine under the ordinary Touraine AC.

Vouvray White wine made on the north bank of the Loire, just east of Tours. The vineyards are on the plateau above the river on chalk soil. The cliff facing the river and the small side valleys are riddled with caves and cellars – some people still live in troglodyte houses half built into the cliff. There are three styles of still Vouvray – dry, semi-dry and sweet (*moelleux*). The only grape variety is the Chenin Blanc (Pineau de la Loire). The sweeter – and even some of the better dry – wines can age seemingly for ever. They can be luscious but also with the hard edge of acidity that the Pineau provides which gives them long life. At its best, one of the finest Loire wines, but much inferior Vouvray is bottled elsewhere by *négociants*. Much better are the local bottled wines from the top estates. Vintages (for sweet): '69, '71, '76, '83, '85, '88, '89.

Vouvray Mousseux or Pétillant The *méthode champenoise* sparkling Vouvray, normally dry but sometimes semi-sweet or even sweet. Must be white. Vintages (for dry): '88, '90.

Touraine VDQS

Cheverny White, red and rosé wines from 500 hectares, from a district southwest of Blois. The major production is of a very dry white, from the local Romorantin grape. Other whites come from Chenin Blanc, Sauvignon, Chardonnay and Pineau Menu (Arbois). Red comes mainly from Gamay, as does the rosé. Some sparkling wine is also made.

Coteaux du Vendômois Just to the east of the Coteaux du Loir AC is this larger (40-hectare) area, around the town of Vendôme on the Loir. Red (from Cabernet Franc, Gamay and Pinot Noir), rosé (from Pineau d'Aunis and Gamay), white (from Chenin Blanc and Chardonnay).

Valençay Mainly red Gamay-based wine from a small area to the south of the Cher in southeast Touraine. Some rosé is also made from the Gamay, while white comes from Pineau Menu, Chardonnay or Sauvignon. A little Romorantin is also planted.

Anjou AC

Anjou The general AC for the vineyards of the whole region not covered by more precise *appellations*. White, red and rosé are made under this name. There are around 17,000 hectares making wine – 15 percent red, 55 percent rosé, 30 percent white. Reds are from Gamay (wine called Anjou Gamay) and the two Cabernets (wine called Anjou). Rosé (which is semi-sweet) is mainly made from Groslot (Grolleau), with some Cabernet Franc, Cabernet Sauvignon, Gamay, Pineau d'Aunis and Malbec. White mainly from Chenin Blanc (Pineau de la Loire) with some Chardonnay or Sauvignon. The style of white ranges from dry to sweet.

Anjou Coteaux de la Loire White wines from the area just south of Angers. Can be dry or semi-sweet. The grape used is the Chenin Blanc (Pineau de la Loire).

Anjou Gamay Red wines from the general Anjou AC made from the Gamay grape.

Anjou Pétillant and Mousseux Semi-sparkling (*pétillant*) and *méthode champenoise* sparkling wines made in the general Anjou AC area. Can be from Chenin Blanc or from red grapes (pressed to make white wine). Tiny production.

Anjou Villages *Appellation* covering 46 villages within the main Anjou *appellation* area. It can be used only for red wines made from Cabernet Franc and Cabernet Sauvignon.

Bonnezeaux One of the two great sweet white wine ACs (*see
also* Quarts de Chaume). The small vineyard area is in the
commune of Thouarcé, part of the larger Coteaux du
Layon AC (*qv*). 121 hectares of clay and limestone soil. The
grapes should ideally be left to develop noble rot – certainly
they need to be harvested late to give the required
sweetness and intensity, and the wine can be made only in
good years (the better producers sell it as Coteaux du Layon
in bad years). Vintages: '76, '79, '82, '85, '88, '89, '90.

Cabernet d'Anjou A rosé wine made throughout the Anjou
AC area from Cabernet grapes. It can be sweet or dry. The
wine can be attractive when properly made (without too
much sulphur) but sweet varieties tend to become cloying
quite easily; the dry style is often poorly vinified.

Cabernet de Saumur Rosés from the Saumur AC area,
normally semi-sweet and made from the two Cabernet
grapes. Small production of wines which tend to be better
than ordinary Cabernet d'Anjou.

Coteaux de l'Aubance Small-production white-wine area to
the east of Coteaux du Layon, due south of Angers on the
Aubance river. The delimited area is large but only about
80 hectares make the wine. Normally a medium-dry white
wine made from ripe Chenin Blanc grapes which have been
fermented slowly. Good examples can age well, although
they are not too harsh when young.

Coteaux du Layon The modest river Layon runs southwest to
northeast towards the Loire, making a wide valley. On the
southwest-facing slopes are around 1,616 hectares of Chenin
Blanc making sweet white wines from very ripe grapes,
some with noble rot. Coteaux du Layon is the general AC
and there are smaller ACs with an even higher quality as
enclaves in the area (Quarts de Chaume, Bonnezeaux). The
wines are remarkable value.

Coteaux du Layon Villages Seven communes are allowed to add their name to the main Coteaux du Layon AC. Their wines are generally better with a higher alcoholic level and there are lower yields in one commune (Chaume) as well. The seven are: Beaulieu-sur-Layon, Faye d'Anjou, Rablay-sur-Layon, Saint Aubin de Luigné, Rochefort-sur-Loire, Saint-Lambert-du-Lattay, Chaume.

Coteaux de Saumur Semi-sweet wine from Chenin Blanc made in tiny quantities in the Saumur AC area. It has similar qualities to some Vouvray or Montlouis with a rich, full-bodied, slightly honeyed flavour, balanced by a touch of bitter acidity.

Crémant de Loire *See under* Touraine.

Quarts-de-Chaume Along with Bonnezeaux (*qv*) the other great sweet wine area of Anjou. The vineyard area covers 48 hectares on four fingers of hilly land which stretch out towards the Layon valley in the centre of the Coteaux du Layon AC area. The higher plateau behind protects the vineyards from winds. The wine is sweet, made from late-harvested grapes, in good years infected with noble rot but always picked to be as ripe as possible. The wine tastes surprisingly fresh in its youth (rather like young Sauternes) but between three and ten years becomes quiescent. It is at its greatest between ten and 20 years – but fine wines will last longer. Good Quarts de Chaume ranks with Sauternes and German Trockenbeerenauslesen as one of the world's great sweet wines. Vintages: '76, '79, '82, '83, '85, '88, '89, '90; older vintages if you can find them.

Rosé d'Anjou Medium-sweet rosé wine made anywhere in the general Anjou region (*see under* general Anjou AC).

Rosé d'Anjou Pétillant Rarely found semi-sparkling medium-sweet Rosé d'Anjou.

Saumur White and red still wines from 38 communes around

Saumur. The bone-dry white is made from Chenin Blanc with up to 20 percent Chardonnay or Sauvignon and is normally rather tart and acid. The red comes mainly from Cabernet Franc with Cabernet Sauvignon and Pineau d'Aunis.

Saumur-Champigny A red wine, also from Saumur, but from seven communes in the best part of the area for reds on a plateau above St-Cyr-en-Bourg. A finer wine than ordinary red Saumur, it is in great demand and prices are rather too high. Like Chinon and Bourgueil it has characteristic bitter cherry and vanilla flavours. Vintages: '85, '88, '89, '90.

Saumur Pétillant and Mousseux While only small quantities of *pétillant* are made, Saumur Mousseux is the second AC sparkling wine to champagne in France, producing around 12 million bottles a year. Made in the same way as champagne, much of the production is now linked to champagne companies. Chenin Blanc, Chardonnay and Sauvignon are white grapes used; the two Cabernets, Gamay, Groslot, Malbec, Pineau d'Aunis and Pinot Noir are the red (which are pressed as white). The soil is generally chalk. Most Saumur is made by big *négociant* houses and, like champagne, blending ensures continuity of house style. While not an exciting wine, Saumur is reliable and easy to drink and is much cheaper than champagne. There is also rosé *mousseux* made from any of the combination of red grapes. The wine is now known in publicity as Saumur d'Origine.

Savennières From a small area on the north bank of the Loire west of Angers, opposite Rochefort-sur-Loire and the Coteaux du Layon vineyards. Made from Chenin Blanc, the wine can be sweet or dry, but is now normally dry. Only about 60 hectares in production. Grapes are picked very ripe and fermented dry, giving high alcohol. In the rare good years, the wine is superb, combining a dry palate with a peaches and cream bouquet. Like many great

Chenin Blanc wines, they age well. Vintages: '78, '83, '85, '88, '90.

Savennières-Coulée-de-Serrant The Coulée-de-Serrant vineyard is the heart of Savennières with six hectares making fine dry white wines with an immensely long life. Vintages: '78, '83, '85, '88, '90; older wines will probably survive better.

Savennières-Roches-aux-Moines Second great Savennières vineyard. Six hectares under production. The wines tend to be lighter than Coulée-de-Serrant. Vintages: '78, '83, '85, '88, '90.

Anjou VDQS

Vin du Haut-Poitou While this area is not in Anjou, it is normally linked in for convenience. It is an isolated pocket of winemaking away from the main area, near Vienne in the province of Poitou to the south. Nothing would be known about Haut-Poitou were it not for the cooperative, which is making delightful varietal wines from Chardonnay and Sauvignon – Sauvignon being the more successful variety here. But Chenin Blanc is also permitted for whites. Reds and rosés are made from Gamay, Pinot Noir, Cabernet Sauvignon and Grolleau (Groslot). The wines are fresh and fruity and should be drunk young.

Vin du Thouarsais Red, rosé and dry white wines from the Deux-Sèvres *département*, south of Angers and west of Poitiers. The red and rosé come from Cabernet Franc and Cabernet Sauvignon; the white, which is normally medium-dry, from Chenin Blanc. The wines should be drunk young.

Western Loire AC

Muscadet This is the basic AC for the white wines of what is called the Pays Nantais – the region south of the city of Nantes, almost at the mouth of the Loire. Simple Muscadet made from the Muscadet grape (also called Melon de Bourgogne) comes mainly from the area around the Lac du Grand Lieu on about 808 hectares of vineyard. The area used to be larger, but the Muscadet de Sèvre et Maine (*qv*) area has been enlarged to take in some of the simple Muscadet country. The straight Muscadet very rarely reaches the character or the freshness and fruit of a Muscadet de Sèvre et Maine – and it is normally worth paying the extra to buy the superior wine.

Muscadet des Coteaux de la Loire A small area of 400 hectares of vineyards on chalky soil along the banks of the Loire east of Nantes in the same area as the Coteaux d'Ancenis. The different soil produces a fuller, somewhat coarse wine, which rarely leaves its native area.

Muscadet de Sèvre et Maine This is the biggest Muscadet area by far, covering 8,100 hectares south of Nantes. The best vineyards are generally agreed to be in Saint-Fiacre and Vallet, but much of the production is bought by *négociants*, either local or from Saumur and points west. The area has been vastly expanded to take in what was simple Muscadet vineyard – a classic French sleight of hand when they saw the difference in price the two wines could command.

Superior Muscadet de Sèvre et Maine is described as being bottled *sur lie*, that is, straight from the unracked, unfiltered cask or tank, giving a slight prickle and extra freshness to the taste.

This should be done on the spot in the place where the wine was made (*mis en bouteille au château* will tell you this has happened). But increasingly the wine is taken off the lees and then transferred elsewhere for bottling, and a little carbon dioxide added to give the prickle. Muscadet has been an immense success story. From humble origins as the

local wine for Breton seafood, it has conquered the world
as an easy-to-drink dry white that is sufficiently anonymous
to suit most occasions. No Muscadet can, or should, be
pretentious: the character of the Melon de Bourgogne grape
cannot take it.

Western Loire VDQS

Coteaux d'Ancenis White, rosé and red wines made in the
same area as Muscadet Coteaux de la Loire AC. Only a
little white is made from the Chenin Blanc (Pineau de la
Loire) and Malvoisie (Pinot-Beurot) which makes both dry
and sweet wines. Gamay and Cabernet Franc produce the
red and rosé. Small production from 214 hectares. All
Coteaux d'Ancenis wines have to carry the name of the
grape variety on the label: Pineau de la Loire, Chenin
Blanc, Malvoisie, Pinot-Beurot, Gamay, Cabernet.

Gros Plant or Gros Plant du Pays Nantais This is an
extremely dry white wine from the lesser grape of the
Muscadet area. The Gros Plant (or Folle Blanche) grape
covers 2,430 hectares mostly in the same area as the simple
Muscadet. It is more acid than Muscadet and not a wine to
drink by itself, but it goes well with shellfish. It can be
bottled *sur lie*. A little sparkling wine is also made.

Fiefs Vendéens Red, dry white and rosé wines from the
Vendée, south of the Pays Nantais. Red and rosé from
Cabernet Franc, Cabernet Sauvignon, Gamay, Pinot Noir,
Pineau d'Aunis. Whites from Chenin Blanc, Chardonnay,
Gros Plant and Sauvignon. Only a little white is made. The
wine is simple and should be drunk young.

Vins de Pays

Regional Vin de Pays

Vin de Pays du Jardin de la France While covering the whole of the Loire Valley, the Vin de Pays du Jardin de la France region is actually centred on the Touraine area. Production is of white wines from the Sauvignon and Chardonnay grapes (30 percent), and red wines mainly from the Gamay (60 percent). A small amount of rosé is also made. The total production is considerable, and mostly of single-variety wines.

Other regional *vins de pays*: Vin de Pays des Comtes Rhodaniens (*see* the Rhône), Vin de Pays du Puy-de-Dôme.

Departmental Vins de Pays

Vin de Pays de l'Indre-et-Loire Wines from the Tours region; principally whites from the local Touraine grapes, with a smaller proportion of reds. Production is limited by the greater success of the Vin de Pays du Jardin de la France.

Vin de Pays du Loir-et-Cher Situated around Blois and Vendôme, the wines of this region are made from Pinot Noir and Pineau Menu (or Arbois), for the reds and whites respectively. Much of the *vin de pays* production here goes into Vin de Pays du Jardin de la France.

Vin de Pays du Maine-et-Loire This *vin de pays* covers the area of Anjou and Saumur. Ninety percent of the production is of red and rosé wines from the Gamay, Cabernet Franc, Cabernet Sauvignon and Grolleau grape varieties. White wine is produced in small quantities from Sauvignon Blanc, Chenin Blanc, Pinot Blanc and Grolleau Gris grapes.

Other departmental *vins de pays* are: Vin de Pays du Cher, Vin de Pays des Deux-Sèvres, Vin de Pays de Loire-Atlantique, Vin de Pays du Loiret, Vin de Pays de la Nièvre, Vin de Pays de la Sarthe, Vin de Pays de la Vendée and Vin de Pays de la Vienne.

Zonal Vins de Pays

Vin de Pays des Marches de Bretagne A zone to the east of
Nantes in the Muscadet region, making white wine from
the Muscadet and Folle Blanche, and reds from the unusual
l'Abouriou grape, which originally came from Gascony.

Vin de Pays de Retz Produced south of the Loire, in the
region between Nantes and the Atlantic, these are mainly
red and rosé wines. A speciality of Vin de Pays de Retz is a
rosé made from Grolleau.

Vin de Pays d'Urfé A wide area in the Loire *département*, near
the source of the river. The grapes used are Chardonnay,
Gamay and Pinot Noir, with some Aligoté and Viognier.
Production is small.

Other zonal *vins de pays* are: Vin de Pays du Bourbonnais, Vin
de Pays des Coteaux Charitois, Vin de Pays des Coteaux du
Cher et de l'Arnon.

Upper Loire Producers
Ménétou-Salon AC

Georges Chavet et Fils
**GAEC des Brangèrs, 18510 Ménétou-Salon. Vineyards
owned: Ménétou-Salon: Sauvignon 5·5ha; Pinot Noir
5·5ha. 70,000 bottles. VP-R**
For those who want large bottles of Ménétou-Salon – especially
reds – this is where to come. The red wine inside is a well-balanced
product, made half from grapes that have been pressed and half
from maceration, with some ageing in wood. The whites are very
fresh and full of grape fruit. A small amount of attractive, lively rosé
is also made. The firm goes back to the 18th century and has only
slowly begun the change to modern vinification techniques for
white wines. *Open: Mon–Sun 8am–8pm. Appointments necessary for
groups.*

Bernard Clement et Fils (Domaine de Châteney)
18510 Ménétou-Salon. Vineyards owned: Ménétou-Salon Sauvignon 12ha; Pinot Noir 8ha. 100,000 bottles. VP-R
Family firm dating back to 1560. The estate at the Domaine de Châtenay is much larger than the present vineyard planting, and expansion is going on. The white tends to a full style, pleasantly perfumed but a little heavy to my taste. The red is much more interesting – vinified traditionally and aged for up to a year in new barrels, giving a wine that needs time to mature and has life of anything up to ten to twelve years. *Open: Appointments preferred.*

Jean-Paul Gilbert
18110 St-Martin d'Auxigny. Vineyards owned: 16ha
The Gilbert family has been producing Ménétou-Salon since the 18th century. They make white, red and rosé, getting colour for the red by use of long maceration on the skins.

Domaine Henri Pelle et Fils
Morogues, 18220 Les Aix-d'Auguillon. Vineyards owned: Sauvignon 13ha; Pinot Noir 2ha. 50,000 bottles. VP-R
The mayor of Morogues, Henri Pelle, is another of the best producers of Ménétou-Salon. Most of his production is of a very fine white, but he also makes red and rosé. The red is sometimes aged for a year in wood. He uses the village name of Morogues as a brand name. *Open: By appointment only.*

Pouilly-Fumé AC and Pouilly-sur-Loire AC

Michel Bailly
Les Berthiers, Les Loges, 58150 Pouilly-sur-Loire. Vineyards owned: 7ha. VP-R
This small estate is the result of a division of land between the sons of Maurice Bailly. Jean-Louis took one portion, while Michel took the other. Michel makes very good wine from land in the Champ de Gris, Les Griottes and Les Perriers. *Open: Appointments preferred.*

Bernard Blanchet
Les Berthiers, St-Andelain, 58150 Pouilly-sur-Loire.
Vineyards owned: 5ha. VP-R
The house of M Blanchet is close to the main N7 road, and his cellars are housed in newly excavated underground workings. He produces both Pouilly-Fumé and Pouilly-sur-Loire, which is bottled early and untreated, giving it extra flavour.

Patrick Coulbois
58150 Pouilly-sur-Loire
Patrick has broken away from his father, Gerard, and set up on his own. Relations are amicable, however, and he sends the Chasselas from his vineyard to make sparkling wine, under the Pouilly-sur-Loire *appellation*. Patrick's still Pouilly-Fumé, made in cellars beneath a modern bungalow, is full, traditional in style, and an assembly from all his vineyards.

Didier Dagueneau
Les Berthiers, 58150 Pouilly-sur-Loire. Vineyards owned:
Les Berthiers 6ha. 40,000 bottles. VP-R
One of the most original and innovative producers of Pouilly-Fumé, influenced by developments among the younger generation of Burgundy winemakers. Fermentation now takes place in small new oak barrels, using specially selected yeasts. Some of this wine is later blended with wine fermented in stainless steel. Much of the land is on high-quality flinty *silex* soil, and this name is used on his finest wine. All his wines age well and should not be drunk too young. *Open: By appointment only.*

Jean-Claude Dagueneau
58150 Pouilly-sur-Loire. VP-R
Of the three Dagueneau firms in Les Berthiers, this is the largest, and bears the name of Domaine des Berthiers. Serge Dagueneau, Jean-Claude's cousin, has premises next door, while his son Didier (*qv*) works just down the road. Jean-Claude's wines include a top *cuvée*, Cuvée d'Eve, from old vines.

Paul Figeat
Les Loges, 58150 Pouilly-sur-Loire. Vineyards owned:

8ha. VP-R
This is a traditional firm making wines that need some ageing in bottle. The family has been in business for at least 200 years. A small proportion of Pouilly-sur-Loire is also made.

Denis Gaudry
Tracy-sur-Loire, 58150 Pouilly-sur-Loire. VP-R
One of the many historic family firms in Pouilly-sur-Loire. This firm has extensive premises in the village of Boisgibault, with vineyards in Tracy-sur-Loire. While some of his wine is exported and sold within France, some is also sold to *négociants* in bulk.

Domaine Masson-Blondelet
1 Rue de Paris, 58150 Pouilly-sur-Loire. Vineyards owned: Pouilly 9ha; Sancerre 3ha. 70,000 bottles. VP-R
Modern cellars and vinification produce some very reliable wines and one or two fine ones. The best wines from Masson-Blondelet are from Les Bascoins vineyard in Pouilly, and there is a top *cuvée* from old vines called Tradition Cullus. Red and white Sancerre are also made here. *Open: By appointment if possible.*

Château de Nozet
58150 Pouilly-sur-Loire. Vineyards owned: 52ha. 1·5 million bottles. VP-R and N
By far the largest producer in Pouilly-sur-Loire, Patrick de Ladoucette owns a magnificent 19th-century château in the centre of his vineyard on high ground above the village of Pouilly-sur-Loire. He buys in much of his needs, reserving his own estate for top wines like Baron de L (made only in good years). He also owns the Sancerre firm of Comte Lafond, apart from other interests elsewhere on the Loire and in Chablis. The quality is good, even if the wines from this estate are not the most exciting Pouilly-Fumé around. *Open: By appointment only.*

Didier Pabiot
Les Loges, 58150 Pouilly-sur-Loire. Vineyards owned: Les Loges Sauvignon 4ha; Chasselas 0·5ha. 30,000 bottles. VP-R
A small production from a young *vigneron* who prefers traditional

techniques. The wines are becoming better each year and the Pouilly-Fumé (some sold under the brand Les Champs de Cri) is in a full, rich style. *Open: By appointment only.*

Roger Pabiot
Tracy-sur-Loire, 58150 Pouilly-sur-Loire. VP-R
Wines are sold here under two labels: Les Champs de la Croix and Les Girannes, depending on the market. Vines are on pebble soil in Tracy-sur-Loire, and M Pabiot uses a harvesting machine. A tiny proportion of Pouilly-sur-Loire is made.

Michel Redde et Fils
La Moynerie, 58150 Pouilly-sur-Loire. Vineyards owned: Pouilly 27ha. 250,000 bottles. VP-R
One of the larger estates in Pouilly run by the sixth generation of the Redde family. They make only Pouilly-Fumé, mainly from flinty soil which gives the wine ageing potential. Their finest wine is called Cuvée Majorum, made only in better years (the last four were '82, '83, '85 and '86). All their wine is made in stainless steel and bottled as quickly as possible. *Open: By appointment if possible.*

Guy Saget
58150 Pouilly-sur-Loire. Vineyards owned: Pouilly 18ha; Sancerre 1ha. 2·5 million bottles. VP-R and N
An old-established family firm which has expanded into a *négociant* business from vineyard holdings. The wines are made by low-temperature, controlled vinification which gives them good fruit but not-too-high acidity. Their vineyard holdings are in Chanta-louettes, Les Loges, Les Bascoins, Château de la Roche for Pouilly; Clos du Roy for Sancerre. Their wines are generally soft and very accessible. Their *négociant* business includes wines from Touraine and Anjou. *Open: By appointment only.*

Château de Tracy
Tracy-sur-Loire, 58150 Pouilly-sur-Loire. Vineyards owned: Tracy and Les Loges 24ha. 80,000 bottles. VP-R
Traditional family firm, owned by the Comte d'Estutt d'Assay and run by his two sons. The estate has been in the family since the 16th century. The wines are full of character, tending towards a

considerable heaviness and richness and can age well in good years. Poor years are to be avoided, since their old-fashioned techniques cannot cope with poor fruit. *Open: By appointment only.*

Château de Tracy – Tracy-sur-Loire

Quincy AC

Claude Houssier
Domaine du Pressoir, 18120 Quincy. Vineyards owned: 8ha. 30,000 bottles. VP-R
Only white from Sauvignon Blanc is produced here. The wines are made naturally dry, without chaptalization, and are designed to age well over a period of four or five years. Sold locally and in Paris.

Raymond Pipet
Quincy, 18120 Lury-sur-Arnon. Vineyards owned: Quincy 14ha. 86,000 bottles. VP-R
As little treatment as possible is meted out to the white Quincy wines of M Pipet. He filters only after a brief period in glass-lined tanks. The result is a wine with full flavour and only moderate acidity which is one of the best from Quincy. He also makes a little rosé Vin de Pays des Coteaux du Cher et de l'Arnon from a small holding of Pinot Gris. Both the white and the red should be drunk young. *Open: Mon–Fri 9am–noon; 2–6pm. Appointments preferred.*

Reuilly AC

Olivier Cromwell
Reuilly, 18120 Lury–sur–Arnon. Vineyards owned:
Reuilly: Sauvignon 2·8ha; Pinot Gris 1·2ha. 30,000 bottles.
VP-R
For English readers the name reeks of history and derives, so M Cromwell believes, from one of the Scots guards at the French court during the Middle Ages. Today, his tiny holding makes excellent clean, sharp white Reuilly and an attractive, quite full-bodied rosé. *Open: By appointment only*.

Claude Lafond
Le Bois St–Denis, 36260 Reuilly. Vineyards owned:
Reuilly: Sauvignon 3·5ha; Pinot Gris 1ha; Pinot Noir
1·6ha. 40,000 bottles. VP-R
This young grower makes a very dry white Reuilly from the vineyard of La Raie; a slightly sweet rosé from Pinot Gris grown in La Grande Pièce vineyard; and a light, fresh red from Pinot Noir in Les Grands Vignes. A certain amount of the wine for the rosé and red is matured in wood. Claude Lafond is one of the more dynamic producers in the Reuilly area and he is vice-chairman of the local Syndicat Vinicole. *Open: By appointment only*.

Guy Malbête
Le Bois–St–Denis, 36260 Reuilly. Vineyards owned:
Reuilly: 5·5ha of Sauvignon, Pinot Gris, Pinot Noir.
25,000 bottles. VP-R
A small-scale producer making some quality wines using trad-itional techniques. The red is aged in wood to give it some structure, while retaining the wild strawberry bouquet and taste. The rosé is a crisp wine with an attractive salmon–pink colour. The white is quite rounded for a Reuilly, with a lingering fragrance. *Open: By appointment only*.

Didier Martin
30 Route d'Issoudun, 36260 Reuilly. Vineyards owned:
Reuilly 4ha. 13,000 bottles. VP-R
Sauvignon Blanc makes the white wines on this small-holding,

while Pinot Gris is used to make an attractive rosé and Pinot Noir a light red. M Martin vinifies in wood. *Open: By appointment only.*

Sancerre AC

Pierre Archambault
Caves du Clos la Perrière, Verdigny, 18300 Sancerre.
Vineyards owned: Verdigny (Sancerre): Sauvignon 27ha;
Pinot Noir 3ha. 600,000 bottles. VP–R and N
This *vigneron* and *négociant* makes a wide range of single-vineyard Sancerre, producing red, rosé and white wines from his own vineyard and from bought-in grapes. His finest wine is the very dry white Carte d'Or la Perrière. White wines are made in stainless steel, but wood is used to age the reds. A small amount of Pouilly-Fumé La Toge aux Moines is also made from bought-in grapes. *Open: Mon–Fri 2:30–6pm; Holidays (April–Sept) 2:30–7pm. Appointments necessary for groups.*

Bernard Bailly-Reverdy et Fils
Bué, 18300 Sancerre. Vineyards owned: Sancerre:
Sauvignon 10ha; Pinot Noir 7ha. 75,000 bottles. VP–R
Red wines are a speciality with this firm, aged partly in new wood, giving a surprisingly spicy, rich result, which is sold two years after the vintage. The white wine, Clos du Chêne Marchand, is fermented slowly at a controlled temperature, giving considerable flavour and fruit. Other wines sold under Domaine de la Mercy-Dieu. *Open: By appointment only.*

Bernard Balland et Fils
Bué, 18300 Sancerre. Vineyards owned: Sancerre:
Sauvignon 13ha; Pinot Noir 4ha. 100,000 bottles. VP–R
An old-established firm (1730) with new ideas. Treatment of the wine is kept to a minimum with modern equipment. Two whites – Le Grand Chemarin and Le Clos d'Ervocs are bottled separately; a red, Les Marnes, is in a modern style. The whites are fresh and very fragrant, the red less interesting. *Open: By appointment only.*

Joseph Balland-Chapuis
La Croix St-Laurent, Bué, 18300 Sancerre. Vineyards owned: 17ha.
A relation of Bernard Balland, Joseph Balland-Chapuis sells single-vineyard Sancerre: Grand Chemarin, Clos le Chêne Marchand and Clos d'Ervocs. He makes red and rosé called Les Marnes. There is a prestige *cuvée* called Comte Thibault.

Philippe de Benoist
Domaine du Nozay Sancerre
The owner of this estate is related to Aubert de Villaine, co-owner of Domaine de la Romanée-Conti in Burgundy. His style of Sancerre is elegant, light rather than too full. The domaine was set up in 1970.

Roger Champault (Domaine de Colombier)
Crézancy en Sancerre, 18300 Sancerre. Vineyards owned: Sauvignon 6·8ha; Pinot Noir 3·8ha. 80,000 bottles. VP-R
An old-established vineyard which has been in the Champault family for generations. They produce traditional wines, which see some wood before bottling. Domaine de Colombier is the main vineyard, but the family also owns land in Clos du Roy, Moulin à Vent and Côte de Champtus (all in Crézancy). *Open: By appointment only.*

François et Paul Cotat
Chavignol, 18300 Sancerre. 12,000–18,000 bottles
Top-quality wines are made here in small quantities. The wines are fermented in wood and are not fined or filtered before bottling.

Lucien Crochet
Place de l'Eglise, Bué, 18300 Sancerre. Vineyards owned: Bué, Crézancy, Sancerre: Sauvignon 15ha; Pinot Noir 5ha. 250,000 bottles. VP-R and N
A family firm with holdings in some of the best Sancerre vineyards: Chêne Marchand and Grand Chemarin for white; Clos du Roy for red. About 40 percent of production is from bought-in grapes and must, 60 percent from their own vineyards. The quality of the wines is sound rather than exciting, but the single-vineyard Chêne

Marchand has great character.

Vincent Delaporte
Chavignol, 18300 Sancerre. Vineyards owned: Chavignol
and Sancerre: Sauvignon 10ha; Pinot Noir 3ha. 80,000
bottles. VP-R
A top-quality producer, especially for his whites from Chavignol,
which age unusually well for Sancerre. One of his best wines comes
from the Clos Beaujeu. The reds tend to be quite tannic when
young, and benefit from some ageing. White wines are produced
in modern stainless steel, the reds are aged in wood. *Open: By
appointment only.*

Fournier Père et Fils
Verdigny, 18300 Sancerre. Vineyards owned: Sauvignon
12ha; Pinot Noir 3ha. 480,000 bottles. VP-R and N
Cave des Chaumières is the brand name for the estate white, red
and rosé Sancerre made by this firm of growers and *négociants.* They
use only stainless steel and their wines are light, fruity and
immediately attractive. The *négociant* wines go under a whole range
of marques: Léon Vatan, Célestin Blondeau, Patient Cottat, Henry
de Chanvre, Charles Dupuy. They also use Sauvignon grapes to
make Vin de Pays du Jardin de la France. *Open: Appointments
preferred.*

Gitton Père et Fils
Chemin de Lavaud, Ménétréol, 18300 Sancerre. Vineyards
owned: Sancerre: Sauvignon 18·7ha; Pinot Noir 1·6ha.
Pouilly-sur-Loire: Sauvignon 9ha. 280,000 bottles. VP-R
One of the larger landowners in the area, from holdings built up
since World War II. The firm specializes in separate bottlings for
different holdings. Fruit from young vines is vinified in stainless
steel, that from old vines in wood. There are ten Sancerres
(including two reds) and five Pouilly-Fumés. The wines retain the
characteristics of the different vineyards to a considerable degree.
Open: Mon–Fri 8am–noon; 2–6pm. Sat 9am–noon.

Château de Maimbray
Sury-en-Vaux, 18300 Sancerre. Vineyards owned:

Sancerre: Sauvignon 8·4ha; Pinot Noir 3·6ha. 70,000 bottles. VP-R
The château is owned by the Roblin family, who produce an absolutely true-to-type white, clean, racy and full of flavour. Vinification takes place in stainless steel, with some wood-ageing for the small production of reds. Some impressive winemaking. *Open: By appointment only.*

A Mellot
18300 Sancerre. Vineyards owned: 42ha. VP-R and N
One of the largest firms in Sancerre, acting both as grower and *négociant*. The top wine is Domaine de la Moussière, from what is agreed to be the largest single vineyard in Sancerre. Mellot also produces wines in Ménétou-Salon, Quincy and Reuilly and in Pouilly-Fumé.

Paul Millérioux
Champtin, 18300 Crézancy-en-Sancerre. Vineyards owned: Sauvignon 10ha; Pinot Noir 3ha. 100,000 bottles. VP-R
A top-class producer whose Clos du Roy white has a surprising ability (for a Sancerre) to age. M Millérioux's vineyards are ideally situated in the northern slopes of Sancerre facing south and southwest. His red Sancerre, Côte de Champtin, also has good ageing ability. Both red and white mature for a while in wood. *Open: Mon–Sat 8am–noon; 2–8pm.*

Roger Neveu (Domaine du Colombier)
18300 Verdigny-en-Sancerre. Vineyards owned: Sancerre: Sauvignon 8ha; Pinot Noir 2ha. 55,000 bottles. VP-R
Established in the 18th century, a family firm run by father and two sons. The white is Clos des Bouffants, the red Domaine du Colombier. The white tends to be quite delicate in style. As with many other producers in Sancerre, old and new techniques are combined in the winery. *Open: Mon–Fri, during working hours.*

Lucien Picard
Bué, 18300 Sancerre. Vineyards owned: 7ha. VP-R
Wine from the Clos du Chêne Marchand is the most prestigious

from this family firm. They also produce another *cuvée* called Clos du Roy, as well as Pinot Noir red and rosé. The style is traditional and the wines can age well.

Paul Prieur et Fils
Verdigny, 18300 Sancerre. Vineyards owned: Sancerre:
Sauvignon 6ha; Pinot Noir 4ha. 80,000 bottles. VP-R
Family firm which owns one part of the best Sancerre vineyards, Les Monts Damnés, giving a particularly elegant wine from chalky soil. The red and rosé come from the gravelly Pichon vineyard in Verdigny and they place great emphasis on the red, which they exported to England in the last century. I prefer the white. *Open: By appointment only.*

Jean Reverdy et Fils (Domaine des Villots)
Verdigny, 18300 Sancerre. Vineyards owned: Sancerre:
Sauvignon 5·5ha; Pinot Noir 2ha. 60,000 bottles. VP-R
This family firm was established in 1646. Today, it owns the whole of the Clos de la Reine Blanche vineyard at Verdigny. The white wines age attractively and their smooth fruit can certainly sustain four or five years' cellaring. The red also gives plenty of fruit and a surprising depth of colour. *Open: By appointment only.*

Pierre and Etienne Riffault
Chaudoux, Verdigny, 18300 Sancerre. Vineyards owned:
Verdigny: Sauvignon 9ha; Pinot Noir 1ha. 90,000 bottles.
VP-R
Soft fruit characterizes the wines from this small family firm. The wines are attractive if unexciting; the red, with a touch of new wood on the palate, has more character than the white. Modern, low-temperature fermentation is used for the white wine, while the red is partly aged in stainless steel, partly in wood. *Open: By appointment only.*

Domaine Jean-Max Roger
Bué, 18300 Sancerre. Vineyards owned: Sancerre:
Sauvignon 10·4ha; Pinot Noir 2·6ha. Ménétou-Salon:
Sauvignon 4ha. 200,000 bottles. VP-R and N
Forty percent of the production from this firm is from grapes and

wines that are bought in. Principal holdings in Sancerre are in Le
Grand Chemarin and Le Chêne Marchand. In Ménétou-Salon, the
small-holding is at Morogues in Le Petit Clos. Quality is average,
with Le Grand Chemarin the best Sancerre. But the Ménétou-
Salon is probably the most attractive white wine. *Open: By
appointment only.*

Château de Sancerre
**18300 Sancerre. Vineyards owned: Sauvignon 19ha. 150,000
bottles. VP-R**
The old château at Sancerre is now owned by the company that
produces the Grand Marnier liqueur. Here, though, they make a
white Sancerre, using mainly stainless steel, with 20 percent of the
wine matured briefly in wood. The style is modern with few
pretensions.

Domaine Thomas et Fils
**Chaudoux, Verdigny, 18300 Sancerre. Vineyards owned:
Verdigny: Sauvignon 6·8ha; Pinot Noir 1·2ha. 60,000
bottles. VP-R**
The best wine from this house is the white Clos de la Crele, while
the Clos Terres Blanches is flintier and more austere. The '83 red,
aged in wood, was mellow and soft and had good colour. White
wines, made in stainless steel at a low temperature, are bottled
immediately. *Open: By appointment only.*

Domaine Vacheron
**1 Rue du Puits Poulton, 18300 Sancerre. Vineyards owned:
Sancerre 20ha. 130,000 bottles. VP-R**
Top-quality wines come out of the Vacheron cellars in the centre of
Sancerre, one of the most popular visits for tourists. Wines can be
tasted at le Grenier à Sel in the town during the summer months.
The reds are the stars with this firm, although the whites are of high
quality as well. The reds can age remarkably – a 1975 was still
tasting too young at 11 years old. Some red is aged in new wood
and all red is kept in small barrels for a year. *Open: Mon–Fri 9am–
noon; 3–7pm. Appointments necessary for groups.*

André Vatan
Chaudoux, Verdigny, 18300 Sancerre. Vineyards owned:
St-Satur 2ha; Verdigny 2ha. 20,000 bottles. VP-R
Unusually among Sancerrois, M Vatan makes only white wine, using modern stainless steel equipment. His wines are full of life and fruit and he has obviously learnt much from his father, Jean Vatan, with whom he has also worked. *Open: By appointment only.*

Côtes du Forez VDQS

Les Vignerons Foreziens
Trelins, 42130 Boen-sur-Lignon. Vineyards owned: Côtes du Forez 200ha; Vin de Pays d'Urfé 100ha. 800,000 bottles.
Coop (250 members)
The cooperative dominates the tiny Côtes du Forez VDQS region. The red, mainly from Gamay, is made using some carbonic maceration in a sub-Beaujolais style, to be drunk young and chilled. The two top wines are a Cuvée de Prestige and the explosively named Cuvée Volcanique. A small amount of rosé is made from Pinot Noir, some of it medium-dry. *Open: By appointment only.*

Côtes de Gien VDQS

Alain Paulat
Villemoison, Saint-Père, 58200 Cosne-sur-Loire.
Vineyards owned: Villemoison 5·5ha. 45,000 bottles. VP-R
M Paulat practises organic farming and winemaking in his small-holding, while using modern equipment in his cellars. He makes a light, fresh white from Sauvignon and a rosé from Pinot Noir and Gamay (80 percent). The red Réserve Traditionnelle is a more serious affair, made from Pinot Noir and aged for up to 18 months in large barrels. It needs at least four to five years to mature. If any wines will ensure the survival of this small *appellation*, they are here. *Open: Mon–Fri 8am–9pm. Appointments necessary for groups.*

Jean Poupat et Fils
47 Rue Georges Clemenceau, 45500 Gien. Vineyards
owned: Gien 7ha. 35,000 bottles. VP-R
A Gamay-based red is the main production here, with small
amounts of rosé and white. The white, from Sauvignon, is the best
of the three and has something of the character of Sancerre in its
crispness and liveliness. *Open: By appointment only.*

Côte Roannaise VDQS

Pierre Gaume
Les Gillets, 42155 Lentigny. Vineyards owned: Lentigny
1·5ha. 10,000 bottles. VP-R
Simple Gamay wines are made using both stainless steel and wood.
M Gaume makes a red and rosé from the VDQS Côte Roannaise
and also a Gamay rosé Vin de Pays d'Urfé. All his wines are lively,
with plenty of cherried fruit. *Open: By appointment only.*

Maurice Lutz (Domaine de Pavillon)
42820 Ambierle. Vineyards owned: Côte Roannaise 5ha.
24,000 bottles. VP-R
A Gamay wine, made using semi-carbonic maceration techniques
to give plenty of strawberry fruit and colour, is the bulk of M Lutz's
production. He also makes a little soft, fruity rosé, also from
Gamay. *Open: Mon–Sun.*

Saint-Pourçain VDQS

Union des Vignerons
Quai de la Ronde, 03500 St-Pourçain-sur-Sioule.
Vineyards owned: 300ha of Gamay, Pinot Noir,
Chardonnay, Sauvignon, Tressalier. 1·5 million bottles.
Coop (200 members)
This is by far the biggest production unit in St-Pourçain and,
luckily, methods are good and the wines reliable examples. The
bulk of production is of red, made from Gamay and a little Pinot
Noir. Rosés include a *vin gris* from Gamay. Standard whites are

made using the local Tressalier grape, but the top-quality wine is made from Sauvignon and Chardonnay (50/50). There is also a *méthode champenoise* sparkling, Anne de Bourbon. *Open: Mon–Fri 8am–noon; 2–4pm. Appointments preferred.*

Ray Père et Fils
Saulcet, 08600 St-Pourçain-sur-Sioule. Vineyards owned: Saulcet 8ha in red and white. 65,000 bottles. VP-R
One of the best Saint-Pourçain producers, concentrating on a Gamay/Pinot Noir red which takes two or three years' ageing. The white is soft with a high Chardonnay content (50 percent) and a touch of Sauvignon to balance the rather bland Tressalier. The rosé, from Gamay, is a very fresh style, which needs to be drunk young. Modern winemaking techniques are used in the cellars. *Open: By appointment only.*

Touraine Producers
Bourgueil AC and Chinon AC

Claude Ammeaux
La Contrie, St-Nicolas-de-Bourgueil, 37140 Bourgueil. Vineyards owned: St-Nicolas-de-Bourgueil 4·5ha. 25,000 bottles
This estate has a small production of high-quality St-Nicolas-de-Bourgueil, made from 30-year-old vines. Fermentation is in stainless steel, but the wines are aged in wood, giving them considerable flavour and quite high alcohol. Consequently the wines need more time to mature than is usual in St-Nicolas. However, the wine is worth the wait. *Open: By appointment only.*

Bernard Baudry
37500 Cravant-Les-Coteaux
The Baudry name is important in Chinon. Apart from Bernard there are also Jean Baudry and Jean's uncle Gaston Angelliaume.

Pierre Caslot
Le Domaine de la Chevalerie, Restigné, 37140 Bourgueil.

Vineyards owned: Bourgueil 18ha. 53,000 bottles. VP-R
This family firm has been making wine here since 1650, passing
down from father to son. Today, they have introduced some
stainless steel into their attactive old cellars, and do half the
fermentation in the new style, and half still in wood, blending
together later. The wine is traditional in style and ages well, rich and
with a good colour. *Open: Appointments preferred.*

Caslot-Galbrun
La Hurolaie, Benais, 37140 Bourgueil. Vineyards owned:
11ha. 30,000 bottles. VP-R
A long-established producer whose wines have considerable depth
and quality. Although fermentation is now in stainless steel, all the
wines see some wood. They always seem to need some years before
being attractively drinkable; in their youth they have deep colour
and a fair amount of stalky tannin. *Open: By appointment only.*

Max Cognard-Taluau
Chevrette, St-Nicolas-de-Bourgueil, 37140 Bourgueil.
Vineyards owned: St-Nicolas 7ha. 50,000 bottles. VP-R
There are two qualities of wine coming from this producer: a
standard St-Nicolas wine – red or rosé – firm but full of fruit, for
reasonably early drinking; and a more serious red, from older vines,
called Les Malgagnes. With the latter wine, too, the fruit comes
through well. *Open: By appointment only.*

Anne-Marie Donabella (Domaine du Roncée)
Panzoult, 37220 Ile-Bouchard. Vineyards owned: Chinon
25ha. 130,000 bottles. VP-R
A considerable holding, established in 1964, making light soft reds
and rosés, most of which are for early drinking. Some, from older
vines in Le Clos des Marronniers and Le Clos des Folies, are aged in
wood for a short period to give greater longevity and some depth.
Open: By appointment only.

Couly-Dutheil
12 Rue Diderot, 37502 Chinon. Vineyards owned: Chinon
39ha. 700,000 bottles. VP-R and N
Mainly modern-style wines, from the flat plain of Chinon under

the names Domaine de Turpenay and Domaine René Couly. But there are quantities of finer wines, for ageing, from Clos de l'Echo and Clos de l'Olive on the higher plateau vineyards. Vinification techniques are modern here, and the only traditional sights are the 11th-century *caves*. The winemaker, Jacques Puisais, is a local consultant who works for other producers. The firm acts as *négociant* for other Touraine red and white wines and Saumur-Champigny. *Open: By appointment only.*

René Gouron et Fils
Cravant-les-Coteaux, 37500 Chinon. Vineyards owned:
Chinon 18ha. 100,000 bottles. VP-R
Stainless steel fermentation and ageing in wood keeps these wines clean and ready to drink quite young. Quality is high. Sparkling and still rosé are also produced. *Open: By appointment only.*

Anselme et Marc Jamet
Clos du Vigneau, 37140 St-Nicolas-de-Bourgueil.
Vineyards owned: St-Nicolas 20ha. 40,000 bottles
The low production figure from the comparatively large vineyard gives a clue to the age (25 years) of the vines in this old family holding, founded in 1847. While they are attractive in a cool, stalky way when young, the wines (all red St-Nicolas) improve with some ageing. Methods are traditional with some fermentation in wood, although stainless steel has also put in an appearance. *Open: By appointment only.*

Pierre Jamet et Fils
Le Fondis, St-Nicolas-de-Bourgueil, 37340 Bourgueil.
Vineyards owned: St-Nicolas 20ha. 80,000 bottles. VP-R
Of the two Jamet firms (*see above*), this is the more modern, operating only since 1970 and making wines that can be drunk young and fresh. A small quantity of Cabernet Sauvignon tends to give the wine some body and tannin. The firm is likely to expand into the *négociant* business. *Open: Mon–Fri, appointments preferred.*

Charles Joguet
Sazilly, 37220 L'Ile Bouchard. Vineyards owned: 12ha
The major producer in the village of Sazilly, Charles Joguet is very

much the Renaissance man: artist, poet, sculptor as well as wine producer. He sells wines under four different names: Cuvée du Clos de la Cure, Clos du Chêne Vert, Clos de l'Haute Olive and Les Varennes du Grand Clos. There is also a wine from old vines, Clos de la Dioterie. M Joguet's wines are of the highest quality.

Lame–Delille Boucard
37140 Ingrandes de Touraine. Vineyards owned: Bourgueil 28ha. 150,000 bottles
A traditional firm using wood for vinification and leaving the red Bourgueil for up to three years in wood. They have been experimenting with new clones of Cabernet Franc to improve quality at the expense of yield (a rare phenomenon and one that should be applauded). A small amount of Bourgueil rosé is made from Cabernet Sauvignon, and a Rosé de Touraine is made from Grolleau and Gamay. A red Vin de Pays du Jardin de la France is also produced by the firm. The brand name is Domaine des Chesnaies.

Jean–Claude Mabileau
La Jarnoterie, St–Nicolas-de-Bourgueil, 37140 Bourgueil. Vineyards owned: St–Nicolas 10ha. 25,000 bottles. VP–R
M Mabileau makes a light red, from vineyards on the St–Nicolas *coteaux*, using carbonic maceration techniques and vinifying in cement tanks, subsequently passing them through wood for a short period. Although they can be drunk young, he argues that they will age for anything up to 30 years and has old vintages in his spectacular tufa cellars back to 1893 to prove his point. *Open: By appointment only.*

Paul Maître
SCEA Domaine Raguenières, Benais, 37140 Bourgueil. Vineyards owned: 12ha. 60,000 bottles
Rosé as well as red is made here. The wine is claimed by M Maître to have considerable ageing qualities: certainly the level of tannin in young wine would suggest this.

Marc Mureau
37140 Bourgueil

M Mureau has five sons in wine production, so there are plenty of Mureaus in Bourgueil. Marc himself makes wines which appear to have a remarkable ability to age. The cellars, in a former quarry, provide perfect conditions in which to age in bottle. A large proportion of wines are exported elsewhere in Europe and to America.

James Morisseau
Domaine de la Caillardière, St-Nicolas-de-Bourgueil,
37140 Bourgueil. Vineyards owned: St-Nicolas 12ha. 20,000 bottles
An old-established (1840) firm with vineyards on the *coteaux* of St-Nicolas, which has just moved into the modern age with temperature control and some stainless steel. The wines tend to have some tannin when young and need at least four to five years before they open out. M Morisseau makes only a red wine. *Open: By appointment only.*

Plouzeau et Fils (Château de la Bonnelière)
37500 Chinon. Vineyards owned: Touraine 20ha; Chinon 3ha. 900,000 bottles. VP-R and N
The biggest firm in Chinon, making wines from all over Touraine and Anjou. Their own vineyards (once owned by the Duc de Richelieu) produce Sauvignon de Touraine and Cabernet de Touraine, plus a small quantity of an early-drinking Chinon. Other wines they handle are Saumur-Champigny, Cabernet d'Anjou, Vouvray, Saumur and Coteaux du Layon. There are few excitements here. *Open: Mon–Fri 9am–noon; 2–6pm. Appointments necessary for groups.*

Jean-Maurice Raffault
La Croix, Savigny-en-Véron, 37420 Avoin. Vineyards owned: Chinon 35ha. 200,000 bottles. VP-R
One of the great characters of Chinon (and one of its chief propagandists), M J-M Raffault specializes in wines with considerable ageing ability. His enormous tufa *caves* are stacked high with old casks – dating back to the 1940s and 1950s – that are still extraordinarily drinkable in a mature way. M Raffault's family vineyard holdings date back to 1693. He vinifies, matures and

bottles wines separately from his different holdings. *Crus* include Les Picasses, Domaine d'Isore, Le Close du Gallon and Le Clos des Lutinières. *Open: Appointments preferred.*

Joel Taluau
Chevrette, St-Nicolas-de-Bourgueil, 37140 Bourgueil.
Vineyards owned: 10ha. 18,000 bottles

M Taluau has set up in business separately from his father, Albert. He goes against tradition in St-Nicolas by not using wood for ageing. He bottles wines under three labels: Jeunes Vignes from young vines, Domaine de la Chevrette and Vieilles Vignes from the old vines of the vineyard.

Domaine Thouet-Bosseau
37140 Bourgueil. Vineyards owned: Bourgueil 12ha. 70,000 bottles. VP-R

The firm owns two estates, of which the more famous is the Clos de l'Abbaye. Here vines (average age 38 years) produce excellent Cabernet Franc Bourgueil. Made partly in wood and partly in stainless steel it is then blended and can age for up to ten years. In Restigne, the five-hectare Domaine Thouet-Bosseau makes a lighter style of wine, using more stainless steel and extracting considerable freshness. *Open: By appointment only.*

Jasnières AC

Joel Gigou
72340 La Charte-sur-Loir

In the Domaine de la Charrière, M Gigou makes a typical Chenin wine, muted when young, needing some years to open out. His wine is called Cuvée Clos Saint-Jacques.

Jean-Baptiste Pinon
12 Promenade du Tertre, 41800 Montoire-sur-le-Loir.
Vineyards owned: Jasnières 4·5ha; Coteaux du Vendômois 1ha; Vouvray 1ha. 25,000 bottles. VP-R

This may be a small holding of Jasnières but it represents about a tenth of the *appellation* total. M Pinon's wine is dry, almost harsh when young, and matures slowly. The small portion of Coteaux du Vendômois produces a red from Gamay and Pineau d'Aunis, with a little medium-dry Vouvray completing the range. *Open: By appointment only.*

Touraine AC

Jacques Bonnigal
17 Rue d'Enfer, Limeray, 37530 Amboise. Vineyards owned: Limeray 10ha. 40,000 bottles. VP-R
M Bonnigal's traditional techniques produce an excellent red, Touraine-Amboise Cuvée François I, a blend of Gamay, Cot (Malbec) and Cabernet Franc, which needs three or four years for maturity. He also makes an average Sauvignon and a honeyed medium-sweet still white from the Chenin Blanc. A small proportion of this production is of a *méthode champenoise* wine from Chenin. He has planted Chardonnay which has improved the wine. *Open: Mon–Fri 8am–7pm. Appointments necessary for groups.*

Bougrier
41400 St-Georges-sur-Cher. VP-R and N
The family-owned vineyard of Domaine Guenault produces a wide range of AC Touraine wines: Sauvignon Blanc, Cabernet Franc, Gamay and Chenin Blanc. The bulk of production, however, is from the *négociant* side of the business.

Philippe Brossillon
Domaine de Lusqueneau, Mesland, 41150 Onzain.
Vineyards owned: Mesland 18ha; Mouteaux 10ha; Onzain 2ha. 150,000 bottles. VP-R
A 200-year-old family firm which still relies on traditional practices, apart from mechanical harvesting. All the Domaine de Lusqueneau lies in the Touraine-Mesland AC area and most of the production is of red, with small amounts of rosé and white, and two sparklers – a rosé and a white. Some of the reds (90 percent Gamay, 10 percent Cot and Cabernet) are now aged in wood, giving extra longevity. *Open: Appointments preferred.*

Pierre Chainier (Château de la Roche)
Chargé, 37530 Amboise. Vineyards owned: Chargé 30ha; Pocé 35ha. 8 million bottles. VP-R and N
Besides owning two estates in the Amboise district, this firm runs a big *négociant* business, buying in 80 percent of its requirements. A full range of Touraine wines is made, of which the Touraine-Amboise from the Château de Pocé is the best. Also made is Vin de Pays du Jardin de la France, the general Loire *vin de pays*. Another name used is Philippe de Guerois.

Confrérie des Vignerons de Oisly et Thesée
Oisly, 41700 Contres. Vineyards owned: 275ha. 1·8 million bottles. Coop (50 members)
This is generally regarded as the best cooperative on the Loire, and one of the best in France. It was started in 1961 in an attempt to improve the quality of the Touraine wines. Strict quality control is practised, with below-standard grapes being sold off. The wines – especially the Gamay de Touraine, Cabernet de Touraine and white Sauvignon de Touraine – are top-quality examples of what Touraine can produce given a little more effort. Vinification is mainly in stainless steel, but some reds do spend a time in wood. Blended wines carry the brand name Baronnie d'Aignan. A creamy white sparkling Crémant de Loire is made using Pinot Noir, Cabernet Franc and Chenin Blanc. *Open: By appointment only.*

Domaine Dutertre
20/21 Rue d'Enfer, 37530 Limeray. Vineyards owned: Touraine Amboise 30ha. 100,000 bottles. VP-R
Most of the wines from this firm come under the Touraine Amboise AC, although there is also a sparkling Touraine Crémant. The style for the whites and rosés – made using the full range of Loire grapes – is modern, clean and fresh. Reds, however, are made traditionally and see some time in wood, which gives them good ageing potential. Cot, Cabernet Franc and Gamay are used in the blend. *Open: By appointment only.*

Jean-Mary Duvoux
Le Pernas, Ange, 41400 Montrichard. Vineyards owned: Ange 10ha. 40,000 bottles. VP-R

The best wine to come from Duvoux is his Cabernet, which is made traditionally with a long, slow fermentation. Lots of cherry-like fruit and some tannin: a wine that needs time to develop. He also makes a semi-carbonic maceration Gamay which needs to be drunk young, a Cabernet Rosé and an attractive grassy Sauvignon. White and rosé *méthode champenoise* (white from Chenin Blanc) also come out of this small family firm. He has just set up a group of 20 small producers from along the Loire to coordinate export activities. *Open: By appointment only.*

Domaine de la Gabillière
13 Route de Blere, 37400 Amboise. Vineyards owned: Touraine–Amboise and Touraine 15ha. 60,000 bottles. VP-R
The domaine, set around an 18th-century château, is one of the French Ministry of Agriculture's viticultural training schools. A red and white are made in the Touraine-Amboise AC area, the red mainly from Gamay and Malbec with a little Cabernet Franc, the white from Chenin Blanc. A *méthode champenoise* Crémant de Loire is made from Chenin and Chardonnay and a sparkling Touraine from ten percent Chenin. All the wines are (as expected) extremely correct. *Open: By appointment only.*

Vincent Girault (Clos Château Gaillard)
41150 Mesland. Vineyards owned: Mesland 6ha. 70,000 bottles. VP-R
Red wines of the Touraine-Mesland AC are the speciality of this house. The best red is Vieilles Vignes Tradition, a blend of Gamay, Cabernet Franc and Malbec; 100 percent Gamay wines tend to be rather short and light, although well made. A small amount of rosé is also made. One of M Girault's stars is his dry Crémant de Loire, Les Doucinières, full of soft, smooth Chenin fruit. *Open: Mon–Fri 8am–noon; 2–6pm.*

Domaines Girault-Artois
7 Quai des Vioiettes, 37400 Amboise. Vineyards owned: Mesland 28ha. 250,000 bottles. VP-R
Modern techniques dominate this large estate which makes the full range of Touraine-Mesland wines. Stainless steel, mechanical

harvesting and temperature control are all brought into play. They are best in a crisp Sauvignon white, Domaine des Buttelières, and the Gamay Jeunes Vignes, Domaine d'Artois – produced by carbonic maceration. *Open: Appointments preferred.*

Château Luynes – one of the Loire valley's many stunning châteaux

Lucien Launay
Ange, 41400 Montrichard. Vineyards owned: Ange 10ha. 80,000 bottles. VP-R
A full range of Touraine wines are made by this firm, of which the majority is from Cabernet Franc and Gamay. Other grape varieties are Pineau d'Aunis and Sauvignon. M Launay also makes *méthode champenoise* wines. *Open: Mon–Sun.*

Jean Louet
3 Rue de la Paix, Monthou-sur-Bièvre, 41120 Les Montils. Vineyards owned: 8ha. 30,000 bottles
Out of this tiny vineyard come a top-class Cabernet/Gamay/Cot red, Tradition, and a clean, fragrant Sauvignon Blanc. The red is definitely a wine to keep for two or three years. M Louet makes the full range of Touraine AC wines, including a Chenin-based *méthode champenoise* and a rosé from Gamay. He is president of the Syndicat of the Touraine AC. *Open: By appointment only.*

Henry Marionnet (Domaine de la Charmoise)
Soings, 41230 Mur-de-Sologne. Vineyards owned: Soings 45ha. 400,000 bottles. VP-R

Gamay and Sauvignon are the two principal vine varieties on this large estate, and they make a red from the Gamay and a still white. A rosé is blended from Pineau d'Aunis, Cot and Cabernet Franc. The approach is modern and the Gamay is treated to carbonic maceration to bring out the colour. Everything is done in stainless steel. *Open: By appointment only.*

Domaine Christian Mauduit
Le Mechimière, Mareuil-sur-Cher, 41110 St-Aignan.
Vineyards owned: 14ha. 100,000 bottles. VP-R
Modern techniques of temperature control are used to make a clean-tasting Sauvignon, and future vineyard expansion will concentrate mainly on this vine variety. The reds and rosés are less successful. *Open: Mon–Fri. Appointments preferred.*

J-M Monmousseau
41400 Montrichard. Vineyards owned: 62ha. 1·7 million bottles. VP-R and N
Most of the production from this firm, now owned by the Champagne house of Taittinger, is of sparkling wine made by the *méthode champenoise.* Brand names used include Brut de Mosny, JM Rosé and the top *cuvée* JM93. The wines are aged in large chalk cellars dug out of cliffs above the river Cher at Montrichard. *Open: During working hours.*

Domaine Yves Moreau
Fleuray, Cangey, 37530 Amboise. Vineyards owned:
Touraine-Amboise 4·9ha; Touraine-Mesland 3ha; Touraine 1·85ha. 30,000 bottles
The Touraine-Amboise red, Cuvée Françoise I, made from Gamay (60 percent), Cabernet (20 percent) and Cot (20 percent), is the star from this old family firm, founded in 1847. The Touraine-Mesland, from 100 percent Gamay, is well made, but just misses that top quality. M Moreau also makes a small quantity of a white Sauvignon Touraine. These are true holy wines: vinification is in the former village church. *Open: By appointment only.*

Gaston Pavy
La Basse-Chevrière, Saché, 37190 Azay-le-Rideau.

Vineyards owned: 3ha. 13,500 bottles. VP-R
The top name in the Touraine-Azay-le-Rideau AC, operating since 1890. M Pavy makes only two wines. A white from Chenin Blanc can be dry but is also in good years lusciously sweet. A rosé made in tiny quantities is from a blend of Grolleau, Cot and Cabernet Sauvignon which ages well. Both wines are matured in wood for two to three months which brings out considerable depths – especially in the whites. *Open: By appointment only.*

Gaston Pibaleau
Luré, 37190 Azay-le-Rideau. Vineyards owned: Azay-le-Rideau 7·2ha. 12,000 bottles
This is a young firm that has adopted traditional techniques such as vinifying in wood. This approach benefits the white and rosé as much as the red: the white, especially, is a wine that needs some ageing, being characteristically acid in youth and developing honeyed depths in older vintages. A small amount of white and rosé *méthode champenoise* is also made. *Open: Appointments preferred.*

Jacky Preys
Le Bois Pontois, 41130 Meusnes. Vineyards owned: Touraine 46ha; Valençay 20ha. 300,000 bottles. VP-R
With vineyard holdings in the Touraine AC and Valençay, this large grower is able to produce a full range of wines, using Sauvignon and Pinot Blanc in white; Gamay, Cabernet Franc, Cot in red and rosé. They also make a Crémant de Loire. Pinot Noir and Chardonnay have been planted. *Open: By appointment only.*

Jean-Jacques Sard
La Chambrière, 37320 Esvres. Vineyards owned: 1ha. 3,000 bottles. VP-R
M Sard makes only one wine; a fine dry rosé, Noble Joué, described by the producer as a *vin gris*, made from free-run juice which is then put back onto the skins for 24 hours and fermented in wood. It is pale salmon-pink and very fresh to taste. Noble Joué is an old term for this style of wine and a number of producers in the area are aiming to revive it. Pinot Meunier is the main grape, with Pinot Gris and Pinot Noir. M Sard has another 14 hectares (owned since 1976) which he is developing. *Open: By appointment only.*

Vouvray AC and Montlouis AC

Domaine Daniel Allias
Le Petit Mont, Vouvray. Vineyards owned: 10ha
As with many Vouvray producers, M Allias's cellars are carved out
underneath his vines. The vineyard, called Le Clos du Petit Mont, is
at the highest point of the Vallée Coquette. In good years he makes
moelleux wines which age superbly, while the bulk of production is
of dry and sparkling wines. The present owners of the vineyard are
the fourth generation on the same land.

Berger Frères
135 Rue de Chenonceaux, St–Martin–le–Beau, 37270
Montlouis. Vineyards owned: St–Martin 20ha. 100,000
bottles. VP-R
A well-run, modern firm which makes some attractive wines. The
demi-sec Montlouis is particularly good in better years, and the
pétillant is lighter than the same style of wine in Vouvray. They
make a Crémant de Loire from Chenin Blanc, Chardonnay and
Cabernet Franc, which is aged for two to three years in bottle
before release. *Open: Appointments preferred.*

Claude Boureau
1 Rue de la Résistance, St–Martin–le–Beau 37270
Montlouis. Vineyards owned: Montlouis 5ha. 25,000
bottles. VP-R
A traditional producer who ferments his wine in wood, and makes
high-quality still and sparkling Montlouis. The wine can be either
dry or medium-sweet (in good years) and it ages well: 'the more it
ages, the better it is', says M Boureau. He also produces Touraine
rouge from Cabernet Franc, rosé (Cot and Grolleau) and white
(Sauvignon). *Open: By appointment only.*

Marc Brédif
Rochecorbon, 37210 Vouvray. N
This is purely a *négociant* firm, but is responsible for much of the
history of Vouvray: it was first to develop sparkling Vouvray. It is
now owned by the de Ladoucette family of Pouilly-Fumé fame.
The firm's cellars in Rochecorbon are quite spectacular.

G Delétang et Fils
St-Martin-le-Beau, 37270 Montlouis. Vineyards owned: Montlouis 12ha; Touraine 6ha. 100,000 bottles. VP-R
The cellars of M Delétang in the centre of St-Martin-le-Beau are filled with old bottles of wine gathering cobwebs. But modern techniques have been applied to fermentation. His still Montlouis can be dry or sweet, depending on the quality of the vintage. The sparkling wine is aged for two years in bottle before sale and is slightly off-dry and full. He also makes Touraine AC wines from Sauvignon, Cabernet Franc, Gamay and Grolleau. *Open: Mon–Sat 10am–noon; 3–6pm.*

André et Philippe Foreau (Domaine du Clos Naudin)
37210 Vouvray. Vineyards owned: Vouvray 12ha. 50,000 bottles. VP-R
One of the top Vouvray producers, now in its third generation, making still and sparkling wines. All the still wines are fermented and aged in wood, the *méthode champenoise* in stainless steel. They age their still wine for a considerable time – especially the sweet wine, made only in good years. The results are well worth the wait. *Open: By appointment only.*

Domaine Freslier
37210 Vouvray. Vineyards owned: 4ha. 25,000 bottles. VP-R
A small, traditional producer, making still and sparkling Vouvray, using wood for fermentation. The vineyard, known as the Quarts de Moncontour, is near the Château Moncontour, in one of the top sites of Vouvray. The Fresliers make a little of the rare Vouvray *pétillant. Open: Mon–Fri 9am–7pm. Appointments necessary for groups.*

Sylvain Gaudron
59 Rue Veuve, Vernou, 37210 Vouvray. Vineyards owned: Vernou, Noizay, Chançay 9·4ha. 30,000 bottles
Typical Vouvray cellars, carved out of rock in the 14th century. M Gaudron is a traditionalist who vinifies at least part of his wine in wood. He makes all the Vouvray styles – from dry through to *méthode champenoise*. His '85 sweet wines will be classics – in about 15 years' time. *Open: Mon–Sat, during working hours.*

Benoit Gautier et Germain Gautier-Peltier
La Recauderie, Parçay-Meslay, 37210 Vouvray. Vineyards owned: Rochecorbon: Chenin Blanc 20ha; Grolleau 1·5ha. 80,000 bottles. VP-R
The domaine is first recorded in the family in 1669 and it is now divided between Germain (the father) and Benoit (the son), although the cellars are still shared. Both men work in a traditional way, using the natural cool air of the *caves* to control fermentation. Over half the production goes into a *méthode champenoise* wine. Like other Vouvray producers, the finest year recently for sweet wines was 1985. They have only recently started bottling and selling – previously the wine was sold to *négociants*. *Open: Mon–Fri 8am–8pm. Appointments necessary for groups.*

Gaston Huet
Domaine du Haut-Lieu, 37210 Vouvray. Vineyards owned: Vouvray 32ha. 130,000 bottles. VP-R
M Huet is Mayor of Vouvray and a great propagandist for the wines. Luckily he is also one of the best producers in the area, making wines from some of the finest sites – Le Haut-Lieu, Le Clos du Bourg and Le Mont, which are vinified and sold separately. He uses a judicious mix of traditional techniques and modern stainless steel equipment, but his best wines are all matured in small wood casks. The extensive cellars, carved out of the tufa rock of Vouvray, are crammed with half a million bottles, and some of the sweet still wines are of amazing antiquity; the most recent vintages are '76 and '85. M Huet also makes sparkling and *pétillant* medium-dry wines. He makes very little dry, believing that Vouvray's vocation is as a sweet wine. *Open: Mon–Fri 9am–noon; 2–6pm.*

Mme Claude Metivier
51 Rue Neuve, 37210 Vernou-sur-Brenne. Vineyards owned: Vernou 7ha. 15,000 bottles. VP-R
Most of Mme Metivier's production is of sparkling and *pétillant* wines. Of the still wines, most are dry and medium-dry. Her Vernou vineyards are about five kilometres to the east of Vouvray where the tufa cliffs draw further back from the Loire. *Open: Afternoons only; by appointment only.*

Château Moncontour
Rochecorbon, 37210 Vouvray. Vineyards owned: 108ha
One of the new names of Vouvray, Château Moncontour was acquired in 1985 by entrepreneur Charles Rolin, who now makes a full range of Vouvrays from dry to sparkling to sweet. The *demi-sec* has achieved considerable success and has certainly done much to show the quality of which Vouvray is capable.

Dominique Moyer
2 Rue de la Croise des Granges, Husseau, 37270 Montlouis. Vineyards owned: Husseau 12ha. 40,000 bottles. VP-R
The Moyer family have been in the wine business since 1830, and some of their vines have been around since the 1920s, giving them wines with great intensity. They take great care in picking, going through the vineyard a number of times to ensure that the fruit is as ripe as possible: this is the old tradition in Montlouis but is now only carried out in a few of the best properties. Virtually all their production is of dry or medium-dry still wines – the medium-dry wines coming from the oldest vines. Fifteen percent of their production is of *méthode champenoise* or *pétillant* wine. Their house is a hunting lodge dating from 1620. *Open: By appointment only.*

Prince Poniatowski
Le Clos Baudoin, Vallée de Nouys, 37210 Vouvray. Vineyards owned: Le Clos Baudoin 3·8ha; Aigle Blanc 18·3ha. 150,000 bottles. VP-R
Prince Poniatowski is from an ancient Polish family which has lived in France for many years – the Vouvray estate has been in the family for 70 years. Wines tend to be on the dry side, of great elegance and finesse, with intense fruit, taking some time to mature. Clos Baudoin is one of the best sites in Vouvray, on the top of a sheltered valley facing south. Aigle Blanc is a brand for both still and sparkling wines – with more sparkling being made in less ripe years. The house, like so many in Vouvray, is half carved out of the rock. *Open: By appointment only.*

Cheverny VDQS

Bernard et François Cazin
Le Petit Chambord, 41700 Cheverny. Vineyards owned:
Cheverny 12ha. 50,000 bottles. VP-R
The bulk of production is of a fruity carbonic maceration Gamay,
but there is also a small quantity of the rare white from the
Romorantin grape. Look also for the well-made *méthode champe-
noise* from Chardonnay. Other wines made include still whites
from Sauvignon and Chardonnay, and a rosé and red from Pinot
Noir. *Open: By appointment only.*

Maison Père et Fils
41700 Cheverny
Half of production here is of white, from Sauvignon and
Chardonnay, half of red from Gamay, Cabernet Franc, Pinot Noir
and Cot. The reds are better, with excellent fruit flavours: the
whites tend to be a little too soft.

Vignobles de Nozieux
41700 Cheverny
François Huguet produces some excellent Romorantin, which
seems to need four or five years' ageing, a fresh-tasting Sauvignon
Blanc, and a Cheverny red that is a blend of Pinot Noir and Gamay.

Domaine Sauger Père et Fils
41700 Cheverny
There is a wide range of wines form this 17-hectare vineyard.
Chardonnay and Sauvignon are used for white wines; Gamay, Cot,
Cabernet Franc for reds; and Pineau d'Aunis for rosés. There is also
a vintage-dated sparkling wine, made for the first time in 1989,
from Chardonnay.

Philippe Tessier
41700 Cour-Cheverny
The third generation to run the family vineyard, M Tessier is full of
ideas and enthusiasm. He is particularly keen on Romorantin,
which makes a wine that can age well. He is better at whites than
reds, and his Sauvignons show good, grassy freshness.

Coteaux du Vendômois VDQS

Colin et Fils
41100 Vendôme
One of the 15 growers in this out-of-the-way corner of the Loir (*sic*)
valley, Patrice Colin makes excellent crisp rosé from Pineau
d'Aunis, a Chenin Blanc which is fermented in wood, and a
surprisingly colourful red from a blend of Gamay, Pinot Noir and
Pineau d'Aunis.

Anjou Producers
Anjou AC

Bonnin et Fils
Domaine la Croix des Loges, 49540 Martigné-Briand.
Vineyards owned: Anjou 30ha. 200,000 bottles. VP–R
Modern techniques dominate this large estate which covers mainly
wines from the AC Anjou, but also produces a small quantity of
fine sweet white Bonnezeaux. The Anjou Rouge from Cabernet
Franc is a well-made wine with plenty of youthful raspberry fruit,
but also some ageing potential. Other wines include Anjou Rosé,
Cabernet Rosé, a medium-dry Anjou Blanc and Rosé de Loire. A
certain amount of sparkling Saumur is also made. *Open: Appointments preferred.*

Brault Père et Fils
Domaine de Ste–Anne, Ste–Anne, 49320 Brissac–Quincé.
Vineyards owned: Anjou 48ha. 140,000 bottles. VP–R
This estate has adopted the high vine training of the Lenz Moser
method for the most part and although yields (which are supposed
to be higher under this system than conventional vine training) are
controlled by the AC laws, the quality of the fruit is certainly good.
This quality is clear in the well-made wines which cover the range
of Anjou ACs, and include some Coteaux du Layon and Coteaux
de l'Aubance. Just under half the production is bottled, the
remainder being sold in bulk to *négociants*. Their best wines tend to
be the reds. *Open: Appointments preferred.*

Les Caves de la Loire
19320 Brissac. Vineyards owned: 2,000ha. 4 million bottles. Coop (500 members)

One of the largest cooperatives on the Loire, Les Caves de la Loire has made a big name for itself in supplying reliable well-made wines on an own-label basis. In an ultra-modern winery, the full range of Anjou wines is made: Anjou Rouge, Anjou Blanc, Rosé d'Anjou, Cabernet d'Anjou, Rosé de Loire. They also make sparkling Crémant de Loire and Saumur Mousseux, and some good-quality sweet Coteaux du Layon. *Open: By appointment only.*

Jean Douet (Château des Rochettes)
Concourson-sur-Layon, 49700 Doué-la-Fontaine. Vineyards owned: Anjou and Coteaux du Layon 25ha. 80,000 bottles. VP-R

A long-established family firm which makes the full range of Anjou wines, plus some Coteaux du Layon made from old vines. They tend to use a mixture of traditional techniques for the reds (with wood-ageing) and temperature-controlled fermentation for other wines. The bulk of the production is of Anjou red. *Open: Appointments preferred.*

Domaine Gaudard
Chaudefonds-sur-Layon, 49290 Chalonnes-sur-Loire. Vineyards owned: 15·1ha. 100,000 bottles. VP-R

They have been expanding plantings of the noble varieties – Chardonnay and Cabernet Franc – on this estate and cutting back on the local Grolleau and Chenin. The Chardonnay is used as a *cépage ameliorateur* in a *méthode champenoise* Anjou sparkler. Cabernet Franc goes into the Anjou Rouge, a well-made, long-lasting wine. Other wines include the range of Anjou wines, plus some Coteaux du Layon. *Open: Mon–Fri 8am–5pm.*

Guy Gousset (Clos de l'Aiglerie)
St-Aubin-de-Luigné, 49190 Rochefort-sur-Loire. Vineyards owned: 12ha. 60,000 bottles. VP-R

M Gousset makes a range of wines: Anjou Rouge and Rosé from Cabernet Franc; sweet Coteaux du Layon; and some Vin de Pays de Maine et Loire. Techniques are traditional, with fermentation in wood for all wines. Quality is reliable, with a few pleasant surprises, especially in the reds. *Open: Working hours.*

Yves Leduc (Château Montbenault)
Faye d'Anjou, 49380 Thouarcé. Vineyards owned: Anjou 20ha. 35,000 bottles. VP-R

M Leduc specializes in sweet wines of the Coteaux du Layon Faye AC. These wines are made cleanly using stainless steel for vinification and tend not to last as long as some other sweet wines of the area. Part of his Coteaux du Layon from the Clos Poirier Bourgeau vineyard is vinified and bottled separately. He also makes Anjou Rouge and Blanc, Rosé d'Anjou, Cabernet d'Anjou, Rosé de Loire and sparkling Anjou *méthode champenoise. Open: Mon–Sat 9am–noon; 2–5pm.*

Vins Mottron
Rue d'Anjou, 49540 Martigné-Briand. Vineyards owned: Anjou 25ha. 1 million bottles. VP-R and N

One of the largest *négociants* in the Anjou AC area. From their own vineyards they make red and rosé wines in their modern winery, using the Cabernet d'Anjou, Rosé d'Anjou and Anjou Rouge ACs, plus Vin de Pays du Jardin de la France. They also produce other Loire wines: Muscadet, Saumur, Chinon, Bourgueil, Touraine, Sancerre and Pouilly-Fumé. Brands include: Caves de Bel Air, Caves de Petit Colombier, Pierre Frain, Louis Bret, Roger Lefèvre. *Open: By appointment only.*

Domaine Richou
Chauvigné, Mozé-sur-Louet, 49190 Rochefort-sur-Loire. Vineyards owned: Anjou 28ha. 90,000 bottles. VP-R

The white Anjou Blanc is the star from this old-established firm. This blend of Chenin (80 percent) and Chardonnay (20 percent) makes a dry, full-of-fruit, clean wine, best drunk in the year following the vintage. They also make a Cuvée de Printemps from young vines – a blended red of Cabernets which is designed to be drunk early. From old vines, quantities of Anjou Rouge and Cabernet d'Anjou are made, plus some sweet Coteaux de l'Aubance. *Open: By appointment only.*

Les Vins Touchais
49700 Doué-la-Fontaine. Vineyards owned: 16ha. VP-R and N

One of the remarkable discoveries of the 1980s was the vast quantity of old wines held in the cellars of Touchais in Doué-la-Fontaine. Most of the wines were of Coteaux du Layon and Anjou, and all were sweet. They came from the family vineyards, Les Vignobles Touchais. There is also a *négociant* business which deals in Anjou Rosé and other local wines.

Coteaux du Layon AC, Quarts de Chaume AC, Bonnezeaux AC

Domaine des Baumard
8 Rue de l'Abbaye, 49190 Rochefort-sur-Loire. Vineyards owned: Quarts de Chaume 3·5ha; Savennières 12·4ha; Coteaux du Layon 1ha; Anjou 12ha. 100,000 bottles. VP-R

Quarts de Chaume and Savennières are inevitably the top two wines from this producer. But the quality throughout the range is high and M Baumard makes some of the best and most consistent wines in the region. His Quarts de Chaume has the true intensity of this great sweet wine and only really develops after ten years in bottle. His Savennières (he owns part of the Clos du Papillon), on the other hand, is a faster developer than Savennières from other producers and is very drinkable after four to five years. Clos de Sainte-Catherine Coteaux du Layon is a lovely contrast between intensity and lightness. Other wines made are a Crémant de Loire from Chardonnay and a red Anjou, Logis de la Giraudière, from Cabernet Franc. *Open: Appointments preferred.*

Domaine Beaujeau
Champ-sur-Layon, 49380 Thouarcé. Vineyards owned: 10ha

From cellars near the church of Champ-sur-Layon, the Beaujeau family makes long-lived Coteaux du Layon. The wines age well.

Jacques Boivin (Château de Fesle)
49380 Thouarcé. Vineyards owned: 33ha. VP-R
One of the top producers of Bonnezeaux, which is fermented and aged in small barrels. The wine in good years can be superb. M Boivin also makes standard Anjou wines: red and white, plus Vin de Pays du Jardin de la France using Chardonnay. The Château de Fesle itself is built on an 11th-century foundation, and the Boivin family has been there for many generations. *Open: By appointment only.*

Jean-Pierre Chéné
Impasse de Jardins, Beaulieu-sur-Layon, 49190 Rochefort-sur-Loire. Vineyards owned: 21ha
A family vineyard in Beaulieu-sur-Layon producing red wines from Cabernet Franc as well as Coteaux du Layon Beaulieu. There are a number of named vineyards: Clos du Paradis Terrestre, Clos des Mulonnières and Clos des Ontinières. They use a long slow fermentation process to achieve maximum fruit.

Fardeau-Robin (Domaine des Hauts Perrays)
49290 Chaudefonds-sur-Layon. Vineyards owned: Coteaux du Layon 12ha; Anjou 13ha. 80,000 bottles. VP-R
The actual Domaine des Hauts Perrays produces an Anjou Blanc from Chenin Blanc and Chardonnay (20 percent), the Chardonnay cutting the natural harshness of the Chenin. They also make about 40,000 bottles of a soft, medium-sweet Coteaux du Layon. Red wines include an Anjou Rouge – also Domaine des Hauts Perrays – from Cabernet Franc (70 percent) and Cabernet Sauvignon (30 percent). *Open: By appointment only.*

Vignobles Laffourcade (Château de Suronde)
49190 Rochefort-sur-Loire. Vineyards owned: Quarts de Chaume 20ha. 60,000 bottles. VP-R
The largest producer by far in the Quarts de Chaume. They use fermentation in stainless steel before maturation in wood to make fine examples of this superb sweet wine. Do not expect to enjoy their wine before ten years, but then savour every mouthful. Names they use are Château de Suronde and Château de l'Echarderie. *Open: By appointment only.*

Jacques Lalanne (Château de Belle Rive)
49190 Rochefort-sur-Loire. Vineyards owned: Quarts de Chaume 17ha. 20,000 bottles. VP-R
Expense is no object in the vineyard: picking is done over a number of weeks in a series of passes, gathering only the ripest, most nobly-rotten grapes each time. Fermentation takes place in large barrels and bottling in the spring after the vintage. This means that Quarts de Chaume matures in bottle, taking upwards of ten years to do so. The rewards are there for those willing to wait. Quarts de Chaume is the only wine made. *Open: By appointment only.*

Fernand Moron
8 Rue de Perinelle, St-Lambert du Lattay, 49190 Rochefort-sur-Loire. Vineyards owned: Coteaux du Layon 11ha; Anjou 12ha. 120,000 bottles. VP-R
M Moron makes a whole range of wines: from the sweet Coteaux du Layon St-Lambert and Coteaux du Layon, through Anjou Blanc and Rouge and Rosé Cabernet d'Anjou and Rosé de Loire. Half the vineyard is of Chenin Blanc, but he also has Cabernet Franc, Chardonnay, Grolleau and Gamay. His best wine is inevitably the Coteaux du Layon St-Lambert which shares some of the intensity of Quarts de Chaume in good years and ages well. *Open: By appointment only.*

René Renou
Place du Champ de Foire, 49380 Thouarcé. Vineyards owned: Thouarcé 18ha. 100,000 bottles. VP-R
Top of M Renou's production is his Bonnezeaux, made in wood and matured in bottle. This is a family firm – the seventh-generation René Renou is now eight years old – and methods are traditional, especially for the sweet wines. M Renou is president of the Bonnezeaux growers and a keen supporter of his *cru*, joining with others in marketing it, and luckily his wines live up to its reputation. He also makes dry Anjou Blanc, Rosé de Loire, Rosé d'Anjou and Anjou Rouge. *Open: By appointment only.*

Henri Rochais et Fils (Château de Plaisance)
49190 Rochefort-sur-Loire. Vineyards owned: Coteaux du
Layon Chaume 13·5ha; Anjou 1·5ha. 50,000 bottles. VP-R
Not to be confused with Quarts de Chaume, Coteaux du Layon
Chaume is nevertheless one of the best of the Coteaux du Layon
Villages from vineyards just up the hill from Quarts de Chaume
and sharing some of the microclimate. M Rochais picks the grapes
ripe during successive passes through the vineyard, vinifies in tank
then gives the wine a short period in wood before bottling. He also
makes dry Anjou Blanc and Anjou Rouge from Cabernet
Sauvignon (60 percent) and Cabernet Franc (30 percent). *Open:
Appointments preferred.*

André Sorin (Domaine de la Motte)
31 Avenue d'Angers, 49190 Rochefort-sur-Loire.
Vineyards owned: Rochefort 17ha. 130,000 bottles. VP-R
While Rosé d'Anjou is M Sorin's largest production, he also makes
a Coteaux du Layon Rochefort from a south-facing slope, which is
a fine example of this sweet white wine – and one with which he
obviously takes considerable care. Apart from these wines, he
makes the usual range of Anjou wines, including an Anjou Sec Clos
des Belles Mères from Chardonnay and an Anjou Mousseux from
Chenin Blanc. *Open: By appointment only.*

Pierre-Yves Tijou (Domaine de la Soucherie)
Beaulieu-sur-Layon, 49190 Rochefort-sur-Loire.
Vineyards owned: 35ha. 200,000 bottles. VP-R
A large landowner in an area of small holdings, the bulk of M
Tijou's wine is of Coteaux du Layon and Coteaux du Layon
Chaume. However, he tends not to use wood for his white wines,
preferring to make a wine that is fresher and quicker to mature
than some of the sweet wines of the area. He also makes the full
range of Anjou AC wines, including a superior Crémant de la
Soucherie. *Open: By appointment only.*

Saumur AC and Saumur-Champigny AC

Ackerman-Laurance
St-Hilaire-St-Florent, 49400 Saumur. Vineyards owned:
None. 3·3 million bottles. N
A *négociant* and producer specializing in sparkling wines. The oldest
producer of Saumur, and still one of the largest. The bulk of
production is of good-quality sparkling white and rosé Saumur, all
made in stainless steel, but in a range of qualities, including the top
Cuvée Privilège and Cuvée Privée. They also make considerable
quantities of very good Crémant de Loire. *Open: Mon–Fri 9:30am–
noon; 2:30–5pm. Appointments necessary for groups.*

Bouvet-Ladubay
St-Hilaire-St-Florent, 49400 Saumur. Vineyards owned:
none. 1·6 million bottles. N
Producers of some of the best sparkling Saumur, the firm has
contracts with 150 growers in the Saumur region, from which it
draws all of its wine requirements. They make two qualities of
Saumur – a standard range and the Excellence range, which
includes the Crémant Brut Saphir and the vintage Crémant d'Or.
Other wines in their portfolio include white, red and rosé *brut*
sparkling using the general Anjou AC. Overall, the standard is
high. The firm is part of the Taittinger Champagne group. *Open:
Mon–Fri 8am–noon; 2–6pm.*

Domaine Vinicole de Chaintres
Dampierre-sur-Loire, 49400 Saumur. Vineyards owned:
Saumur 20ha. 130,000 bottles. VP-R
The Château de Chaintres is a red-wine estate, producing wine for
the firm's classic Saumur-Champigny. Methods are traditional and
wood is used for maturation, giving wines with some lasting power
and extra tannin. The style seems to have become lighter in recent
years, probably because stainless steel is being used as well. Owner
Bernard de Tigny also makes a white Saumur Blanc. *Open: By
appointment only.*

Claude Daheuiller
28 Rue du Ruau, Varrains, 49400 Saumur. Vineyards

owned: Saumur 23ha. 130,000 bottles. VP-R
Main production here is of a good Saumur-Champigny made from
the estate of Domaine des Varinelles. Half the wine is made in
wood, the other half in stainless steel, then the two are blended,
giving some firmness and structure but allowing for early drinking
and plenty of instant fruit. They also make still white Saumur and a
little sparkling Saumur Brut. Small amounts of Sauvignon and
Rosé de Loire are also produced. *Open: By appointment only.*

Denis Duveau
27 Rue de la Mairie, Varrains, 49400 Saumur. Vineyards
owned: Saumur-Champigny 10ha. 50,000 bottles. VP-R
Producer of one of the more intense, rich Saumur-Champigny,
principally because at least 20 percent of the wine comes from old
vines. Vinification and maturation are all in wood. The family has
been on the land for four generations and sticks entirely to the one
wine. *Open: By appointment only.*

Domaine Filliatreau
Chaintres, Dampierre-sur-Loire, 49400 Saumur. Vineyards
owned: 30ha
This is the largest producer of Saumur-Champigny, made in a
modern way with controlled fermentation at 24°C (low for red
wines). Some of the *cuvées* see wood: Vieilles Vignes and Lena
Filliatreau for example, while the Jeunes Vignes is bottled straight
from tank. The wines are excellent examples of the *appellation* and
have done much to promote its virtues.

J-L et B Foucault
Chacé, 49400 Saumur
The Foucault brothers are the latest in the family's many
generations of wine production in Saumur-Champigny. They
make wines which are designed for ageing: so much so that they
have matured some of them in casks from Château Margaux in
Bordeaux. They certainly do age well, as do their whites under the
Coteaux de Saumur *appellation*.

Gratien, Meyer, Seydoux
Château de Beaulieu, Route de Chinon, 49400 Saumur.

Vineyards owned: Saumur 20ha. 2·5 million bottles. VP-R and N

Gratien & Meyer is the brand name for a range of sparkling Saumur wines – brut, demi-sec and rosé. They also make a red sparkling wine from 100 percent Cabernet Franc. The quality is very reliable (they consider that 'behind the mousse there should be a pleasant wine') and the wines are widely distributed throughout the world. The firm owns the champagne house of Alfred Gratien. *Open: Mon–Sat 9am–noon; 2–6pm.*

Langlois–Château
BP6, 3 Rue Léopold Palustre, St-Hilaire-St-Florent, 49416 Saumur. Vineyards owned: Saumur 27ha; Sancerre 15ha. 200,000 bottles. VP-R and N

One of the famous names in sparkling Saumur, Langlois–Château also produce red and white still wines from the same AC and Sancerre red and white wines from their estate at Château Fontaine-Audon. Production is quite modern in approach, using stainless steel. The firm is owned by the Champagne house of Bollinger. *Open: Summer only, Mon–Fri 10:30am–12:30pm; 3–6:30pm.*

Sylvain Mainfray
Rue Jean Jaurès, 49400 Saumur. 360,000 bottles. N

A firm of *négociants* which sells wines from Anjou, Saumur and Touraine. Unusually, they have the wines bottled by the growers rather than doing the *élevage* and bottling at a central cellar. This certainly enhances the individual characteristics of each wine.

De Neuville
St-Hilaire-St-Florent, 49400 Saumur. Vineyards owned: 40ha

Producers of sparkling Saumur, partly from their own vineyards and partly from purchased grapes. Quality is reliable.

Edouard Pisani-Ferry (Château de Targé)
49730 Parnay. Vineyards owned: Saumur-Champigny 20ha. 100,000 bottles. VP-R

The château has been in the family since 1655, but methods are modern, with stainless steel and temperature control used for fermentation. The total production is of Saumur-Champigny, which is then matured for six months in wood. The blend employs ten percent Cabernet Sauvignon to top up the Cabernet Franc and the results are a wine which is most attractive in the second year after vintage. *Open: Mon–Fri, during working hours.*

Rémy-Pannier
St-Hilaire-St-Florent, 49400 Saumur. Vineyards owned: none. 15 million bottles. N
Probably the largest *négociant* in the Loire Valley, buying in all their requirements. They make wines from virtually every AC in the Loire, all to a standard, if uninspiring, quality. Their Saumur wines are probably their best. Their marketing techniques are highly sophisticated.

Philippe et Georges Vatan
49400 Saumur
Based in the Château de Hureau, the Vatan family has been producing wine for three generations. They make just the one wine, the red Saumur-Champigny, which in good years can age remarkably well.

Savennières AC, Coulée de Serrant AC, Roches-aux-Moines AC

Société Bizard (Château d'Epiré)
Epiré, 49170 Savennières. Vineyards owned: Savennières 10ha. 50,000 bottles. VP-R
Stock turnover is obviously not a consideration here. The Savennières is not really drinkable for ten to 12 years, and will last for up to 30 or more. Like other Savennières producers, they need to pass through the vineyard two or three times to get the grapes at their ripest – even though they are making a dry wine. Vinification and maturation of the wines are all in wood. They also make small quantities of Anjou Rouge and Rosé de Loire – probably to keep the money coming in. *Open: Appointments preferred.*

Mme de Jessey (Domaine du Closel)

49170 Savennières. Vineyards owned: Savennières 12ha; Anjou 2ha. 60,000 bottles. VP-R
Mme de Jessey makes a classic, dry white Savennières, vinified and matured in wood and needing a considerable time before it is ready to drink. This is probably the truest Savennières, sometimes lacking the intensity of Coulée de Serrant but with what the French call *nervosité* and poised balance. Mme de Jessey also makes red Anjou from Cabernet Franc and Cabernet Sauvignon, again matured in wood. *Open: By appointment only.*

Mme Joly
Vignoble de la Coulée de Serrant, Château de la Roche-aux-Moines, 49170 Savennières. Vineyards owned: Savennières-Coulée de Serrant 7ha, Savennières-Roche-aux-Moines 2ha; Coteaux de la Loire 2ha. 20,000 bottles
Low yields, intense fruit and high quality are the reasons for the low production at this famous estate. Mme Joly is one of the few owners in France who controls an entire AC (Coulée de Serrant); the other well-known example is Château Grillet on the Rhône. Coulée de Serrant is an ancient monastic vineyard, Roche-aux-Moines was planted first in the 12th century. Wines are treated as naturally as possible with few chemicals. They are vinified in wood and bottled with the minimum of filtration. Despite their dryness, these Savennières wines need a minimum of five years in bottle before drinking, and will survive seemingly for ever. The risks are high: for three years in the 1970s production was well below normal and in 1972 nothing was made at all. Demand, though, is enormous and prices have followed demand upwards. Mme Joly also makes a Coteaux de Loire Rouge from Cabernet Franc and Cabernet Sauvignon – with the same extreme care. *Open: Mon–Sat 8:30am–noon; 2–5:30pm.*

François Roussier
Clos de Coulaine, 49170 Savennières. Vineyards owned: Savennières 8ha. 50,000 bottles. VP-R
About a third of production here is of Savennières, while the rest is of Anjou Rouge made from Cabernet Franc. Like most other Savennières producers, methods are traditional with vinification in wood and long ageing in bottle required. The red is well made, less

interesting than the white but certainly one of the better Anjou Rouges. M Roussier's estate has been in the family since 1860. *Open: By appointment only.*

Pierre et Yves Soulez (Château de Chamboureau)
49170 Savennières. Vineyards owned: Savennières 21ha; Anjou 3ha. 120,000 bottles. VP-R

One of the most technically advanced of the Anjou producers, who yet contrives to make a Savennières that really needs time in bottle. Most of the production is of Savennières and the three sections of the estate are bottled separately: Domaine de la Bizolière, Clos du Papillon, Château de Chamboureau. Of the three, I prefer Clos du Papillon, of which the Soulez family own two hectares. They also make a small amount of the superior Savennières-Roche-aux-Moines, under the Château de Chamboureau name. The other wine they produce is an Anjou Rouge, 50/50 Cabernet Franc/Cabernet Sauvignon. *Open: Mon–Sat 8am–12:30pm; 1:30–6:30pm.*

Haut-Poitou VDQS

Cave Coopérative du Haut-Poitou
32 Rue Alphonse Plault, 86170 Neuville de Poitou. Vineyards owned: 808ha. 3·2 million bottles. Coop (625 members)

This cooperative has revived the fortunes of the Haut-Poitou vineyard area, by making a very good range of varietal wines. The best are from Chardonnay and Sauvignon, but they also make reds from Cabernet Franc and Gamay. Also produced are *méthode champenoise* wines from Chardonnay and a sparkling rosé called Diane de Poitiers. All the wines are made by modern techniques, using stainless steel. *Open: By appointment only.*

Western Loire Producers
Muscadet AC

Auguste Bonhomme
1 Rue de la Roche, Gorges, 44190 Clisson. Vineyards
owned: Muscadet 25ha. 960,000 bottles. VP-R and N
Fief de la Brie and Domaine du Banchereau are the two estate-
bottled wines from this *négociant*. Eighty percent of sales comes
from wine which is bought in from the area, the bulk of it from
Muscadet AC. A smaller amount of Gros Plant is also sold.
Techniques are quite traditional. *Open: Mon–Fri 8am–noon; 2–6pm.*

Pierre et Luc Choblet (Domaine des Herbauges)
Herbauges, 44830 Bouaye. 145,000 bottles. VP-R
New techniques are used to make straightforward, slightly *pétillant*
Muscadet and also some Gros Plant. The vineyard contains some
35-year-old vines. The wines are bottled *sur lie*. There are two
brand names: Domaine des Herbauges and Clos de la Senaigerie.
They also make some rosé Vin de Pays du Jardin de la France from
Grolleau and red from Gamay, plus a *méthode champenoise* called
Perlant Ste-Cecile. *Open: By appointment only.*

René Erraud (Château de la Roulière)
44310 St-Colomban. Vineyards owned: St-Colomban
30ha. 30,000 bottles. VP-R
Muscadet, Gros Plant and *vin de pays* (from Gamay, Cabernet Franc
and Grolleau) are all produced by this traditional grower.
Production is 45 percent Muscadet, 45 percent Gros Plant and ten
percent *vin de pays*. Much of it is sold in bulk to *négociants*. What is
bottled is sold under the Château de la Roulière name. *Open: By
appointment only.*

Muscadet de Sèvre et Maine AC

Aubert Frères
49270 La Varenne. Vineyards owned: Muscadet 59ha;
Anjou 13ha. 7 million bottles. VP-R and N

One of the major *négociants* of the Muscadet/Anjou area, but whose main vineyard holdings are in Muscadet. Their range of wines includes lesser *appellations* like Coteaux d'Ancenis, but their interests cover the whole Loire: from Sancerre and Pouilly-Fumé in the east to Vin de Pays de Maine et Loire and Muscadet in the west. They also produce wines from further afield: Côtes de Provence, Côtes de Duras and Côtes du Rhône. The techniques are modern and their cellars well run. *Open: By appointment only.*

Jérome et André Batard
La Bigotière, 44690 Maisdon-sur-Sèvre. Vineyards owned: Muscadet de Sèvre et Maine: Domaine le Rossignol 15ha. 50,000 bottles. VP-R
Nine-tenths of production is of Muscadet de Sèvre et Maine, with a small amount of Gros Plant. The vineyard has been run by the family for many generations, but now techniques are modern, with stainless steel and temperature controls. There is a *cuvée de prestige*, Carte Noire. *Open: Appointments preferred.*

Guy Bossard (Domaine de l'Ecu)
La Bretonnière, 44300 Le Louroux-Bottereau. Vineyards owned: 17ha
M Bossard has made a considerable name for himself with his entirely organic Muscadet, which regularly shows well at tastings and which demonstrates the high quality of wines bottled from the lees. The wines have the additional quality of ageing well – not normally associated with Muscadet.

Henri Bouchaud
Le Bois Joly, Le Pallet, 44330 Vallet. Vineyards owned: Muscadet de Sèvre et Maine: Le Pallet 13ha. 85,000 bottles. VP-R
Domaine du Bois Joly is the name for the Muscadet de Sèvre et Maine produced here. There is also some Gros Plant VDQS and red Vin de Pays du Jardin de la France Cabernet Franc. *Open: By appointment only.*

Jean Bouyer
49 Rue d'Anjou, La Charouillère, 44330 Vallet. Vineyards

owned: 11·5ha. 20,000 bottles. VP-R
Domaine de la Pingossière and Domaine du Clos Julienne are the
two names used by this young producer. M Bouyer makes
Muscadet de Sèvre et Maine, plus a little Gros Plant and Gamay-
based Vin de Pays des Marches de Bretagne. Fifty percent of
production is sold to *négociants. Open: Appointments preferred.*

André-Michel Brégeon
**Les Guisseaux-Gorges, 44190 Clisson. Vineyards owned:
7·5ha. 48,000 bottles. VP-R**
Traditional techniques (including a short period of wood maturation) are used here and the wines are bottled at the estate *sur lie.*
This gives a fuller style of wine and also an attractive prickle on the
palate. M Brégeon's Gros Plant is a very good example. He also
makes a small quantity of Vin de Pays des Marches de Bretagne
from Cabernet Franc and Cabernet Sauvignon. *Open: Mon–Fri
10am–7pm.*

Robert Brosseau (Domaine des Mortiers Gobin)
**44690 La Haie-Fouassière. Vineyards owned: 9ha. 50,000
bottles. VP-R**
The wines sold under the Domaine des Mortiers Gobin name are
bottled *sur lie* and methods are traditional, with some wood
maturation before bottling. M Brosseau's family has owned the
land 'for ever'. *Open: By appointment only.*

Le Cellier des Ducs
**Rue de Sèvre et Maine, 44450 La Chapelle-Basse-Mer.
1 million bottles. N**
Large-scale *négociant* making a range of wines from the Pays
Nantais. They sell wines from a number of Muscadet de Sèvre et
Maine estates: Domaine des Morines, Château de la Bigotière,
Château de Richebourg and Domaine de Bigotière. *Open: By
appointment only.*

Guy Charpentier
**Les Noues, 44430 Le Loroux-Bottereau. Vineyards owned:
12ha. 40,000 bottles. VP-R**
Three-quarters of production here is of Muscadet de Sèvre et

Maine, with smaller amounts of Gros Plant and Vin de Pays du Jardin de la France (from Gamay), plus Vin de Pays des Marches de Bretagne (from Cabernet Franc). Vineyard holdings are in four communes: Le Loroux-Bottereau, Le Landreau, La Chapelle-Heulin and La Chapelle-Basse-Mer. M Charpentier also makes a *méthode champenoise* called La Belle Folie. *Open: By appointment only.*

Ets Chéreau-Carré
Château de Chasseloir, St-Fiacre-sur-Maine, 44690 La Haie-Fouassière. Vineyards owned: 74ha. 505,000 bottles. VP-R
The Chéreau family is one of the biggest landowners in Muscadet de Sèvre et Maine, with five estates in some of the best vineyard land in the area. Château de Chasseloir (17 hectares) is the centre of operations. The other estates are: Château du Coing (30 hectares); La Bournaire (five hectares); Moulin de la Gravelle (12 hectares); and Château de l'Oiselinière de la Ramée at Vertou (ten hectares). Each estate makes a straight Muscadet de Sèvre et Maine and a *cuvée de prestige*, but all are bottled *sur lie* at the individual estate and sold under the estate name. Quality of the wines is high, although Château de Chasseloir is generally regarded as the best. *Open: Apply to Château de Chasseloir.*

Donatien Bahuaud
La Loge, La Chapelle-Heulin, 44330 Vallet. Vineyards owned: 18ha. 412,000 bottles. VP-R and N
Two main brands come from this firm. Le Master de Donatien is the *négociant* brand, launched with the '84 vintage. This is sold in a specially designed, painted bottle. Quality is reliable if unexciting. More interesting is the estate-bottled Château de la Cassemichère which is bottled *sur lie* and has some wood maturation. The firm has undertaken extensive marketing for its wines and has gained widespread publicity. They also make a good Chardonnay *vin de table*, called Le Chouan. *Open: By appointment only.*

Domaine des Dorices
La Touché, 44330 Vallet. Vineyards owned: 31ha. 200,000 bottles. VP-R
The Boullault family has run this ancient vineyard since the 1930s,

making wines using no chemicals in the winery. They are particularly proud of their Domaine des Dorices which, unusually for Muscadet, needs two years' ageing. They also make a younger-style Muscadet, Château la Touché, plus a Gros Plant and a *méthode champenoise* called Leconte. Quality is high here. *Open: By appointment only.*

Joseph Drouard
La Hallopière, 44690 Monnières. Vineyards owned: 13ha.
80,000 bottles. VP-R
As serious a producer as is possible to find with Muscadet, making wine traditionally and bottling *sur lie* at the domaine. The wine is full-bodied and needs a little time in bottle. M Drouard allows no other wines to distract him. *Open: By appointment only.*

R E Dugast
Domaine des Moulins, Monnières, 44690 La Haie-
Fouassière. Vineyards owned: 9ha
A small estate which makes Muscadet *sur lie* under the names Domaine des Moulins and Cuvée des Grands Quarterons and also some sparkling wines from Gros Plant, which, the producer advises, need to be drunk very cold.

Domaine de la Févrie
La Févrie, Maisdon-sur-Sèvre, 44690 La Haie-Fouassière.
Vineyards owned: 13ha. 70,000 bottles. VP-R
Three generations of the Branger family have worked this land. They now employ modern techniques of temperature control but continue to bottle *sur lie* to protect the wine's 'gaiety and youth'. The result is a classic Muscadet which can take some bottle-ageing. *Open: By appointment only.*

Gabare de Sèvre
Le Pé de Sèvre, Le Pallet, 44330 Vallet. Vineyards owned:
80ha. 160,000 bottles. VP-R
This group of nine small landowners was set up in 1982 and already it has become a powerful force in the region. Each member of the group vinifies and bottles his own wine; the group then sells it. The 70 percent of wine not sold in bottles goes to *négociants*. The bulk of

production is of Muscadet, which goes under the Gabare de Sèvre label; the remainder is of Gros Plant. The name Gabare refers to the barges which used to transport wine along the Sèvre. *Open: By appointment only.*

Château de la Galissonière
Le Pallet, 44330 Vallet. Vineyards owned: 39ha. VP–R
The estate consists of two properties, Château de la Galissonière and Château de la Jannière, both of which produce lively, fresh Muscadet of good quality. The family of Pierre Lusseaud, the owner, has been at the estate since 1912. Modern techniques are very much to the fore here, making wine that is delicious in the summer following the vintage. M Lusseaud also makes Gros Plant and Vin de Pays des Marches de Bretagne from Cabernet Franc and Chardonnay. *Open: By appointment only.*

Marquis de Goulaine (Château de Goulaine)
Haute-Goulaine, 44115 Basse-Goulaine. Vineyards owned: 30·7ha. 350,000 bottles. VP–R and N
The château of Goulaine dates from the 15th century and the estate has been in the family for 1,000 years. When you are that well established, it's a good thing that the wine is setting an example to the neighbours. Much of the wine is of a modern style, which needs early drinking, but the Cuvée du Millénaire, made from old vines, repays a couple of years' keeping. Gros Plant is also made. *Open: The château is open from 2–6pm, the winery by appointment only.*

Guilbaud Frères
Les Lilas, Mouzillon, 44330 Vallet. Vineyards owned: 16·5ha. 2·5 million bottles. VP–R and N
About five percent of production here is from three estates owned by this large *négociant* firm. They bottle Domaine de la Pingossière, Domaine de la Moutonnière and Clos du Pont separately. Other Muscadet de Sèvre et Maine goes under a variety of brand names: Le Soleil Nantais, Cuvée Grand Or, Cuvée du Lion. Wines tend to a soft style. *Open: By appointment only.*

Domaine de la Hautière
44690 St-Fiacre-sur-Maine. Vineyards owned: 10ha. 90,000

bottles. VP-R and N
The Thébaud family have run this small *négociant* and farm for
many generations and today buy in 50 percent of their stock as
grapes from vineyards owned by other members of the family.
They make one estate wine, Domaine de la Hautière, bottled *sur lie*
in the March following vintage; they also make a *négociant*
Muscadet, Les Doyennes, and a Gros Plant. *Open: Appointments
preferred.*

Michel et Jean-Claude Lebas
38 Rue de Bazoges, 44330 Vallet. Vineyards owned: 15ha.
60,000 bottles. VP-R
Domaine de la Rouxière is the estate, but Réserve des Noes Gueréts
is the name of the best wine to come from this small family firm. It is
a comparatively sophisticated wine, quite soft and with an
attractive tingle from being bottled *sur lie*. They also make Gros
Plant. *Open: By appointment only.*

Domaine de la Louvetries (Pierre et Joseph Landron)
**Les Brandières, 44690 La Haie-Fouassière. Vineyards
owned: 22ha**
The vineyards of this estate are on a well-sited slope, Coteaux du
Breil, on schist soil, which gives the wines an ability to age. The
basic *cuvée*, Domaine de la Louvetries, however, is designed for
early drinking. They make a prestige *cuvée*, which is sold in a
satinized bottle, and two *cuvées* (Cuvée Concours and Hermine
d'Or) which are blends designed after blind tastings by other
growers.

Pierre et Rémy Luneau (Domaine de la Grange)
**44430 Le Landreau. Vineyards owned: 30ha. 150,000
bottles. VP-R**
The Muscadet here is bottled *sur lie*. The style is quite traditional
(the family have been *vignerons* since 1680) and tends to fullness.
They also make a small quantity of Gros Plant. Interestingly, they
like to bottle the different sections of the vineyard separately and
label them accordingly: Clos de Rochettes, Clos de la Claretière,
Clos des Allées, Cuvée Domaine. *Open: By appointment only.*

Château de la Mercredière
Le Pallet, 44330 Vallet. Vineyards owned: 36ha. 220,000 bottles. VP-R

The vineyard surrounds a beautiful 14th-century château on the banks of the River Sèvre. The winemaking, though, is modern, with stainless steel and bottling under inert gas. The wine is smooth, not too acid, and with plenty of fruit. It responds to a little ageing. *Open: Mon–Fri 9am–noon; 2–6pm.*

Louis Métaireau
La Fevrie, 44690 Maisdon-sur-Sèvre. Vineyards owned: 107ha. 210,000 bottles. Group of producers

Louis Métaireau has organized a group of nine producers who pool resources and make *cuvées* which are sold under M Métaireau's name. The wines are selected jointly, but bottled *sur lie* at each producer's own cellars. The group also owns one vineyard, the Grand Mouton, as a joint venture. The success of this enterprise lies in the high quality of the wines. *Open: By appointment only.*

Château la Noë
44330 Vallet. Vineyards owned: 60ha. 150,000 bottles. VP-R

The Comte de Malestroit, whose family property this is, produces a classic Muscadet, unusually full-bodied, intended for some ageing. It is not bottled *sur lie*. The estate, set around a classical mansion, has been in the family since 1740. *Open: By appointment only.*

Château de l'Oiselinière Gorges
44190 Clisson. Vineyards owned: 32ha. 200,000 bottles. VP-R

The heart of the estate is a 19th-century Italianate villa, but the Aulanier family has owned the land since 1765. It is divided into four parcels, mainly producing Muscadet de Sèvre et Maine. There is also some Gros Plant. The winemaking is a mixture of traditional and modern. *Open: Mon–Fri 9:30am–noon; 3–6pm.*

Bernard Pichon (Domaine des Croix)
44330 Vallet. Vineyards owned: 17ha. 120,000 bottles. VP-R

Eighty percent of production here is of Muscadet de Sèvre et Maine, with smaller amounts of Gros Plant (15 percent) and Vin de Pays du Jardin de la France (from Gamay and Cabernet Franc). The wines are bottled by Le Cellier du Prieuré at St-George-sur-Loire. *Open: By appointment only.*

Château de la Ragotière
La Regrippière, 44330 Vallet. Vineyards owned: 29ha.
190,000 bottles. VP-R

The château is an old property, with a 14th-century chapel, but the present owners, the Couillaud family, have been in charge since 1979. They are moving away from traditional techniques to stainless steel. The Muscadet de Sèvre et Maine is clean and penetrating, with citrus undertones: it can be very attractive when drunk young. They also make a Gros Plant wine. *Open: By appointment only.*

Clos des Rosiers
44330 Vallet. Vineyards owned: 13ha. 70,000 bottles. VP-R

This is a traditional producer, who uses some wood for maturation, making a fragrant wine with plenty of fruit which takes some ageing. About two-thirds of the production is of Muscadet de Sèvre et Maine, the rest is of Gros Plant. The vineyard's title, Clos des Rosiers, is used as a brand name. *Open: By appointment only.*

Marcel Sautejeau (Domaine de l'Hyvernière)
Le Pallet, 44330 Vallet. Vineyards owned: 70ha. 450,000
bottles. VP-R and N

As the *vigneron* at Domaine de l'Hyvernière, Marcel Sautejeau produces Muscadet de Sèvre et Maine, which is bottled *sur lie* at the estate. As the *négociant*, they handle wines from Anjou, Saumur and Vouvray. The domaine's history goes back to mediaeval times when it was visited by the French King Henri IV when he came to sign the Edict of Nantes in 1598. *Open: By appointment only.*

Sauvion et Fils (Château du Cléray)
44330 Vallet. Vineyards owned: 35ha. 700,000 bottles.
VP-R and N

The Château du Cléray estate is the heart of a *négociant* business which produces a range of qualities of Muscadet. The *négociant* side takes 80 percent of production and they make Carte d'Or and Lauréat brands, as well as Château du Cléray, which is bottled *sur lie*, and the prestige *cuvée*, Cardinal Richard. Quality is high with all these wines, the style generally being soft, with attractive earthy overtones. They pay great attention to the quality of each vineyard from which they buy wine. La Nobleraie is a brand name for that produced from bought-in grapes. *Open: During working hours.*

André Vinet
12 Rue du Progrès Uilbaud, 44330 Vallet. Vineyards owned: None. 3 million bottles. N
A *négociant* specializing in the wines of the Pays Nantais. They make Muscadet de Sèvre et Maine and some Gros Plant, plus a sparkling *blanc de blancs*. The range varies, with the wines from some estates being bottled separately – one of them, Château la Touché, is run on organic lines. *Open: By appointment only.*

Coteaux d'Ancenis VDQS

Jacques Guindon
La Couleuverdière, St-Geréon, 44150 Ancenis. Vineyards owned: Ancenis 8ha; Muscadet Coteaux de la Loire 14ha; Gros Plant 3ha. 200,000 bottles. VP-R and N
Inevitably, Muscadet and Muscadet Coteaux de la Loire *sur lie* are the largest production from the *négociant* side of the firm – representing 20 percent of requirements. But the interest lies in 8,000 bottles of sweet Malvoisie wine made under the Coteaux d'Ancenis VDQS: a honeyed dessert wine with a good balance. They also make rosé Coteaux d'Ancenis from Gamay and red from Cabernet Franc and Cabernet Sauvignon. Some of the red is matured in wood. *Open: Mon–Sat.*

Les Vignerons de la Noëlle
BP 102, 44150 Ancenis. Vineyards owned: 459ha. 2 million bottles. Coop (300 members)
One of the few cooperatives in the Muscadet area, this produces large quantities of simple Muscadet from 220 hectares under a

number of different brand names. Other wines they make include red Coteaux d'Ancenis from 50 hectares of Gamay, Gros Plant and red Vin de Pays du Jardin de la France. They also make some red and white wines under the Anjou AC, plus a small amount of Crémant de Loire from Chardonnay grapes. Standards are improving with the installation of new equipment. *Open: By appointment only.*

Fiefs Vendéens VDQS

Mercier Frères (Domaine de la Chaignée)
La Chaignée, 85770 Vix. Vineyards owned: Fiefs Vendéens Vix 25ha. 9,000 bottles. VP-R
All the wines at this small estate are made in stainless steel. White comes from a blend of Chenin Blanc, Sauvignon and Chardonnay; rosé from Gamay, Pinot Noir and Cabernet Franc. Red wine from Gamay, Cabernet Franc and Cabernet Sauvignon is made by a semi-carbonic maceration method.

Ph et X Coirier
La Petite Groie, Pisotte, 85200 Fontenay-le-Comte.
Vineyards owned: Fiefs Vendéens Pisotte 16ha. 50,000 bottles. VP-R
Over half the production here is of red and rosé wines – a blend of Gamay, Pinot Noir and Cabernet Sauvignon. The red is a light-coloured wine, best drunk chilled and at its best a year after the vintage. The white is a fragrant blend of Colombard with Chenin Blanc and Muscadet. *Open: Appointments preferred.*

Arsene Rambaud
Follet, Bosnay, 85320 Mareuil-sur-Lay. Vineyards owned: Fiefs Vendéens 4ha. 6,000 bottles. VP-R
Red and rosé Fiefs Vendéens are produced from a range of grapes: Gamay, Pinot Noir, Cabernet Franc and Cabernet Sauvignon and Négrette. About 40 percent of production is sold to *négociants*. *Open: By appointment only.*

Provence

Provence was the first area of France to be planted with vines. They were already growing when Greek traders from Asia Minor arrived at the Phoenician city of Marseille in 600 BC. The Greeks set about consolidating what they found and when the Romans arrived in about 125 BC they continued the process. It was from Provence – the Roman Provincia – that vines were carried north up the Rhône valley to the rest of France.

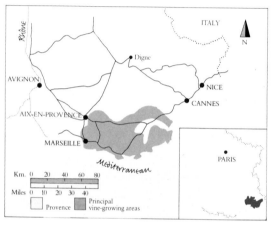

Provence is natural vine-growing country. Long, hot, dry summers and mild winters provide ideal conditions, the cool winds from the sea keep temperatures from soaring too high, while the mountains of Lubéron protect the region from the worst effects of the Mistral wind.

It is a beautiful region to visit. Inland from the strip of resorts along the coast, the landscape is relatively unspoilt. The Massif des Maures looms huge over the vineyards of the Côtes de Provence and the Massif de Sainte-Baume backs the coastal vineyards of Bandol. The vineyards of Les Baux are inside the spectacular circle of jagged mountains called Les Alpilles, with the Alps stretching in a line to the north.

There has always been a market here for the wines. The

Mediterranean coast was colonized first by traders and, more recently, by holidaymakers. Vast quantities of local wine are washed down by the visitors thronging the fashionable resorts of the Côte d'Azur. Because it is so much a part of local society, wine is not treated very seriously in Provence. It is something to be enjoyed and not talked about too much. The general quality of wine is adequate rather than inspiring, although there are a few pockets of vineyards producing high-quality wine. Out of four million hectolitres made each year about 20 percent is of AC status, lower than the French average of 25 percent.

The main concentration of vines is in the *département* of Var, the central part of Provence. Here they cover over half the agricultural land, two-thirds producing rosé, the remainder almost all red. Provence is by far the biggest producer of rosé wine in France, much of it alcoholic, heady stuff with surprisingly little taste but quite a kick. In the past it has been consumed unconcernedly by tourists, but, increasingly, producers are finding a resistance to the old-fashioned heavy style.

Modern equipment has certainly helped to lighten the rosés, giving greater freshness and less risk of oxidation. The ability to control fermentation has also made possible an increase in the planting of vines for white wines, which are undeniably the fashion of the decade. But with 4,500 producers in the Côtes de Provence AC alone, it will take a while for the message to get through that white is in and rosé is out.

Before the creation of AC Côtes de Provence, this vast region was churning out some fairly mediocre wines, with only a few growers aiming for quality. The best wines of Provence came from much smaller areas in the west (Bandol, Cassis and Palette) and east (Bellet), with some decent producers also found around Aix-en-Provence and Les-Baux-en-Provence. Good wine still comes from these areas; but, certainly in Bandol and Bellet, the prices can be unnecessarily high.

Much-needed improvements came with the creation of the AC Côtes de Provence in 1977. Tasting panels were introduced to control the quality, and now taste upwards of 3,000 wines a year. New grape varieties from the north – the Syrah and Cabernet Sauvignon – are being planted to give the wines more taste, and more emphasis has been given to the Tibouren grape, already grown in Provence, which gives a deliciously herby taste to dull rosés based on Grenache and Cinsault.

Other areas of Provence are changing too. The two former VDQS areas of Coteaux d'Aix-en-Provence and Coteaux des Baux-en-Provence have been promoted to AC status, and are probably the best source of good Provençal reds; apart from one or two top estates. They are not too expensive either.

Between Aix-en-Provence and the Côtes de Provence the VDQS Coteaux Varois, established in 1984, is producing some promising wines. The reds have been especially good since the introduction of Cabernet Sauvignon and Syrah. Production is huge – around 30 million bottles – and the price is good. While much of the wine comes from cooperatives, it is the few private estates that are putting in the hard work.

The Appellations
Appellations Contrôlées

Bandol Red, white and rosé wines made in vineyards on the coast between Toulon and Marseille. The total production area is 1,000 hectares, on limestone soil. The approved grape varieties for the reds and rosés include Mourvèdre (about 50 percent of the red vineyards), Grenache, Cinsault, Calitor, Carignan, Syrah and Tibouren. For whites, the grapes are Bourboulenc, Ugni Blanc, Clairette and Sauvignon. The red (by far the greatest production) and rosé wines are the more famous, often commanding high prices. Reds, which have to spend at least 18 months in wood, are deep, intense and spicy and peppery on the palate. Rosés are often aged before bottling and can develop a mature orange colour: they are an acquired taste, but are much appreciated in France. Whites are generally less interesting. Reds can improve in bottle for six years or more, but in general, rosés and whites should be drunk young.

Bellet A tiny AC, to the north of Nice, where most of the wine seems to be consumed. About 40 hectares of vines are planted. The wines can be red, rosé or white, but the white is best. The grapes used for the whites are the local Rolle with Roussanne, Chardonnay, Clairette and Bourboulenc, producing an attractive almondy wine. For reds and rosés, the grapes are the local Braquet (Italian Brachetto) and Folle Noire (Italian Fuella Nera) – this region being close to the Italian border – Cinsault and Grenache. Prices for Bellet wines are high – undeservedly so. Drink young.

Cassis Not to be confused with blackcurrant liqueur. This is an area producing red, rosé and white wines, situated around the small port of Cassis between Marseille and Bandol. There are 150 hectares of vines producing 700,000 bottles each year. The most famous wine of the region is made from a blend of Marsanne, Ugni Blanc, Clairette, Grenache Blanc (locally known as Doucillon) and Sauvignon. The wine is dry, normally pale yellow in colour (because of slight oxidation), and quite tangy – like light *fino* sherry. Reds and rosés are made from Grenache, Cinsault, Mourvèdre and Carignan. Drink whites young. Reds are capable of ageing, but drink sooner than Bandol (*see above*).

Coteaux d'Aix-en-Provence Promoted to AC with the 1985 vintage, this is an area producing some of the best-value wines in Provence. Reds, rosés and whites are all made on 3,000 hectares of chalky soil lying mainly to the south and east of Aix-en-Provence. Reds are made from Cinsault, Grenache, Counoise, Carignan, Mourvèdre, Syrah and Cabernet Sauvignon. The Cabernet has an immense influence on the taste (it can comprise up to 60 percent of the blend) and produces a wine akin to a deep-coloured, intense-tasting Bordeaux. Other reds resemble Côtes du Rhône. The rosés are lighter in colour than Côtes de Provence. Whites (five percent of production) are made from Grenache Blanc, Clairette, Sémillon, Ugni Blanc and Sauvignon: it is the touch of Sauvignon that gives these wines their class, style and freshness, even if they do tend to lack acidity. Age red wines for three to six years. Drink whites and rosés as young as possible.

Coteaux des Baux-en-Provence A much smaller area than Coteaux d'Aix-en-Provence, lying within a circle of mountains near the hilltop resort of Les-Baux-en-Provence. The AC was created for the 1985 vintage. Virtually all the wines are red, although rosé and white are permitted. The general quality of the wine is even higher than that of Aix-en-Provence although they are similar in style. This is partly due to the fact that production is smaller and controlled by private estates. The grape varieties used are the same as for Aix-en-Provence. At the moment prices are very good.

Côtes de Provence By far the largest AC in Provence, covering 18,000 hectares, producing red, rosé and white wines. This huge expanse is divided into three main areas: the coastal vineyards running from St-Tropez to Toulon; the valley north of the Massif des Maures around Les Arcs, and the vineyards further northeast and west of Draguignan. By far the largest production (55 percent) is of rosé wines. The old style was heavily alcoholic and full-bodied, made mainly from Carignan and Grenache grapes. Newer style rosés are lighter and include some Mourvèdre and Tibouren; they are lower in alcohol and cleaner and younger to taste. Reds are the next most important style in Provence. Made from Grenache, Cinsault, Mourvèdre and Carignan, they now also include Syrah and Cabernet Sauvignon to an increasing degree. As with rosés, there has been a change of style and the introduction of these northern grape varieties has led to wines which are fresher and less prone to oxidization. Tannic structure and a firmer, spicy, stalky taste, have replaced the somewhat soft, heavy taste of old-style reds. White wines make up ten to 15 percent of production. Permitted grape varieties are Clairette, Ugni Blanc, Rolle and Sémillon. Early picking and controlled-temperature fermentation are improving these wines beyond all recognition. Reds can age well: try them at between two and five years. Drink rosés and whites as young as possible.

Palette A tiny AC area, just to the east of Aix-en-Provence, that really consists of one property: Château Simone. Here old vines, on 15 hectares of limestone soil, produce red, rosé and white wines. The reds are the finest: made from Mourvèdre, Grenache and Cinsault, they are aged in wood, which makes them austere, lean and quite tannic, needing to be kept for some time before drinking. The rosés are made from the same grape varieties. The white wines are made from Clairette, Grenache Blanc and Ugni Blanc and despite the use of these traditional 'southern' grapes, they are surprisingly lively and steely to taste. Drink as young as possible.

VDQS

Coteaux de Pierrevert Often referred to as the highest vineyard in France – certainly the scenery is Alpine and remote – this is a small area of 400 hectares in the Alps-de-Haute-Provence *département* on the River Durance, north of Aix-en-Provence. Red, rosé and white wines are produced here. The rosé is the best of them, made from Cinsault, Carignan and Grenache, it is fresh, acidic and good when drunk within two years of the vintage. White wines are made from Clairette, Marsanne and Roussanne grapes.

Coteaux Varois A large area of vines around the town of Brignoles, making over 30 million bottles of wine a year. Red, rosé and white wines are made. For the reds the grapes used are: Cinsault, Grenache, Mourvèdre, Carignan, Alicante and Aramon (the grapes that have contributed most to the French portion of the European wine lake), Cabernet Sauvignon and Syrah are also used. These tend to be heavy, slightly too full and a little dull, but quality is improving. Whites come from Grenache Blanc, Ugni Blanc, Clairette and Malvoisie. It is the Malvoisie that gives them character and some fragrance and flavour, but on the whole they lack acidity. The area was promoted from *vin de pays* to VDQS in 1984.

Vins de Pays

Departmental Vins de Pays

Vin de Pays des Alpes-de-Haute-Provence Full-bodied reds
and rosés from the valley of the Durance, made from the
usual mix of southern grapes: Carignan, Grenache,
Cinsault, Syrah and Mourvèdre. There is a small
production of white wines, mainly from Clairette and
Muscat à Petits Grains.

Vin de Pays des Bouches-du-Rhône One of the largest *vin de
pays*-producing areas in Provence. The wines come from
three distinct zones: the Aix-en-Provence area, the main
Côtes de Provence vineyards in the east of the *département*,
and the Camargue. Eighty percent of production is of red
wine, made from the southern grape varieties and some
Cabernet Sauvignon.

Vin de Pays du Var This is the most important *vin de pays*
region in Provence, covering the whole of the Var
département. Côtes de Provence AC is also produced in this
region, although half the rosés made here are classified as
vin de pays rather than AC. Grape varieties used for rosé
wines are: Grenache, Cinsault and Syrah, with some
Roussanne du Var. The red wines are made from the
Carignan, Grenache, Cinsault, Syrah, Mourvèdre and
Cabernet Sauvignon grape varieties. Very little white
wine is made.

Vin de Pays du Vaucluse Another large *vin de pays*, producing
wines from the Côtes du Rhône, Côtes du Ventoux and
Côtes du Lubéron regions, north and east of Avignon. The
red wines are very much in the style of Côtes du Rhône,
although Cabernet Sauvignon is also found in the blend.
There is also a considerable amount of white wine made
from Ugni Blanc grapes.

Other departmental *vins de pays* are: Vin de Pays des Alpes-
Maritimes, and Vin de Pays des Hautes-Alpes.

Zonal Vins de Pays

Vin de Pays d'Argens Wines from 17 communes in the Var
département, in the valleys of the Issole and Argens.
Production is mainly of rosé wines from local grape
varieties; red wines are from the Cabernet Sauvignon, and a
small proportion of white, from the Ugni Blanc, Clairette,
Bourboulenc and Rolle, is also made.

Vin de Pays des Maures Wines from the region of the Massif
des Maures, west of Saint-Tropez in the Var *département*.
The *vin de pays* region stretches inland from the coast as far
as Fréjus. Reds and rosés make up almost the entire
production though a tiny amount of white is also made. All
the usual local varieties are permitted, and Cabernet
Sauvignon may also be used.

Vin de Pays du Mont-Caume A zone producing a small
amount of wine, situated on the coast west of Toulon
around the AC area of Bandol. The majority of production
is of powerful red wines and the rest is of rosé. Very little
white is made.

Vin de Pays de la Petite Crau A small area between Avignon
and Les Alpilles of Baux-en-Provence, its vineyards are on
stony soils and produce fruity red wines with smaller
amounts of rosé and white wine. The area is dominated by
one cooperative.

Producers

Bandol AC

La Bastide Blanche
83330 Ste-Anne-du-Castellet
The star wine at this estate is the white, although the reds can have
good weight and tannin. A high percentage of Grenache is grown.

Domaine de Frégate
Domaines Notre-Dame de Port d'Alon, Route de Bandol,
83270 St-Cyr-sur-Mer. Vineyards owned: Domaine de

Frégate 22ha. 100,000 bottles. VP-R

Red wines make up the major part of production here. They are aged for the statutory 18 months, but not sold until three years old – at their best after five to six years. Whites (ten percent of total production) and rosés are sold in the year after the vintage. The estate is situated next to the sea, with its cellar cut into the rock. *Open: Mon–Fri 8am–noon; 2–6pm.*

Domaine le Galantin
83330 Le Plan du Castellet. Vineyards owned: 14ha. 60,000 bottles. VP-R

M Pascal is only a part-time *vigneron*, but produces a fragrant red wine from 60 percent Mourvèdre, 20 percent Grenache and 20 percent Cinsault (which he buys in) and white and rosé wines too. The latter are vinified in stainless steel vats, from free-run juice only; the red is made in stainless steel, then aged in wood for the 18-month minimum. All the wines tend to be quite light and fresh. *Open: By appointment only.*

Domaine de l'Hermitage
Le Rouve, 83330 Le Beausset. Vineyards owned: 36ha. 180,000 bottles. VP-R

Gerard Duffort, who owns the estate, has completed a thorough restoration since acquiring it in 1974. Half his production is of red wines (including a small proportion of Syrah), with about 45 percent rosé, and five percent white wine (made from Ugni Blanc and Clairette). The equipment used is modern, and the reds are vinified in stainless steel before being wood-aged in an air-conditioned cellar for 18 months. The whole operation is highly professional and the results are expensive. *Open: Mon–Fri 8am–noon; 2–6pm.*

Domaine la Laidière
GAEC Estienne, Ste–Anne d'Evenos, 83330 Le Beausset. Vineyards owned: 18ha. 90,000 bottles. VP-R

Among the secrets behind the very fine wines emerging from this estate are the carefully carried-out destalking and long slow fermentation processes. Stainless steel is used for vinification, but reds (which account for 60 percent of production) are then aged in oak. The red wines last well, and the whites and rosés often have more fruit than the average Bandol. The Estienne family was involved in the creation of the Bandol AC in 1941. *Open: Mon–Fri 8am–noon; 2–6pm.*

Moulin des Costes
Mas de la Rouvière, 83740 La Cadière d'Azur. Vineyards owned: 75ha. 350,000 bottles. VP-R

The Bunan family have owned this estate since 1962 when they returned from Algeria. Red and rosé Bandol is made in equal quantities, with a smaller amount of white. The wines are made using both modern and traditional methods, and some superb wines result. A high percentage of Mourvèdre is used for the red wines, and, unlike many estates in Bandol, a little Cabernet Sauvignon is grown. This is used to produce Vin de Pays de Mont Caume. *Open: Summer: 8am–noon; 2–7pm. Winter: 8am–noon; 2–5:30pm.*

Domaine de la Noblesse
83740 La Cadière d'Azur. Vineyards owned: 15ha. 90,000 bottles. VP-R

Jean-Pierre Gaussen, the owner of this small estate, makes powerful red wines and also a little rosé and white. Stainless steel is used for fermentation, producing wines which are modern in style. *Open: By appointment only.*

Domaines Ott
22 Boulevard d'Aguillon, 06601 Antibes. Vineyards owned: 140ha. 550,000 bottles. VP-R

One of the largest producers in Provence, founded in 1896. Domaines Ott own estates in Côtes de Provence (Château de Selle and Clos Mireille) as well as Bandol (Château Romassan). They are most famous for their highly sought-after Bandol Rosé Coeur de Grain, which is fermented and aged in wood. This is an orange-coloured wine which may lack freshness but compensates with a wide range of flavours. Small amounts of red and white Bandol are also made. The Clos Mireille estate produces a white Côtes de Provence from Ugni Blanc and Sémillon; Château de Selle produces rosé and red from a high proportion of Cabernet

Sauvignon; their white is dominated by Sémillon. *Open: Each estate Mon–Fri 8am–noon; 2–6pm.*

Château de Pibarnon
83740 La Cadière d'Azur. Vineyards owned: 30ha. 130,000 bottles. VP–R

The vineyards of Comte Henri de Saint Victor at Château de Pibarnon are situated on limestone soil, and cover a wide area of the Bandol region. Both modern and traditional winemaking techniques are used, including stainless steel for the vinification. The red wine (60 percent of production) is aged for a maximum of two years in wood and has the typical Bandol richness and tannin, and needs seven to eight years' ageing before it reaches maturity. The rosé, too, is a wine for keeping. The white wine – with 40 percent of its blend from the rare Bourboulenc grape – needs to be drunk young. *Open: Mon–Sat 8am–noon; 2:30–7pm.*

Château Pradeaux
83270 St-Cyr-sur-Mer

The wine from this property is made from 95 percent Mourvèdre, and is aged for anything up to eight years in large wooden barrels. The result is sometimes just too woody, but may also reveal great staying power.

Château Ray-Jane
83330 Le Plan du Castellet

Very traditional wines are made here, full of tannin and powerful fruit. The grapes are not destalked before pressing, and the wines are neither fined nor filtered. They need many years to mature. A small estate by Bandol standards.

Château Romassan
See Domaines Ott.

Château Sainte-Anne
Ste-Anne d'Evenos, 83330 Le Beausset. Vineyards owned: 20ha. 100,000 bottles. VP–R

François Dutheil de la Rochère owns two estates: the 12 hectares and 16th-century building of Château Sainte-Anne, producing

Bandol wines; and the eight-hectare Château de la Tourelle producing Côtes de Provence. Winemaking methods are traditional and the use of chemicals for vinification is avoided. The red wines are wood-aged for up to 22 months. Bandol wines also include a light rosé and some white. The Côtes de Provence is all rosé. *Open: Mon–Fri 8am–noon; 2–6pm.*

Domaine des Salettes
83740 La Cadière d'Azur. Vineyards owned: 29ha. 150,000 bottles. VP-R
Half the production of Jean-Pierre Boyer's Domaine des Salettes, on the slopes of Mal Passe, is of Bandol rosé, a light fresh style of wine. About 45 percent is of a full, smooth red with less Mourvèdre than some others of the area. This is a solid, reliable producer, even if great heights are not reached. The vineyard has recently been expanded by 15 hectares. *Open: By appointment only.*

Domaine Tempier
GAEC Peyraud, Le Plan du Castellet, 83330 Le Beausset. Vineyards owned: 26ha. 90,000 bottles. VP-R
The use of chemicals is minimal in this vineyard, originally established in 1834. Lucien Peyraud, the owner, works hard to support the wines of Bandol, and makes his wines using traditional methods: wood for some of the fermentation, and also for maturing the red wines for up to 30 months. The results are tannic wines, that need plenty of time but mature well, with complex flavours. Red and rosé are the only two wines made. The blend of the rosé includes a little Carignan from old vines. *Open: By appointment only.*

Domaine de Terrebrune
Ollioules, 83330 Ste-Anne d'Evenos
One of the hallmarks of this showpiece estate is the fact that the wines are kept in bottle for two years (after two years in wood) before release. They are put on the market only a year or two before maturity. The cellars used for ageing these wines are carved out of the rock.

Château Vannières
83740 La Cadière d'Azur. Vineyards owned: 27ha. 150,000

bottles. VP-R
The vineyard of Vannières dates back to the 16th century, when it was the property of André de Lombard, Seigneur de Castellet. Today the Boisseaux family run the property using traditional methods, vinifying in wood. They make a red Bandol and a red Côtes de Provence, both with the same *cépages*, including six percent Syrah. The Bandol can be very long-lasting with splendid rich, ripe fruit. *Open: By appointment only.*

Bellet AC

Château de Bellet
St-Roman de Bellet, 06200 Nice. Vineyards owned: 9ha.
30,000 bottles. VP-R
One of a handful of Bellet producers, Ghislain de Charnacé makes white, red and rosé wines at the historic castle of Bellet in the hills above Nice. The whites are made from Rolle and Chardonnay; the reds and rosés from Braquet, Folle Noire, Cinsault and Grenache. Vinification methods are traditional. The white is to my mind the most interesting of the three wines: the Chardonnay gives it considerable depth, balancing the simple, rather bland freshness of the Rolle. The rosé is fruitier than many of the Côtes de Provence rosés – but is also more expensive. *Open: by appointment only.*

Cassis AC

Domaine de La Ferme Blanche
13260 Cassis
The largest estate in the *appellation*, established in 1715, producing mainly white wines, which tend towards lightness and freshness. The blend includes ten percent Sauvignon Blanc. Red and rosé are also made.

Château de Fontcreuse
13260 Cassis
Only white wine is made on this estate, which is dominated by a

splendid château. Both the regular *cuvée* and a superior, limited edition wine are made by Joseph Maffei.

Clos Sainte-Magdelaine
Avenue du Revestel, 13260 Cassis. Vineyards owned: 10ha. 50,000 bottles. VP-R
Three-quarters of the production is of a straw-coloured white wine, with a nutty bouquet and a tinge of greenness from the small amount of Sauvignon in the blend; the remainder is of a rosé, made from Cinsault, Grenache and Mourvèdre. The vineyard lies on a narrow spit of land jutting into the bay of Cassis. *Open: By appointment only.*

Coteaux d'Aix-en-Provence AC

Château Bas
13116 Vernegues
Red and rosé wines are produced on this estate. Grapes used for the red are Syrah, Grenache and Cabernet Sauvignon, while Grenache is the base for the rosé. The best wine is called Cuvée du Temple.

Domaine les Bastides
St-Canadet, 13610 Puy-Ste-Réparade. Vineyards owned: 20ha. 100,000 bottles. VP-R
Organic methods are used in this vineyard, which produces red and rosé Coteaux d'Aix, using traditional grape varieties. The red, Rouge Tradition, is a blend of Grenache, Mourvèdre and Cinsault. There is also a Cuvée Spéciale made from 50 percent Cabernet Sauvignon. The house speciality is a *vin cuit*, a dessert wine made from Grenache, Cinsault, Ugni Blanc and Clairette. *Open: By appointment only.*

Château de Beaulieu
13840 Rognes. Vineyards owned: 300ha. 1·2 million bottles. VP-R
The largest estate in the Aix-en-Provence AC, owned by the Touzet family. A modern winery produces red, white and rosé wines from vines grown on volcanic soil, to the east of Aix. The red

is made from Grenache, Cabernet Sauvignon, Syrah and Mour-vèdre; the rosé from Cinsault and Carignan; and the white from Sauvignon, Clairette, Ugni Blanc and Sémillon. The Touzet family built up this estate during the past decade and now live in the well-restored house. *Open: By appointment only.*

Commanderie de la Bargemone
RN7, 13760 St-Cannat. Vineyards owned: 60ha. 350,000 bottles. VP-R
This estate has been spectacularly restored by the Rozan family, wealthy industrialists from northern France. Winemaking tech-niques rely on tradition, but some carbonic maceration is used for the reds, and stainless steel fermentation for the whites. The best red, Cuvée Tournebride, made with 50 percent Cabernet Sauvig-non, spends some time in wood and the more standard red, Commanderie de la Bargemone, is a blend of Grenache (45 percent), Cinsault, Syrah, Cabernet Sauvignon and Carignan. Rosé is made from Grenache and Cinsault; and white wine is produced from a blend of Sauvignon, Grenache Blanc and Ugni Blanc. High standards have been achieved since the estate was bought by M Rozan in 1977. *Open: By appointment only.*

Château La Coste
13610 Puy-Ste-Réparade. Vineyards owned: 180ha. 1·3 million bottles. VP-R
One of the largest estates in Provence. The Bordonado family owns Château La Coste and two associated estates: Domaine de la Grand Séouve and Domaine de la Boulangère. Winemaking techniques are modern for rosés and whites, but traditional for reds. Nearly half the production is of red, with 40 percent rosé and 15 percent white. For such large-scale production, the quality of the wines is very high – especially for the reds. The Bordonado family also own the 30-hectare estate, Château de Costefriede, whose first vintage was the 1987. *Open: By appointment only.*

Château de Fonscolombe
13610 Puy-Ste-Réparade. Vineyards owned: 160ha. 1 million bottles. VP-R
The Marquises de Saporta have owned this estate since 1720.

Modern equipment is used here and some of the best-value wines from the Coteaux d'Aix AC are produced. The red Château de Fonscolombe makes up the bulk of production: a wine which is fruity, aromatic and can be drunk young, although it will age for some years. Other brands used are Domaine de la Crémade and Marquis de Saporta. Fonscolombe also make a Vin de Pays des Bouches-du-Rhône, called Domaine de Boullery. *Open: Mon–Fri 8am–noon; 2–6pm.*

Château Grand Seuil
13540 Puyricard. Vineyards owned: 47ha. 250,000 bottles. VP-R
This mediaeval château is now owned by the Carreau Gaschereau family, who bought the estate in 1973. Extensive renovations have been carried out and modern equipment installed in a brand new 6,000 hectolitre-capacity cellar. Red, rosé and white wines are produced; the red is a blend of Cabernet Sauvignon, Syrah and Grenache. *Blanc de blancs* (made by the *méthode champenoise*) is also produced. These are wines of reliable quality and the name is worth looking out for. *Open: By appointment only.*

Château Vignelaure
Route de Jouques, 83560 Rians. Vineyards owned: 55ha. 160,000 bottles. VP-R
In the days before Coteaux d'Aix was promoted to AC this was probably the most expensive VDQS wine in France. Now Vignelaure is simply the most expensive wine from Coteaux d'Aix. It is still the best. Georges Brunet, who restored the Bordeaux château of La Lagune, has created the nearest thing to a red Bordeaux in Provence, using a blend of 60 percent Cabernet Sauvignon, 30 percent Syrah and ten percent Grenache. The wine is made using modern technology, and stays in wood for up to 32 months. This results in an elegant wine, with finesse despite its fullness and richness of fruit. In the Bordeaux manner, a second wine, Le Page de Vignelaure, is made from younger vines. *Open: Mon–Sat 8:30am–12:30pm; 2–6:30pm. Sun 10:30am–12:30pm; 2–6:30pm.*

Château Vignerolles
13700 Gignac-la-Nerthe. Vineyards owned: 80ha. 500,000 bottles. VP-R

This property, owned by Charles Sardou, is to the west of Aix-en-Provence, and operates using modern technology and stainless steel for vinification. 65 percent of production is of red wine, with 30 percent rosé and five percent white. The brand names used are Château Saint-Jean de l'Hôpital and Cuvée Margot. The white and rosé wines are better than the red – the white, with its touch of Sauvignon, is especially attractive. *Open: By appointment only.*

Coteaux des Baux-en-Provence AC

Domaines de Lauzières
Le Destet, 13890 Mouries. Vineyards owned: 60ha. 400,000 bottles. VP-R

This well-established family estate produces only one wine: a red Coteaux des Baux, using 70 percent Grenache, with Cinsault, Carignan, Syrah and Mourvèdre. The wine is hard in its youth, but mellows after four to five years. *Open: By appointment only.*

Mas de la Dame
13520 Les Baux-en-Provence. Vineyards owned: 55ha. 300,000 bottles. VP-R

Rosé and red wine is made here in one of the best Baux-en-Provence estates. Stainless steel is used. The high (14 percent) proportion of Syrah in the red wine, Rouge Réserve, gives it good ageing ability, and the introduction of 23 percent Cabernet Sauvignon gives considerable elegance. The rosé has 25 percent Syrah and 25 percent Cabernet Sauvignon. The wines are not expensive for their quality but may become so. *Open: By appointment only.*

Mas de Gourgonnier
Le Destet, 13890 Mouries. Vineyards owned: 35ha. 200,000 bottles. VP-R

A new vineyard on an old family estate, run by Nicolas Cartier who runs the vineyard organically, producing excellent wines, red, rosé and white. His best wine is the Reserve du Mas, a blend of Grenache (40 percent), Cabernet Sauvignon (30 percent) and Syrah (30 percent). His other red introduces ten percent Mourvèdre. The white, a wine fresh in character, comprises 40 percent Sauvignon Blanc. A very serious estate. *Open: Mon–Fri 8am–noon; 2–6pm.*

Mas de Sainte-Berthe
13520 Les Baux-en-Provence. Vineyards owned: 33ha. 25,000 bottles. VP-R

Carbonic maceration and stainless steel vats enable production of easy-drinking fruity wines at this estate, situated in a spectacular position under the cliff-top village of Les Baux. Almost two-thirds of the production is of red wine, one-third rosé, and a few thousand bottles of white. The brand Cuvée Louis David is their best-quality wine, and is designed for some ageing. *Open: Mon–Sun 9am–noon; 2–6pm.*

Domaine des Terres Blanches
RN99, 13210 St-Rémy-de-Provence. Vineyards owned: 40ha. 200,000 bottles. VP-R

Organic farming methods are adopted on this model estate and few chemicals are used for the making of the wine. Noël Michelin, the owner, and his cellarmaster Georges Dutel, are both strong advocates of this method of winemaking which is gaining ground in other Baux-en-Provence estates. They produce a white, a rosé and a red. The red is sometimes described as austere and certainly it needs time; with ageing it becomes very poised and elegant. *Open: Mon–Sat 8am–noon; 2–6pm.*

Domaine de Trévallon
13150 St-Etienne. Vineyards owned: 15ha. 65,000 bottles. VP-R

These vineyards are in the centre of the strange basin surrounded by the Alpilles mountains. Another of the estates in Les Baux that practises organic methods. In the winery, stainless steel is used, but then the wine is aged in wood. The red – the sole wine from this estate – is a blend of 60 percent Cabernet Sauvignon and 40 percent Syrah, a splendid combination, producing a wine that is well-structured, with considerable ageing ability. *Open: By appointment.*

Domaine de la Vallongue
13810 Eygalières. Vineyards owned: 35ha. 130,000 bottles.
VP-R
Red and rosé wine are produced at this estate. The wines are mainly
based on the traditional varieties of the area – Carignan, Cinsault
and Grenache – with only a little amelioration from Cabernet
Sauvignon and Syrah. The red is full-bodied, southern-tasting but
not overblown. The rosé tends to mature quickly and needs to be
drunk young. *Open: By appointment only.*

Palette AC

Château Simone
Palette, 13100 Aix-en-Provence. Vineyards owned: 15ha.
VP-R
By owning three-quarters of the vineyards of the AC area, the
Rougier family are entitled to regard themselves as synonymous
with Palette. They make red, rosé and white wines. To my mind –
on the rare occasions when I have tasted them – the wood-aged red
(from Grenache, Mourvèdre, Cinsault, and local varieties Manos-
quan, Caster, Brun-Fourca and Teoulier) needs six or seven years
before being ready. The white is herbily aromatic. *Open: By
appointment only.*

Côtes de Provence AC

Jean Bagnis et Fils
83390 Cuers. Vineyards owned: 13ha. 3·5 million bottles.
VP-R and N
By far the largest production from this firm is of the brand
L'Estandon Côtes de Provence. It also owns a small vineyard in the
Bellet AC area at Château de Crémat, where red, rosé and white
wines are made. *Open: By appointment only.*

Château Barbeyrolles
Gassin, 83990 St-Tropez. Vineyards owned: 10ha. 65,000
bottles. VP-R

Organic methods are used in this small vineyard owned by Régine Sumeire. Sumeire, who has a PhD in history, has been researching the history of viticulture in this region. She makes very fine red and rosé wines – the red a blend of a third each Grenache, Mourvèdre and Syrah that spends ten to 18 months in wood. The rosé is surprisingly delicate for Provence. A small amount of white is also made from Ugni Blanc, Rolle and Sémillon vines planted in 1983. *Open: By appointment in winter only.*

La Bastide Neuve
Le Cannet des Maures, 83340 Le Luc. Vineyards owned:
12ha. 70,000 bottles. VP-R
Unusually for Provence, M Brochier makes 100 percent varietal wines – red, rosé and white. The reds – from Syrah, Mourvèdre and Grenache – are made traditionally, before ageing for one year in large barrels. His other wines are made in enamel-lined tanks: a Tibouren-based rosé of great character, and a white from Ugni Blanc. *Open: Mon–Sat 8am–noon; 2–7pm.*

La Bernarde
83340 Le Luc. Vineyards owned: 33ha. 200,000 bottles.
VP-R
M and the late Mme Meulnart bought this vineyard in 1974 and invested considerable sums of money in order to produce top-quality wines. The vineyard is situated 300 metres up, north of Les Maures. Reds include the special *cuvée*, Clos Bernarde St-Germain, made from 55 percent Syrah, 40 percent Cabernet Sauvignon and five percent Grenache, and Clos de la Bernarde, which contains 30 percent Grenache. Both reds are matured in bottle rather than wood. The estate produces a delicate rosé made with 30 percent Tibouren with Grenache and Cinsault, and white wines made from Ugni Blanc and Sémillon. *Open: By appointment only.*

Domaine de Bertaud
83990 Gassin
Red wine is the main production from this pretty estate above St-Tropez. The wine has a high proportion of Cabernet Sauvignon as well as Mourvèdre and Syrah, giving considerable complexity.

Domaine Castel Roubine
BP 117, RD 562, 83510 Lorgues. Vineyards owned: 65ha. 300,000 bottles. VP-R
Soundly based red, rosé and white Côtes de Provence, the red is made in wood, the white and rosé in stainless steel. The rosé is made attractive by a touch of Tibouren, and the red has a good percentage of Cabernet Sauvignon, with some Syrah and Mourvèdre. *Open: Mon–Fri 8am–noon; 2–5pm.*

Commanderie de Peyrassol
SCEA Rigord, Flassans, 83340 Le Luc. Vineyards owned: 55ha. 160,000 bottles. VP-R
Modern technology is used at this large estate to make red, white and rosé wine. The red is then aged in new wood, the time varying according to vintage. There are two ranges, the standard being Cuvée Eperon d'Or: *blanc de blancs*, rosé and red (the red with 33 percent Cabernet Sauvignon). The special *cuvée*, Cuvée Marie Estelle, is from lower-yielding vines, the red comprising 60 percent Cabernet Sauvignon. A rosé is also made – Le Rosé d'Art. *Open: Mon–Sun 9am–noon; 2–5pm. Appointments necessary for groups.*

Vignobles Crocé-Spinelli
Domaine des Clarettes, 83460 Les Arcs. Vineyards owned: 31ha. 60,000 bottles. VP-R
M Crocé-Spinelli owns three estates: Domaine des Clarettes near Les Arcs, and Domaine du Saint-Esprit and Domaine de Fontselves near Draguignan. The wine from Domaine du Saint-Esprit has a high percentage of Syrah, while Domaine des Clarettes relies more on Mourvèdre. At Domaine de Fontselves some Cabernet Sauvignon is used. Rosé wines are also made. *Open: Appointments preferred.*

Domaine de la Croix
83420 La Croix Valmer. Vineyards owned: 100ha. 540,000 bottles. VP-R
A long-established vineyard in St-Tropez peninsula which has been completely reconstructed in recent years. They produce red, white, rosé, *blanc de blancs* and a *gris de gris*. They also produce wines of 100 percent Cabernet Sauvignon and 100 percent Mourvèdre. *Open: By appointment only.*

Domaine de Curebeasse
KM 4, Route de Bagnols, 83600 Fréjus. Vineyards owned: 18ha. 100,000 bottles. VP-R
Low-temperature fermentation is used here for rosés and whites: the whites stay on their lees after this to retain their freshness. There are three styles of red and two of rosé. The best red is Roches Noires, which comes from vines on volcanic soil; it is matured in wood and made from 50 percent Mourvèdre, 30 percent Cabernet Sauvignon and 20 percent Syrah. Other reds use Cinsault, Carignan and Grenache. The white is a blend of Rolle and Ugni Blanc: an attractive, fresh wine that needs to be drunk young. *Open: By appointment only.*

Domaine du Deffends
83600 Carnoules. Vineyards owned: 29ha. 50,000 bottles. VP-R
Red and rosé wines make up 90 percent of production at this traditional estate. A white is made from Ugni Blanc and Clairette. Nearly 60 percent of production goes to *négociants* in bulk. *Open: In working hours only.*

Domaine du Dragon
Route de Montferrat, 83300 Draguignan. Vineyards owned: 25ha. 130,000 bottles. VP-R
The three wines – red, white and rosé – produced here all bear the Domaine du Dragon name. The red has 30 percent Cabernet Sauvignon and a proportion of Syrah, and is made using a semi-carbonic maceration method, giving considerable colour though it perhaps lacks depth. The white is slightly sweet and soft, with 30 percent Clairette. The proprietor, M Garro, uses traditional vinification methods. *Open: Mon–Sat 9am–noon; 3–7pm.*

Domaine des Féraud
Route de la Garde Freinet, 83550 Vidauban. Vineyards owned: 60ha. 190,000 bottles. VP-R
High quality winemaking is carried out at this large estate. The red, a blend of 60 percent Cabernet Sauvignon, 25 percent Syrah and 15 percent Grenache, is a strange Bordeaux creature in the middle of Provence, big and tannic and requiring some ageing. The rosé and

white are well made if less unusual. The vineyard has been owned
by the Laudon-Rival family for three generations. *Open: By
appointment only.*

Domaine des Fougues
**83400 Hyères. Vineyards owned: 26ha. 40,000 bottles.
VP-R**
Changes in this vineyard have increased the planting of Syrah,
Tibouren and Grenache. They make red, rosé and white Côtes de
Provence and red and rosé Vin de Pays du Var. The two brand
names are Domaine les Fouques and Les Restanques. *Open: Mon–
Fri 8am–noon; 1–6pm.*

Château de Gairoird
83390 Cuers. Vineyards owned: 30ha. 80,000 bottles. VP-R
Half M Pierrefeu's production is of rosé, for which there is a good
export market. It is made in small refrigerated tanks of epoxy-lined
resin, and is held together by 30 percent of Mourvèdre in the blend,
which also gives some elegance. The white contains 40 percent
Clairette, plus Rolle and Ugni Blanc. Reds contain Syrah and
Grenache. A second label is called Domaine St-Jean. *Open: Mon–Fri
8am–noon; 2–6pm.*

Domaine de Galoupet
**83250 La Londe-les-Maures. Vineyards owned: 65ha.
450,000 bottles. VP-R**
Perhaps the most interesting wine made on this estate is a rosé made
with 95 percent Tibouren, a fresh, very fragrant wine, quite unlike
the traditional dull, heavy Provence rosés. The red Cuvée
Spéciale, made from Mourvèdre, Syrah and Grenache, is aged in
wood. The white is a blend of Rolle and Sémillon. *Open: By
appointment only.*

Vignobles Gasperini
**42 Avenue de la Libération, 83260 La Crau. Vineyards
owned: 15ha. 85,000 bottles. VP-R**
The estate has been in the Gasperini family since 1834 and is now
run by Alain and Guy who preserve traditional methods. The red
wine, Cuvée des Commandeurs, is matured in wood, which

enhances the ageing potential of the Cabernet Sauvignon in the blend. There is also a rosé made from Grenache and Cinsault called Cuvée Dame Jardin. *Open: Mon–Fri 8am–noon; 2–7pm.*

Domaines Gavoty
83340 Le Luc. Vineyards owned: 109ha
There are two vineyards owned by the Gavoty family: Le Grand and Le Petit Campduny. Fruit is the predominant character of all the wines made at the estate. The main production is of rosé, but the youthful, fresh white and the red, made partly by carbonic maceration, are excellent examples of the fresher style of the new Côtes de Provence.

Château Grand'Boise
BP No 2, 13530 Trets. Vineyards owned: 40ha. 165,000 bottles. VP-R
A well-maintained, 17th-century estate southeast of Aix-en-Provence, which has been in the Gruey family since 1879. A combination of techniques is used: cement tanks for white and rosé and carbonic maceration for reds, followed by some wood–ageing. The red is meaty, savoury on the palate, and is quite soft, despite its blend of Cabernet Sauvignon, Syrah and Grenache. Some of the grapes used for the white wine are bought in. *Open: Mon–Sat 8am–noon; 1:30–5:30pm.*

Domaine du Jas d'Esclans
Route de Callas, 83920 La Motte. Vineyards owned: 50ha. 125,000 bottles. VP-R
The red is the best wine from this old-fashioned estate, owned by M Lorgues. It is matured in wood and has smooth, firm fruit, which can take some ageing. The blend is of Mourvèdre, Syrah and Grenache with 50 percent Cinsault. Sémillon and Clairette in the white give the wine an attractively perfumed bouquet, but it tends towards heaviness. The rosé is classic Provençal rosé. *Open: By appointment only.*

Luc et Louis Maille
42 Avenue Ferrandin, 83570 Carces. Vineyards owned: 19ha. 100,000 bottles. VP-R

There are three sections to this estate. Domaine St-Jean, on limestone soil, is the best, and produces a good red based on Syrah, Cabernet Sauvignon and Grenache. The two other vineyards are Domaine de Canebières and Bastide de la Rimade. In total, half the vineyards are now planted with noble grape varieties for red wines, leaving Carignan and Cinsault for the rosés and a little Ugni Blanc and Rolle for whites. They also make Vin de Pays du Var. *Open: By appointment only.*

Les Maîtres Vignerons de la Presqu'ile de Saint-Tropez
83990 St-Tropez. Vineyards owned: 168ha. 2·7 million
bottles. Coop (12 members)
This cooperative chooses only the wines from its members that it wishes to bottle and sell, hence the high quality. Stainless steel is used for whites and rosés, the white (a blend of Ugni Blanc and Rolle) being particularly attractive. The two brand names used are Château de Pampelonne and St-Roch les Vignes. There is also a top-quality range of red wines under the name Cuvée de Chasseur. Distinctive marketing tactics include an association with local Michelin three-star chef Roger Vergé and painted bottles. *Open: Mon–Fri 8am–noon; 2–6pm.*

Domaine de la Malherbe
83230 Bormes-les-Mimosas. Vineyards owned: 25ha.
100,000 bottles. VP-R
A vineyard in a spectacular setting by the sea facing the Fort de Bregançon, an island castle residence of the French President. Mme Serge Ferrari, the owner, has invested considerable sums to create a modern winery which produces wines benefiting from the cool air of the coast. Three brand names are used: Reine Jeanne, Pointe du Diable and, for the top *cuvées*, Domaine de la Malherbe. The rosé is especially fine. *Open: By appointment only.*

Mas de Cadenet
13530 Trets. Vineyards owned: 50ha. 100,000 bottles. VP-R
The Negrel family have owned this pretty estate since 1813. Syrah, Cabernet Sauvignon and Grenache are used for the red, while rosé wines are made from Cinsault and Grenache. Techniques are a combination of traditional and modern. The red is the best wine.

Spicy and rich, it ages well, and also comes through well when young. *Open: By appointment only.*

Château de Mentone
St-Antonin du Var, 83510 Lorgues. Vineyards owned: 29ha. 35,000 bottles. VP-R
Much of the produce from this estate goes in bulk to Lyon and Paris, but a small amount is bottled on the premises. Traditional methods are used by Mme Perrot de Gasquet, whose family has owned the estate for 150 years. The estate has grown quickly recently, from ten hectares to the present 30 or so. *Open: By appointment only.*

Château Minuty
Gassin, 83990 St-Tropez. Vineyards owned: 80ha. 160,000 bottles. VP-R
There are two estates owned by the Farnet family: Château Minuty and Châteauneuf à Vidauban, which is sold under the Domaines Farnet name. Grenache, Cinsault, Mourvèdre and Syrah are used in the red Château Minuty, aged in wood to produce an elegant wine. Rosé and white are also made under the Château Minuty name. A sparkling *blanc de blancs* is made under the Domaines Farnet name. *Open: Mon–Sat 9am–noon; 2–7pm.*

Château Miraval
83143 Le Val. Vineyards owned: 19ha. 40,000 bottles. VP-R
85 percent of production is rosé, the rest red and white. They use Carignan, Cinsault and Syrah for red; Cinsault for rosé; and Ugni Blanc for some white. Some Vin de Pays du Var is also made. Jacques Loussier, the owner, is also a well-known jazz pianist. *Open: By appointment only.*

Clos Mireille
See Domaines Ott, Bandol.

Domaine de Peissonnel
Route de la Garde Freiner, 83550 Vidauban. Vineyards owned: 15ha. 60,000 bottles. VP-R
Unusually for Côtes de Provence, this estate produces only red

wines. And, even more unusually, they make a wine from 80 percent Merlot with 15 percent Cabernet Franc: a combination which works best in cooler years, when the wine's structure shows through. The Domaine de Peissonnel red *cuvée* is a blend of 50 percent Syrah and 50 percent Cabernet Sauvignon: a strongly tannic wine which needs at least four years before drinking. *Open: By appointment only.*

Domaine des Planes
83520 Roquebrune sur Argens. Vineyards owned: 25ha.
150,000 bottles. VP–R
Ilse and Christophe Rieder have owned this estate since 1980. They also own vineyards in Germany and Switzerland, and have obviously learnt much of modern techniques from those two countries. All fermentation is by grape variety in stainless steel, although the red is then aged in wood for up to 18 months. They make a full range of Côtes de Provence AC wines, including a rosé from 100 percent Tibouren. They also produce Vin de Pays du Var, red and rosé, and a sweet 100 percent Muscat. Names include Domaine des Planes, Grives des Planes and Coulée du Fournel. *Open: By appointment only.*

Vignobles Poussel
Domaines le Val d'Anrieu, BP4, 83590 Gonfaron.
Vineyards owned: 35ha. 60,000 bottles. VP–R
The vineyards are in the valleys of Anrieu, la Pellegrine and Sableu, the first two on limestone soil, the third on sandier soil. The white is made from Rolle and Ugni Blanc; the rosé Cuvée Jean Rémy from Grenache and Cinsault with a little Mourvèdre, Syrah, Carignan and Tibouren. Red grapes include Grenache, Mourvèdre, Syrah, Cabernet Sauvignon and Cinsault and the top red wine is called Cuvée Caroline. *Open: By appointment only.*

Pradel
06270 Villeneuve Loubet. Vineyards owned: none. 15·6
million bottles. N
This *négociant* is a large-scale merchant, making large-scale Côtes de Provence, Bellet and Bandol. *Open: By appointment only.*

Domaine de la Pugette
Le Thoronet, 83340 Le Luc. Vineyards owned: 23ha. VP-R

M Petit makes a red, rosé and white at his estate near Brignoles in
the central Côtes de Provence. The vineyards stretch up to the ruins
of the Abbey of Thoronet, which was a Cistercian monastery. The
red, made from Grenache, Syrah and Cabernet Sauvignon, is the
best: aged in wood, it has firm tannin when young and needs time
to mellow. *Open: By appointment only.*

Vignobles F Ravel (Château Montaud)
83390 Pierrefeu. Vineyards owned: 404ha. 2 million bottles. VP-R

One of the largest estates in Provence, built up by M Ravel since the
1960s. He makes a mix of Côtes de Provence red, rosé and white
and Vin de Pays des Maures, using Cabernet Sauvignon for the red
and Tibouren for the rosé. Château Montaud is the estate name for
Côtes de Provence. Rosé forms the bulk of production and is light
with plenty of acidity. The red is from Syrah and Mourvèdre, an
attractive wine which needs some ageing. The white is less
interesting. *Open: Mon–Thur 8am–noon; 1:30–5:30pm. Fri 8am–
noon; 1:30–4:30pm.*

Domaine Richeaume
13114 Puyloubier. Vineyards owned: 22ha. 100,000 bottles. VP-R

M Hoesch's vineyards are on the slopes of Mt Sainte-Victoire in the
east of the Côtes de Provence. He makes a red from Cabernet
Sauvignon and Syrah, which is aged for two years in wood, and
maintains that even his rosé and white are wines for keeping. A *blanc
de blancs* from Clairette is certainly well made in a traditional way.
Open: By appointment only.

Domaine de Rimauresq
83790 Pignans. Vineyards owned: 26ha. 80,000 bottles. VP-R

This vineyard is planted with ancient vines and has small yields but
high quality. The wood-aged red, a blend of Syrah, Mourvèdre,
Grenache, Carignan and Cinsault, is particularly fine, with a
warmth balanced by structure and some tannin. The rosé is 100

percent Tibouren, while the white is a blend of Ugni Blanc, Clairette and Rolle. A top producer in an estate which is one of the oldest in the region. *Open: By appointment only.*

Saint-André de Figuière
83250 La Londe les Maures. Vineyards owned: 15ha. 60,000 bottles. VP-R
An organically run vineyard with modern equipment in the winery producing some deliciously refreshing wines. The white is light and fresh, a blend of Sémillon, Ugni Blanc and Rolle. The red Cuvée Spéciale is a soft, rich wine, a blend of Mourvèdre and Carignan, which needs three to four years. The estate also produces a Vin de Pays du Var. *Open: Mon–Fri 9am–noon; 2–6pm.*

Domaine de Saint-Baillon
83340 Flassans-sur-Issole. Vineyards owned: 28ha. 150,000 bottles. VP-R
Stainless steel for vinification and wood for maturing the reds sit side by side in this new winery, owned by Hervé Goudard since 1974. As much as 60 percent of the vineyard is devoted to Cabernet Sauvignon and Syrah, which are blended into the spicy, peppery Cuvée de Roudaï, and are joined by Cinsault and Grenache in the Rouge Traditionnel. Rosé is also made, and a *blanc de blancs* of Rolle and Ugni Blanc. Domaine du Pradon is another brand name. *Open: By appointment only.*

Château Sainte-Roseline
83460 Les Arcs-sur-Argens
The red is the best wine made at this estate, based around an ancient monastery. It is made from 60 percent Mourvèdre, 30 percent Cabernet Sauvignon and ten percent Syrah, a potent combination which gives considerable power, good structure and longevity.

Château de Selle
See Domaines Ott, Bandol.

Domaine de la Source Sainte-Marguerite
Le Haut Pansard, 83250 La Londe les Maures. Vineyards

owned: 14ha. 65,000 bottles. VP-R
M Fayard produces red, rosé and white wine from his estate,
acquired in 1977. He uses the name of La Source Sainte-Marguerite
for his standard wines and Oustau de Baumanière for his special
cuvée. Open: By appointment only.

Coteaux Varois VDQS

Domaine du Deffends
83470 St-Maximin. Vineyards owned: 10ha. 40,000 bottles.
VP-R
Two reds and a rosé – all VDQS Coteaux Varois – are produced
from this small estate. Clos de la Truffière (made from 40 percent
Cabernet Sauvignon, 45 percent Syrah; 15 percent Grenache and
Cinsault) and Rouge du Deffends (20 percent Cabernet and Syrah,
80 percent Grenache and Cinsault) are the two reds. The Rosé de la
Nuit is made from 80 percent Cinsault and 20 percent Grenache. A
form of carbonic maceration is used to bring out colour in the red.
The rosé is almost blush pink in colour. *Open: By appointment only.*

Domaine de Saint-Jean
83930 Villecroze. Vineyards owned: 31ha. 130,000 bottles.
VP-R
This modern winery, founded in 1975, produces Coteaux Varois
and Vin de Pays du Var from a large vineyard containing a
considerable proportion of Cabernet Sauvignon and Syrah as well
as the more usual Cinsault (used for rosé) and Grenache. A sparkling
blanc de blancs is made from Ugni Blanc, using the *méthode
champenoise*. The Vins de Pays du Var are 100 percent varietals
(from Syrah and Cabernet Sauvignon). The Coteaux Varois red is a
blend of Cabernet Sauvignon, Syrah and Grenache. Red and rosé
wines are also sold in bulk. The vineyard is unusual because of the
training system on wires and the use of California T-budding
techniques for the Cabernet Sauvignon. *Open: Mon–Fri 8am–noon;
1–6:30pm.*

Corsica

Corsica is a land of mountains and rugged splendour. The best vineyards are in the difficult terrain of the west coast, the north tip and the south. On the eastern plain, large vineyards produce basic blending wines.

In this hot climate, the finest wines produced are heady reds and full-bodied rosés. Whites are either over-oxidized or modern and nondescript. Some Vins Doux Naturels are also made.

While imported southern French grape varieties – Carignan, Cinsault, Mourvèdre and Grenache – produce the bulk of the wine, mostly as Vin de Pays de l'Ile de Beauté, the native Corsican varieties – Vermentino and Malvoisie for whites, Nielluccio and Sciacarello for reds and rosés – are used in the AC wines. Noble varieties – Cabernet Sauvignon, Merlot, Chardonnay, Chenin Blanc – are being made into varietal wines under a *vin de pays* label.

The new technology of southern France has been late arriving in Corsica. But major producers and some of the top estates have improved vinification and selection, and are now making some acceptable wines. The most interesting are those made from traditional Corsican grape varieties.

The Appellations
Appellations Contrôlées

Of 28,000 hectares planted, 4,000 are AC. There are eight AC zones:

Vin de Corse	**Vin de Corse Figari**
Vin de Corse Calvi	**Vin de Corse Porto**
Vin de Corse Coteaux	**Vecchio**
d'Ajaccio	**Vin de Corse Sartène**
Vin de Corse Coteaux du	**Patrimonio**
Cap Corse	

All can produce red, dry white or rosé wines. All except Vin de Corse Coteaux d'Ajaccio, Vin de Corse Figari, Vin de Corse

Porto Vecchio and Vin de Corse Sartène can also make semi-sweet whites.
Best vintages: (reds) '78, '81, '84, '85; (rosés) '84, '85; (whites) '85.

Vin de Pays

Regional Vin de Pays

Vin de Pays de l'Ile de Beauté A *vin de pays* classification covering the whole island, this is designed to enable the production of wines from 'foreign' grape varieties, including Cabernet Sauvignon and Chardonnay, as well as local varieties grown outside AC areas. Production is of 58 percent red, 26 percent rosé and 16 percent white wines.

Producers

Clos Capitoro
Bianchetti Frères et Fils, Pisciatella, 20166 Porticcio.
Vineyards owned: Cauro 28ha. 90,000 bottles. VP-R
Producing wines under the Clos Capitoro (AC Coteaux d'Ajaccio) and Leitizia (AC Vin de Corse) names. Clos Capitoro red is full-bodied and heady (13° alcohol); the rosé and white are made in a modern style. Half the vineyard is being replanted, and new land is being purchased. *Open: Mon–Fri 8am–noon; 2–7pm.*

Domaine Peraldi
20167 Mezzavia. Vineyards owned: Ajaccio 40ha. 200,000 bottles. VP-R
Old established firm, and largest producer in the Ajaccio AC, whose Maison Peraldi in the centre of Ajaccio is a local landmark. Modern vinification for all wines is followed by ageing in new wood *barriques* for reds, giving them a general life span of around ten years. Whites and rosés are bottled quickly for freshness. *Open: Mon–Fri 8am–noon; 2–6pm. Appointments necessary for groups.*

Domaine de Torraccia (Christian Imbert)
20137 Lecci de Porto Vecchio. Vineyards owned: Lecci 40ha. 250,000 bottles. VP-R

A large estate outside Porto Vecchio on the east coast. The tower in the name dates back to 1,500 BC. The vineyard is treated biologically, giving a low yield. Local grapes are supplemented by Grenache, Cinsault and some Syrah to give a red with generous ripe, herby fruit which takes some ageing. Top red *cuvée* is a Réserve Oriu. White and rosé are produced in a more modern fruity style. *Open: Mon–Sat 8am–noon; 2–6pm. By appointment only.*

Union des Vignerons Associés du Levant
Rasignani, 20290 Borgo. Vineyards owned: St-Florent, Marana, Bravone, Aghione 2,000ha. 500,000 bottles. Coop

This cooperative specializes in a range of varietal wines. Under the AC Vin de Corse it makes a 100 percent Nielluccio wine. *Vins de pays* include 100 percent Cabernet Sauvignon and Chardonnay. Particular emphasis is put on white wines and new equipment has been installed. The resulting wines are full of fruit, but lack regional character. Brand names include L'Ile aux Pièves and St-Florent. *Open: Sat 9–11am. By appointment only.*

The Midi

Languedoc – the land of the French wine lake – and Roussillon occupy the stretch of Mediterranean coast that sweeps in a great arc from Marseille down to the Spanish frontier. A wide coastal plain in Languedoc is bounded by the mountains of the Massif Central to the north. In Roussillon, the mountains are closer to the sea. What is not harsh, rugged hill country is flat alluvial plain interspersed with marshy tracts.

From the mountains, small rivers run down to the sea. Torrents in winter and dry in the long, hot summers, they have long ago carved out valleys on whose slopes vineyards are the natural form of agriculture.

This is the hottest part of France. The heat is dry, tempered with the winds of the Mistral and Tramontane which blow, for days on end, across the wide open spaces of the plains. Although the coastal strip is now becoming built up with the growth of tourism, inland the landscape is empty, scattered with red-roofed villages and a few larger, often walled, towns commanding the heights.

Nearly 40 percent of all French wines comes from these two regions. Much of it is virtually undrinkable plonk – all red which goes less and less to quench the thirst of the French peasant or factory worker and more and more to increase the EC surplus of industrial alcohol.

But it was not always such a sad tale. Before phylloxera, the majority of vineyards were on the hills, where decent if fairly ordinary wine was made. However, these vineyards were always precarious economically, and when phylloxera struck, it was not worthwhile to replant them. Vinous activity was transferred to the plain, where enormous yields were possible and cash returns were greater. Alicante and Aramon as well as Carignan were planted – giving yields of up to 200 hectolitres per hectare of thin, watery wine which sold well to the poor and thirsty of the industrial towns of the north.

Fashions change and the traditional industries have waned in France as elsewhere. The thirst for cheap wine after a day's work in a dusty steel mill or coal mine has gone. The French want better-quality wine – and are drinking less of it. The call has gone out for a return to the hill vineyards and the abandonment of those on the plains. And, slowly but surely, this is what is happening.

The authorities are now trying to encourage quality rather than quantity. One way of doing this is to create AC and VDQS zones in the hills, which has the effect of pushing up prices – from almost nothing to not very much. And the government has also paid the farmers on the plains to grub up their vineyards and plant other crops such as cereals. The authorities have encouraged local traditional vineyards, especially those in Roussillon, where there is a long history of quality winemaking. And in Languedoc, they have worked at the introduction of the noble grape varieties such as Cabernet Sauvignon, Syrah, Mourvèdre – even Chardonnay – to blend with local grapes to give more flavour, style and aroma to often dull wines.

The authorities are also paying out grants for new equipment in the wineries. Temperature-controlled vinification and stainless steel are coming to Languedoc and Roussillon, where they are at last creating the possibility of decent white wines and unoxidized reds. The techniques of carbonic maceration, which bring out colour and flavour from the grapes, have been introduced and encouraged. The region boasts one of the biggest viticultural and winemaking research centres at SICAREX near Montpellier, and ideas are being disseminated from there.

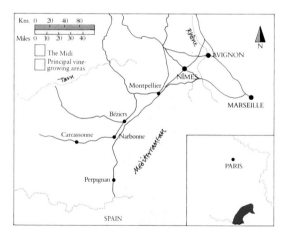

The message is getting through to the conservative French farmers in a number of ways. Cooperatives are important. 60 percent of the region's wines go through cooperatives. Most farmers have tiny holdings on which they can scarcely survive, let alone become involved in the high-tech of wine. A few big *négociant* firms – Nicolas and Chantovent among them – are also buying wine from smallholders, the best of which they bottle under individual domaine names. And a few of the larger estates are dominating their areas by example.

What this means for wine drinkers is that here we have an area which is currently producing some of the best-value wines around, certainly in France, almost certainly in Europe. While there is rarely anything to take one's breath away, there are pockets of very good quality and larger areas where standards are getting better all the time.

It does not just mean, luckily, that what is now being offered is simply well-made 'modern' wines. Some of the new AC and VDQS areas recognize long traditions. There have been vines here since the second century BC, and Narbonne was one of the first major cities of Roman Gaul. The French are good at recognizing local character, and small vineyard areas have been given separate ACs in cognizance of their differences in style and quality.

The region also produces a range of sweet, fortified wines which, though highly popular in France, are virtually unknown outside the country. These are potentially high-alcohol wines whose fermentation is stopped by the addition of about ten percent eau-de-vie, leaving a strong, rich sweet wine. They can be either Vins Doux Naturels (made from grape brandy from any French source) or Vins de Liqueur (made with spirit from the region of production) and can be either red or white. Those made from the Muscat grape are most attractive.

The Appellations
Gard AC

Clairette de Bellegarde White wine only, made from the
Clairette grape in two small areas within the larger

Costières de Nîmes. Up to 3,000 hectolitres are produced
on red, pebbly soil. The wines are often fragrant, if full,
with a pale gold colour. They lack acidity and tend towards
flabbiness unless made with care.

Costières de Nîmes Red, white and rosé wines from a large
area southeast of Nîmes and north of the Camargue
marshes. The 4,000 hectares of vineyard are on flat land,
much of it quite barren, some of it sandy, partly also
planted with olive, lemon and orange groves. Red wines
form around 80 percent of production, rosé about 15
percent and white around five percent. Red and rosé wines
are made from Carignan (which can constitute up to 50
percent of the wine, although better producers use less),
Cinsault, Grenache, Mourvèdre, Syrah, Counoise and
Terret Noir. Syrah or Mourvèdre must make up at least 15
percent. The reds can be attractively simple, with southern
warmth and nuttiness, topped up with a Rhône-like spicy
pepperiness. Whites are made from Clairette, Bourboulenc,
Grenache Blanc and Ugni Blanc. Modern vinification and
the picking of underripe grapes is helping to improve their
quality and make fresh if undistinguished wines. This is a
new name for the Costières du Gard AC.

Gard Vins de Pays

Departmental Vin de Pays

Vin de Pays du Gard Production is large and consists mainly
of standard red wines from local grape varieties. A small
amount of rosé, and an even smaller amount of white, are
also made.

Zonal Vins de Pays

Vin de Pays des Coteaux de Cèze Production of a small
amount of red wine and an even smaller amount of white,
from a large area in the north of the *département*.
Vin de Pays des Coteaux Flaviens Near Aïgues-Mortes, this
zone produces mainly red wines from a mixture of

southern French and Bordeaux grapes.

Vin de Pays des Coteaux du Pont du Gard Mainly red wines
from the local grape varieties, though Cabernet Sauvignon
may also be used. The wines come from 19 communes
around the famous Pont du Gard.

Vin de Pays des Coteaux du Salavès Red and rosé wines
made from a variety of grapes, including Merlot, Cabernet
Sauvignon and Cabernet Franc, in the region west of
Nîmes.

Vin de Pays des Coteaux du Vidourle On the western edge
of the *département*, in the valley of the Vidourle around
Sommières, the production of this zone is mainly of red
wines from a mixture of local southern and Bordeaux grape
varieties. A small amount of white, using Ugni Blanc,
Grenache Blanc and Clairette, is also made. Some Cabernet
wines are produced as 100 percent varietals.

Vin de Pays du Mont Bouquet Situated southeast of Alès, this
is another *vin de pays* producing mostly red wines. Here a
high percentage of Syrah is introduced to the blend to give
well-coloured, characterful wines.

Vin de Pays des Sables du Golfe du Lion A virtually single-
company *vin de pays*, dominated by the huge Salins du Midi
firm, producing wines under the brand name of Listel. A
wide range of wines is made from local grapes, though a
considerable proportion of Chardonnay, Sauvignon Blanc
and Cabernet Sauvignon are also used.

Vin de Pays de l'Uzège Around the town of Uzège, 26
communes produce red, rosé and some white wines. The
usual southern grape varieties are used.

Other zonal *vins de pays* are: Vin de Pays des Coteaux Cévenols, Vin
de Pays des Côtes du Libac, Vin de Pays de la Vaunage, Vin de Pays
de la Vistrenque.

Hérault AC

Clairette du Languedoc Dry, medium and sweet white wines
made exclusively from the Clairette grape in communes

around Cabrières, Aspiran and Clermont l'Hérault in the valley of the Hérault. Much of the 10,000 hectolitres produced is sold for vermouth, but other wines are aged to produce Rancio – what some might call an oxidized wine, but which others describe as maderized and profess to enjoy. High in alcohol, Clairette du Languedoc is best drunk on its own or before or after a meal.

Coteaux du Languedoc A highly complicated region producing red and rosé wines throughout Hérault. The grapes used are Carignan, Cinsault, Counoise, Grenache, Mourvèdre, Syrah and Terret Noir. White wines are not permitted the basic Coteaux du Languedoc AC, although certain communes (*see below*) also produce dry white wines using Clairette, Picpoul and Bourboulenc (locally known as Malvoisie). Standards are improving right across the region and one or two producers are outstanding.

    12 communes are allowed to add their name to the general AC. Two – La Clape and Quatourze – are in the Aude *département*, the rest are in Hérault. They are also allowed to use the village name without the Coteaux du Languedoc prefix – just to confuse us all!

Coteaux du Languedoc-Cabrières Rosé wines from vineyards just outside Béziers, mainly from Carignan and Cinsault with a little Grenache.

Coteaux du Languedoc-La Clape In the Aude *département*, on the edge of the Corbières AC area, a large mound-shaped hill supports the vineyards of La Clape. Red, dry white and rosé wines are made on chalk soil. Red and rosés are made from Carignan, Grenache, Cinsault and Terret Noir, whites from Clairette, Picpoul and Bourboulenc.

Coteaux du Languedoc-Coteaux de la Méjanelle or La Méjanelle Red wines from Carignan, Cinsault and Grenache from near Montpellier. A small amount of dry white is also made.

Coteaux du Languedoc-Coteaux de Saint-Christol Vineyards northeast of Montpellier producing simple red wines from Carignan, Cinsault and Grenache.

Coteaux du Languedoc-Coteaux de Vérargues Red and rosé

wines, from vineyards northeast of Montpellier. Carignan, Cinsault, Grenache and some Aramon are used.

Coteaux du Languedoc-Montpeyroux Red and rosé from schist soil north of Béziers. The reds include some Syrah in the *cépage*, which gives them some style.

Coteaux du Languedoc-Picpoul de Pinet Dry white wines made from Picpoul, Clairette and Terret Blanc in a small vineyard area just inland from the Bassin de Thau. The wines tend to flabbiness quite quickly and need to be drunk young and very fresh.

Coteaux du Languedoc-Pic-Saint-Loup Red, rosé and dry white from north of Montpellier. Fairly ordinary, straightforward wines.

Coteaux du Languedoc-Quatourze Vineyards around Narbonne in the Aude *département* producing red, dry white and rosé wines on stony soil. The red is particularly powerful and traditionally was used to strengthen weaker brews. Now generally bottled in its own right.

Coteaux du Languedoc-Saint-Drézéry Just west of Saint-Christol, vineyards producing red and a small amount of rosé. The usual grape varieties are used, but Carignan tends to be in higher proportion.

Coteaux du Languedoc-Saint-Georges d'Orques Red and rosé wines from northwest of Montpellier. A high proportion of Cinsault is used, and the wines age well.

Coteaux du Languedoc-Saint-Saturnin Stylish wines from Grenache, Cinsault, Carignan and Mourvèdre and Syrah to give the extra quality. Red and rosé are made in the hills north of the Hérault river.

Faugères Red, rosé and dry white wines coming from seven communes in the foothills of the Cevennes north of Béziers. The vineyards are on steep hillsides and are difficult to work. Between 40,000 and 50,000 hectolitres are made each year. Grapes for the red wines are principally Carignan and, increasingly, Grenache and Cinsault. Full-bodied and best described as hearty with intense colour, it is a wine which needs the accompaniment of rich food. A little white is made from the Clairette grape.

Minervois A large area of vineyards, in 61 communes, which crosses the departmental boundary between Hérault and Aude. The best vineyards are in the Hérault around Minerve and St-Jean-de-Minervois. Red and rosé are produced from Carignan (over 50 percent), Grenache and Cinsault with some Syrah and Mourvèdre. A small amount of white is also made. The reds are characterized by spicy, ripe southern fruit which makes them attractive when young, although the producers who use some wood make wines that can age. The area received the AC in 1985.

Saint-Chinian One of the most promising AC areas in the Hérault, producing red and rosé wines in a large area to the southwest of the Faugères AC. The vineyards, on slate soil with limestone, cover the hillsides on both banks of the Orb river. 80,000 hectolitres are made each year. The grapes are Carignan, Grenache, Cinsault, Mourvèdre and Syrah, with the better producers having only a small proportion of Carignan. The wines are lighter and more elegant than other reds from Languedoc and the growth of prestigious single-domaine wines is encouraging.

Hérault Vins Doux Naturels (VDN) and Vins de Liqueur

Clairette du Languedoc Made from the same grapes that also produce the dry white Clairette du Languedoc.
Frontignan Red VDN made from the Grenache grape in an area north of Sète. Also known as Vin de Frontignan. Can be a VDN or Vin de Liqueur.
Muscat de Frontignan In the same area as Frontignan, this is a white wine, one of the best VDNs from the Muscat grape. Can be either a Vin Doux Naturel or a Vin de Liqueur.
Muscat de Lunel From the Muscat grape in the area around Saint-Christol northeast of Montpellier.
Muscat de Mireval A small area just north of Frontignan.
Muscat de Saint-Jean-de-Minervois A small area at the northern extremity of the Minervois.

Hérault Vins de Pays

Departmental Vin de Pays

Vin de Pays de l'Hérault One of the biggest *vin de pays*-producing regions in France (1·1 million hectolitres on average). 85 percent of these wines are red, made from Carignan, Grenache Noir, Cinsault and Syrah, with Cabernet Sauvignon and Merlot also permitted. Small amounts of white and rosé are made.

Zonal Vins de Pays

Vin de Pays de l'Ardailhou Carignan, Grenache and Cinsault are the principal grape varieties used in this area on the coast southeast of Béziers. Once again the production is mainly of red wines.

Vin de Pays de la Bénovie A region of 15 communes around Saint-Christol, producing red, rosé and white wines from the usual southern grape varieties.

Vin de Pays du Bérange Red and rosé are predominant among the wines of this *vin de pays*, with only six percent of white; production is small. Some Bordeaux grape varieties may be used. This zone is situated northwest of Montpellier.

Vin de Pays de Bessan Another small area which, unusually, is dominated by rosé and white wine production. Local grape varieties are used, although the small amount of red produced may also include Cabernet Sauvignon.

Vin de Pays de Cassan An increasing amount of white wine is made in this small area in the centre of the *département*, although the majority continues to be of red. Cabernet Sauvignon and Merlot may be added to the blend.

Vin de Pays de Caux The wines of this *vin de pays* are mostly rosés, with some reds produced in a small area in the centre of the *département*. Syrah is used to give some character.

Vin de Pays des Collines de la Moure A large area along the coast between Sète and Montpellier. Reds and rosés make up the main proportion of production and Syrah is used in their blend, along with the southern grape varieties. Cabernet Sauvignon and Merlot are made into 100 percent varietal wines.

Vin de Pays des Coteaux de Bessilles Another small zone in
the centre of the *département*, producing red and rosé wines.
There has been an increase in the proportion of whites
made, revealing that some interest is being taken in the
wines of this area.

Vin de Pays des Coteaux d'Enserune 13 communes near
Béziers, producing red wines and some rosé. The grape
varieties used are standard for the region.

Vin de Pays des Coteaux de Fontcaude Situated west of
Béziers, this *vin de pays* zone covers six communes making
small amounts of white and rosé wines, and larger amounts
of red.

Vin de Pays des Coteaux du Libron Predominantly red wines
from the Béziers region. Technical specifications for
production help keep the standards reasonably high.

Vin de Pays des Coteaux de Murviel A *vin de pays* of the
valleys of the Libron and Orb, northwest of Béziers; the
wines are mostly red, either including Bordeaux grape
varieties in their blend or as 100 percent varietal wines.

Vin de Pays des Côtes du Brian Red wines from the
Minervois region. Many AC Minervois producers also
make this *vin de pays*, usually adding some of the permitted
Cabernet Sauvignon.

Vin de Pays des Côtes de Thau *Vin de pays* from around the
shores of the Etang de Thau in the south of the *département*.
The production here is divided almost equally between red,
rosé and white wines. Traditionally a region supplying base
wine for vermouth, the local cooperatives have lately
developed an interest in bottling their own wine.

Vin de Pays des Côtes de Thongue In the basin of Thongue,
east of Béziers, this is predominantly a red wine area,
although white is becoming increasingly important. 100
percent varietal wines are also made here, with Cabernet
Sauvignon and Chardonnay both planted for this purpose.

Vin de Pays des Gorges de l'Hérault *Vin de pays* from south
of the popular tourist destination of Saint-Guilhem-le-
Desert; production is mainly of red wine in small quantities.

Vin de Pays du Mont Baudile On the slopes of Mont Baudile, this is principally red wine country, but with an increasing amount of white.

Vin de Pays de Pézenas Small production from one commune. This area specializes in 100 percent varietal wines from Cabernet Sauvignon and Merlot, while also making blends from the normal southern varieties.

Vin de Pays du Val de Montferrand Wines from a large stretch of the northern Hérault (and one commune in the Gard *département*); production is mainly of red wines. There is also a local speciality known as Vins de Café; red wines made using a short maceration to give a fruity style.

Vin de Pays de la Vicomté d'Aumelas Wines from 13 communes in the valley of the Hérault, producing a fairly standard mixture of 85 percent red, 12 percent rosé and three percent white wines.

Other zonal *vins de pays* are: Vin de Pays de Cessenon, Vin de Pays des Coteaux du Salagou, Vin de Pays des Côtes du Ceressou, Vin de Pays de la Haute Vallée de l'Orb, Vin de Pays des Monts de la Grage.

Aude AC

Blanquette de Limoux Hilly region southwest of Carcassonne centred on the town of Limoux, producing sparkling white wine made by the *méthode champenoise* from the Mauzac Blanc, Clairette and Chardonnay. The name Blanquette comes not from the colour of the wine but from the white film that covers the underside of the leaves of the Mauzac. The producers in the area – dominated by a cooperative – claim that their sparkling wine used the *méthode champenoise* before Dom Pérignon introduced it in Champagne. Whether or not that is true, today the Blanquette de Limoux is one of the very best sparklers in France outside Champagne. There are moves to change the name of the wines to Crémant de Limoux, in order to emphasize the sparkling nature of the wine.

Corbières The largest AC area in Languedoc and Roussillon, covering 92 communes from the coast right back to the high land of the Hautes-Corbières. Up to 600,000 hectolitres of wine are produced in an average year, of which 90 percent is red, one percent rosé, the rest white. Grapes for the red and rosé are Carignan, Cinsault, Grenache, Mourvèdre, Terret Noir and Syrah with a little white Picpoul. For white, grapes are Clairette and Bourboulenc. Similar in style to Minervois (*see under* Hérault), the wines are possibly softer and heavier with less ability to age. But with so much wine being made the range of quality from good to bad is enormous. New equipment and better practices in the vineyards are improving standards all the time. The area became an AC in 1985. Maybe in retrospect some of the vineyards should have been declassified at the same time.

Corbières Supérieures White wine only from the same region as Corbières, but with higher minimum alcohol than straight Corbières.

Fitou An area of vineyards within the larger Corbières AC, by the coastal lagoon of Salses. The AC applies to red wine only, made from a minimum of 70 percent Carignan with Grenache and Cinsault. The result is a powerful, full-bodied red which has to be aged for a minimum of nine months in wood. They have recently achieved some popularity on the export market. The AC is one of the oldest in the Aude – established in 1948.

Aude VDQS

Cabardès or Côtes du Cabardès et de l'Orbiel Red and rosé wines produced to the north of Carcassonne on the slopes of the Minervois. Grapes are Carignan, Cinsault, Grenache, Mourvèdre and Syrah with Cabernet Sauvignon, Cot, Fer and Merlot from the southwest region just across the hills. The reds, quite tannic in youth, are better than the rosés.

Côtes de la Malepère Vineyards to the southwest of
Carcassonne on the western side of the Aude Valley. Red
and rosé wines are made principally from Cinsault, Cot and
Merlot with smaller amounts of Cabernet Sauvignon,
Cabernet Franc, Grenache and Syrah: a heady brew which
actually produces some comparatively sophisticated wines.
Rosés are from Grenache and Cinsault and are better than
many rosés from surrounding areas. An area to watch.

Aude Vins de Pays

Departmental Vin de Pays

Vin de Pays de l'Aude Wines mainly from the centre and east
of the *département*. 90 percent of production is red, made
from Carignan, Grenache, Cinsault and Syrah. A small
production of white wine uses Sémillon, Chardonnay and
Chenin Blanc grapes. This is classic supermarket wine.

Zonal Vins de Pays

Vin de Pays de la Cité de Carcassonne Wines from 11
communes around the mediaeval city of Carcassonne; most
of these are red, and of a higher quality than many other
vins de pays in the region. This *vin de pays* also benefits from
the touristic connotations of Carcassonne.

Vin de Pays des Coteaux de la Cabrerisse This is a zone
covering three communes in the middle of the Corbières
region. The grape varieties are strictly controlled, in
contrast to AC Corbières; the main permitted varieties are
Bordeaux *cépage nobles*: Cabernet Sauvignon, Cabernet
Franc, Merlot; southern French varieties also appear.

Vin de Pays des Coteaux du Littoral Audois On the coast to
the east of the Corbières hills, this is an area producing
almost entirely red wines. They are mainly sold in bulk on
the French internal market, by cooperatives.

Vin de Pays des Coteaux de Miramont Wines from nine
communes around Capendu in the east of the *département*,
between Minervois and Corbières. Distribution is largely in
the hands of a group of independent producers.

Vin de Pays des Coteaux de Narbonne A *vin de pays*
producing a comparatively small amount of red wine in the
region around Narbonne. Merlot and Cabernet Sauvignon
are permitted, as are the usual southern varieties.

Vin de Pays des Coteaux de Peyriac Wines from the centre
of the Minervois region, from 17 communes in the Aude
and two in the Hérault, producing red and rosé from both
Bordeaux and southern grape varieties. About 90 percent is
produced by local cooperatives.

Vin de Pays des Côtes de Lastours Northwest of
Carcassonne, on the edge of the Minervois, this zone
combines characteristics of the Mediterranean and Atlantic
climates. These are also reflected by the grape varieties:
Jurançon Noir, Mauzac and the other Mediterranean
grapes.

Vin de Pays des Côtes de Lézignan This is another zone in
the heart of the Corbières. The vines are grown on stony
soil and most of the production is of red grapes – some
from Gascony and some from the Mediterranean. Formerly
known as Coteaux du Lézignanais.

Vin de Pays des Côtes de Pérignan Part of the Massif of La
Clape (*see* Coteaux du Languedoc AC). Production is
almost entirely of red wine, from three local cooperatives.

Vin de Pays de Cucugnan On the southern edge of the
département, covering a small area in the commune of
Cucugnan. Most of the wines produced in this zone are red.
Production is controlled by the cooperative of Tuchan.

Vin de Pays d'Hauterive en Pays d'Aude Wines from a
straggling zone, extending southwest of Narbonne between
the Aude and the plateau of Corbières. Eight communes are
entitled to make this wine.

Vin de Pays de la Haute Vallée de l'Aude Centred on the
sparkling wine town of Limoux, this is one of the rare *vin
de pays* zones where the predominant production is of white
wine. Varietal wines of 100 percent Chardonnay, Merlot
and Cabernet Sauvignon grapes are also important.

Vin de Pays du Torgan Formerly known as Vin de Pays des
Coteaux Cathares, this zone extends over ten communes in
the Hautes-Corbières. Production is almost entirely red.

Vin de Pays du Val de Cesse In the north of the *département*, this zone is based around the canton of Ginestas in the Minervois. Merlot and Cabernet Sauvignon are among the permitted grape varieties. Some whites are made, from a blend which includes Maccabeo.

Vin de Pays du Val de Dagne A wide range of grape varieties are permitted for this zone in the centre of the *département*, which produces mainly red wines.

Vin de Pays du Val d'Orbieu 12 communes between Narbonne and Lézignan are permitted to make this *vin de pays*, which is 96 percent red. Marketing is controlled by an efficient central organization, which has ensured wide distribution of the wine.

Vin de Pays de la Vallée du Paradis Wines from ten communes around Durban, this is one of the most widely exported *vin de pays* of the *département* – probably helped by its name. 95 percent of the production is of red wine; grape varieties include Cabernet Sauvignon and Merlot.

Other zonal *vins de pays* are: Vin de Pays des Coteaux du Termenès, Vin de Pays des Côtes de Prouille and Vin de Pays des Hauts de Badens.

Pyrénées-Orientales AC

Collioure Tiny AC area right by the Spanish border, covering the same area as the Banyuls Vin Doux Naturel AC (*see below*). Red wine from Grenache, Carignan, Mourvèdre, Syrah and Cinsault are made in baking hot vineyards on the slopes of the Monts Albères as they drop down to the sea. Potentially a fine wine, especially from the old-established vineyards, it is a declining area with only about 50 hectares.

Côtes du Roussillon Red, rosé and dry white wines from a large area of the Pyrénées-Orientales. The Côtes du Roussillon spread south from Perpignan and vines are found on the coast and stretching inland to the foothills of the Pyrenees. Reds and rosés are made from Carignan, Cinsault,

Pyrenees. Reds and rosés are made from Carignan, Cinsault, Grenache, Mourvèdre and the local Ladoner Pelut plus the white Spanish Maccabeo in small amounts. Whites are from Maccabeo and Malvoisie. Of the four large AC areas in the Midi – including Corbières, Coteaux du Languedoc and Minervois – this one has shown the greatest potential.

Côtes du Roussillon Villages The area north of Perpignan in the valley of the Agly is regarded as producing superior wine. The soil is gravelly with some granite and schist which gives the wines a backbone and elegance as well as a range of styles. Only red wines are covered by this AC. Two villages – Caramany and Latour-de-France – are allowed to add their name to the Villages AC.

Pyrénées-Orientales Vins Doux Naturels (VDN) and Vins de Liqueur

Banyuls Red and tawny VDN occupying the same area as the red Collioure, stretching down to the Spanish frontier. The wines are made from Grenache Noir, Grenache Gris, Grenache Blanc, Maccabeo, Malvoisie and Muscat. The more Grenache, the better the wine seems to age.

Banyuls Rancio Banyuls VDN which has been aged in barrels in the open air under the sun to concentrate the wine. The best Banyuls Rancio is called Banyuls Grand Cru, and is considered by some to rival tawny port.

Grand Roussillon VDN red wine from the general area of the Pyrénées-Orientales. Can also be made as Rancio.

Maury Red and rosé VDN from the north bank of the Agly river. It is made only from Grenache Noir. Lighter than Banyuls, it can also be aged in wood to produce Rancio.

Muscat de Rivesaltes A Muscat-based VDN from just north of Perpignan. In the same area as Rivesaltes (*see below*).

Rivesaltes Red, white and rosé VDN made from Grenache Noir, Maccabeo, Malvoisie and Muscat. Only 100 percent Muscat wines can be called Muscat de Rivesaltes. If aged in wood, this is called Rivesaltes Rancio.

Pyrénées-Orientales Vins de Pays

Departmental Vin de Pays

Vin de Pays des Pyrénées-Orientales Predominantly red wines, produced in most areas of this *département* with the exception of the southeast.

Zonal Vins de Pays

Vin de Pays Catalan The most important *vin de pays* zone in the *département*, stretching from the Mediterranean to the western boundary. About 70 percent of production is of red and 20 percent is of rosé wine, from a range of grapes including Cabernet Sauvignon, Mourvèdre and Syrah. Whites are made from Muscat, Maccabeo, Chardonnay and Grenache Blanc.

Vin de Pays des Coteaux des Fenouillèdes High-altitude mountain vineyards in the northwest of the *département*, producing mainly red wines from the usual grape varieties. Smaller amounts of rosé and a tiny amount of white wine is also made.

Vin de Pays des Côtes Catalanes Not to be confused with Vin de Pays Catalan (*see above*), these wines come from the northeast of the *département*, around Rivesaltes and along the coast. 80 percent of the wines are red, made from a mixture that includes Syrah, Merlot and Cabernet Sauvignon.

Vin de Pays Val d'Agly Wines from 16 communes in the area of Haut-Agly. These are mainly traditional reds, but there is an increasing production of whites and rosés.

One other zonal *vin de pays*: Vin de Pays des Côtes Vermeilles.

The Midi: Regional Vin de Pays

Vin de Pays d'Oc Covering the whole of Languedoc-Roussillon, this *vin de pays* is used for wines made from grape varieties not traditional to the region. Thus there are Vin de Pays d'Oc made from Cabernet Sauvignon, Cabernet Franc, Merlot, Syrah and Mourvèdre, with whites from Chardonnay, Sauvignon Blanc, Chenin Blanc, Viognier and Vermentino. 70 percent of production is of single varietal wines.

Gard Producers

Clairette de Bellegarde AC

Domaine de l'Amarine
30127 Bellegarde. Vineyards owned: 37ha. 225,000 bottles. VP-R
Costières de Nîmes and Clairette de Bellegarde are the two styles of wine produced on this large estate. The Costières de Nîmes comes in red, rosé and white from a standard range and special *cuvées* of red (Cuvée des Bernis) and rosé (Cuvée Royal). Grenache predominates in the red with Cinsault, Carignan and Syrah; the white is 100 percent Grenache Blanc. Clairette de Bellegarde is 100 percent Clairette. Some rosé *méthode champenoise* sparkling wine is also made (Cour de Bernis). *Open: By appointment only.*

Costières de Nîmes AC

Château de Belle Coste
30132 Caissargues. Vineyards owned: 53ha. 250,000 bottles. VP-R
Bertrand du Tremblay's family has run this estate for more than a century and they produce red, rosé and white Costières de Nîmes. The red (matured in wood) uses Syrah and Mourvèdre with Grenache Noir, and the rosé uses 100 percent Grenache Noir. There are two whites, one with Ugni Blanc and Grenache Blanc, the other Grenache Blanc alone. *Open: 9am–noon; 2–7pm.*

Château Roubaud
30600 Vauvert. Vineyards owned: Costières de Nîmes 70ha. 150,000 bottles. VP-R
This estate has been owned by the Molinier-Thomas family since 1927. Much of the wine from this estate – out of a total of 4,300

hectolitres each year – is sold in bulk. Red, white and rosé Costières de Nîmes are made, using stainless steel for fermentation. The usual *cépage* includes some Syrah for red and Ugni Blanc for whites. *Open: By appointment only.*

Château Saint-Vincent
Jonquières St-Vincent, 30300 Beaucaire. Vineyards owned: Costières de Nîmes 36ha. 250,000 bottles. VP-R
This is a traditional estate, making red and rosé, using wood for ageing the reds. The grapes for both styles are Grenache, Cinsault, Carignan and some Merlot. *Open: Mon–Fri.* ¸

Domaines Viticoles des Salins du Midi
68 Cours Gambetta, 34063 Montpellier. Vineyards owned: Côtes de Provence 123ha; Coteaux Varois 139ha; Vin de Pays 1,750ha. 25·4 million bottles. VP-R
The largest wine producer in France has vineyards in Côtes de Provence (Château La Gordonne, Domaine de Saint-Hilaire), a *négociant* business (Bernard Camp Romain) and the huge vineyard area in the sand dunes of the Gard *département* making Vins de Pays des Sables du Golfe du Lion. Quality for such vast production is high and the brand name is Listel. *Open: Visits to the Côtes de Provence vineyards only.*

Château de la Tuilerie
30000 Nîmes. Vineyards owned: Costières de Nîmes 74ha. 110,000 bottles. VP-R
An immaculately maintained estate owned by Mme Chantal Comte. The property, which she inherited from her husband, includes another 200 hectares of fruit trees. She makes red, rosé and white Costières de Nîmes, the white with 100 percent Grenache Blanc, the red a blend of Grenache, Syrah and Cinsault and the rosé 100 percent Cinsault. The red is the best of the three and ages well. *Open: By appointment only.*

Hérault Producers
Coteaux du Languedoc AC

Georges Bonfils
20 Quai d'Alger, 34200 Sète. VP-R and N
This firm is mainly a *négociant* for wines from the Coteaux du
Languedoc and the Vin de Pays de l'Hérault. It also has a Coteaux
du Languedoc estate, Domaine de Lavabre, which produces a fairly
standard red from Cinsault, Grenache, Syrah and Carignan. Other
Coteaux du Languedoc wines are estates for which the firm has
exclusive rights: Château de Beauregard and Château de Saint-
Series. The *vins de pays* – especially Chardonnay Vin de Pays d'Oc –
are better than the AC wines. *Open: By appointment only.*

J Boscary (Château Rouquette-sur-Mer)
11100 Narbonne. VP-R
A white from 100 percent Bourboulenc and a rosé from Grenache
are made here. There is also a wood-aged red, made using some
Syrah, which has a high reputation. The vineyard is planted on the
steep slopes of the mountain of La Clape, overlooking the sea.

Château de la Condamine Bertrand
**Avenue d'Ormesson, 34120 Lézignan la Cebe. Vineyards
owned: 100ha. 200,000 bottles. VP-R**
Stainless steel has been installed at this family-owned estate and
whites and rosés are vinified at controlled temperatures. Reds – the
bulk of production – go through carbonic maceration which brings
out the fruit and colour. Red and rosé are made under the Coteaux
du Languedoc AC, the white has the Clairette du Languedoc AC. A
range of wines in the interesting Vin de Pays des Côtes de Thongue
includes reds from Syrah, Mourvèdre, Merlot and Cabernet
Sauvignon. *Open: Mon–Fri 8am–noon; 2–8pm.*

Château de l'Engarran
**34880 Laverune. Vineyards owned: 53ha. 200,000 bottles.
VP-R**
The estate of Château de l'Engarran makes only red Coteaux du
Languedoc-Saint-Georges d'Orques from Carignan, Cinsault,

Grenache and ten percent Syrah. This is aged in wood for 18 months and produces rich, slightly spicy wine which takes some ageing. The Domaine de l'Engarran produces a *blanc de blancs* Vin de Pays d'Oc from Ugni Blanc. *Open: By appointment only.*

Claude Gaujal
BP No 1, 34850 Pinet. Vineyards owned: 60ha. 80,000 bottles. VP-R

The estate has been in the Gaujal family since 1791. Most of the production of wine in bottle is of citrussy Picpoul de Pinet, made using modern techniques, with fermentation at 17°C in stainless steel. Other bottled wines include a Sauvignon Blanc and red Merlot Vin de Pays des Côtes de Thau. *Open: By appointment only.*

Domaine Martin-Pierrat
St-Christol, 34400 Lunel. Vineyards owned: 20ha. 90,000 bottles. VP-R

Red and rosé Coteaux du Languedoc-Saint-Christol are produced on this small estate, using traditional methods. The red is a rich, smooth wine which matures quickly. Some Syrah is used in the blends, including a Cuvée Spéciale. The estate also produces a white Vin de Pays de la Bénovie from Chardonnay, Grenache Blanc and Ugni Blanc. *Open: By appointment only.*

Château de Nizas
34320 Roujan. Vineyards owned: 43ha. 180,000 bottles. VP-R

Red Coteaux du Languedoc Château Carrion-Nizas is produced here using carbonic maceration and some wood-ageing, resulting in a typical southern taste which is improved with a touch of Syrah. Perhaps more interesting is the estate's Vin de Pays de Caux: the red is made from ten percent Cabernet Sauvignon and 15 percent Merlot, plus the usual local varieties. Small amounts of rosé and white *vin de pays* are also made. *Open: Mon–Fri 8am–noon; 2–7pm.*

Château Nôtre Dame du Quatourze
11100 Narbonne. Vineyards owned: 45ha. 180,000 bottles. VP-R

One of the bigger private producers from the small Quatourze area near Narbonne, M Yvon Ortola makes red, white and rosé Coteaux du Languedoc using some stainless steel for vinification and aiming for highly aromatic wines. He has been planting Mourvèdre, Syrah and Grenache to replace the Carignan. The white Coteaux du Languedoc is made from Maccabeo. *Open: Mon–Sat 8am–noon; 2–6pm.*

Château Pech–Céleyran
Salles d'Aude, 11110 Coursan. Vineyards owned: 90ha. 300,000 bottles. VP-R
The vineyard is owned by the Comte de Saint-Exupéry, and produces red and rosé Coteaux du Languedoc-La Clape, some of which has up to two years in wood. Plantings of Cabernet Sauvignon, Merlot and Chardonnay are used as part of the blend for red, rosé and white Vin de Pays des Côtes de Pérignan. A vineyard that obviously takes trouble with its wines. *Open: Mon– Sun 8am-6pm.*

Château Pech–Redon
11100 Narbonne. Vineyards owned: 41ha. 300,000 bottles. VP-R
Cabernet Sauvignon and Merlot form 15 percent of this vineyard, and it shows in the red Coteaux du Languedoc-La Clape which Jean Demolombe makes. He uses two names – that of the château and also Domaine de l'Abbaye de Valfernière; an abbey which was discovered while the vineyard was being created. In addition to the reds, M Demolombe makes a rosé La Clape, using 25 percent Syrah and 25 percent Grenache. He also makes a *blanc de blancs* Vin de Pays des Coteaux de Narbonne from Chardonnay and a *blanc de noirs* from Cinsault. Because the vineyard is high up on the slopes, the vines get a slower, longer growing season than those on the plain. *Open: By appointment only.*

Raoul et ses Fils
Domaine des Grés–Ricards, 34150 St-André-de-Sangonis. Vineyards owned: 23ha. 20,000 bottles. VP-R
A red Coteaux du Languedoc is produced with Syrah (15 percent), Grenache and Cinsault; rather high in alcohol but not unpleasant. Another red is a more unusual Vin de Pays de l'Hérault made from

Merlot (60 percent), Cabernet Sauvignon (30 percent) and Carignan: quite stylish, aged in wood and needing some time in bottle. *Open: By appointment only.*

Château de Ricardelle
Route de Gruissan, 11104 Narbonne. Vineyards owned: 47ha. 400,000 bottles. VP-R
Organic methods in the vineyard – no chemical sprays – and modern equipment in the winery produce some attractive Coteaux du Languedoc-La Clape wines. The vineyard is on the western slopes of the hill of La Clape facing out over the city of Narbonne. The red is a blend of Carignan, Grenache, Syrah and Cinsault. The rosé (or *gris*) omits the Syrah. Vin de Pays de l'Aude red and rosé, which include some Merlot, are also made. *Open: Mon–Fri 8am–noon; 2–6pm.*

Domaine Saint-Jean d'Aumières
34150 Gignac. Vineyards owned: 26ha. 180,000 bottles. VP-R
While the bulk of Daniel Delclaud's production is of *vin de pays*, he also produces some Coteaux du Languedoc from Grenache, Cinsault and Syrah. Modern vinification in stainless steel is used, but M Delclaud's aim, he says, is to produce red wines for keeping. His wines include Vin de Pays de l'Hérault made from 50 percent Cabernet Sauvignon, with Grenache, Cinsault and Syrah. Probably his most interesting wine is a 100 percent Cabernet Sauvignon Vin de Pays des Gorges de l'Hérault, which is matured in wood. *Open: By appointment only.*

Les Vins de Saint-Saturnin
Route d'Arbaras, 34150 St-Saturnin. Vineyards owned: 820ha. 3 million bottles. Coop (182 members)
The main cooperative in the Coteaux du Languedoc-Saint-Saturnin AC area, specializing in the rosé Vin d'Une Nuit brand (a blend of Carignan, Cinsault, Grenache and Syrah), so called because the skins remain on the must for only one night. In addition the cooperative makes a large number of brands of red Coteaux du Languedoc – the best is the Cuvée Spéciale. Vin de Pays de l'Herault and *vin de table* are also made. *Open: Mon–Fri 8am–noon; 2–5pm.*

Château de Salles
Salles d'Aude, 11110 Coursan. Vineyards owned: 28ha.
200,000 bottles. VP-R
The Château de Salles has been in the Hue–Bellaud family since the
18th century. Now they make a range of wines, including Coteaux
du Languedoc-La Clape. The Grenache dominates the blend for
this wine which is partly made by carbonic maceration. There is a
small proportion of Syrah, Terret Noir and Carignan as well as
Cinsault. They also make Vin de Pays des Côtes de Pérignan; the
red version has 80 percent Merlot and ten percent Syrah in the
blend, and is an interesting and successful wine. *Open: By
appointment only.*

Jean Ségura (Domaine de Rivière la Haut)
11560 Fleury d'Aude. Vineyards owned: 13ha. VP-R
A locally renowned white wine – made from Bourboulenc grapes –
is produced at this estate in La Clape. The style is soft, but with
excellent tropical fruit flavours, and it is consumed in quantity
along with local seafood.

Faugères AC

Domaine du Fraïsse
Autignac, 34480 Magalas. Vineyards owned: 17ha. 80,000
bottles. VP-R
Jacques Pons uses carbonic maceration for his red Faugères, made
from Carignan, Grenache, Syrah and Cinsault. He vinifies the
different *cépages* separately, then blends them before bottling.
He now makes white wines as well as red, with plantings of
Bourboulenc, Marsanne and Grenache Blanc grapes. *Open: By
appointment only.*

Domaine de la Grange des Aires
Cabrerolles, 34480 Magalas. VP-R
The classic regional grape varieties – Carignan, Grenache, Syrah
and Cinsault – are planted here to make Mme Platelle's long-lived
reds. The estate, which has passed through the female line for
generations, was established in the last century.

Bernard et Claude Vidal
La Liquière, Cabrerolles, 34480 Magalas. Vineyards owned: 29ha. VP-R
Carbonic maceration techniques are used here to gain maximum fruit from the usual blend of grape varieties. Both a red and a rosé are made, the red soft and well balanced, the rosé somewhat muted and less interesting.

Minervois AC

Domaine Barroubio
St-Jean-de-Minervois, 34360 St-Chinian. Vineyards owned: 10ha: 25,000 bottles. VP-R
A 15th-century estate in the Minervois AC area which produces an attractive red for drinking young. It also makes a Minervois rosé and Muscat de Saint-Jean-de-Minervois. *Open: Mon–Fri 9am–noon.*

Dominique de Berthier (Château de Paraza)
11200 Lézignan. Vineyards owned: 72ha. 440,000 bottles. VP-R
Good red and rosé Minervois, using the Château de Paraza label. There are two *cuvées*: Tradition is made using classic fermentation; Cuvée Spéciale by carbonic maceration.

SCAV Costos Roussos
11160 Trausse-Minervois. Vineyards owned: 430ha. 270,000 bottles. Coop (210 members)
The bulk of the bottled production here is of Minervois, sold under two names: Traussan and Costos Roussos. The methods used are traditional but with some carbonic maceration for the Carignan used in the Minervois. Some Vin de Pays de l'Aude and Coteaux de Peyriac are also made. There is a strong feeling at this estate that time has stood still. *Open: By appointment only.*

Domaine Daniel Domergue
Trausse-Minervois, 11160 Caunes. Vineyards owned: 5ha. 25,000 bottles. VP-R
A small producer who is doing interesting things. Over half the

vineyard is planted with Syrah, which dominates three of M Domergue's wines: Cuvée Noire (100 percent Syrah), Cuvée d'Or (75 percent Syrah) and Cuvée Canteperdrix (80 percent Syrah). Another Minervois, Cuvée des Clos du Bosc, is 100 percent Mourvèdre. Although the quantities are small, the quality is high. *Open: By appointment only.*

Château de Fabas
11800 Laure-Minervois. Vineyards owned: 40ha. 300,000 bottles. VP-R
There is quite a high percentage of Syrah and Mourvèdre in this vineyard – with more being planted. But the red Minervois is dominated at present by Grenache, giving a typical southern taste and warm, rounded finish. Jean-Pierre Ormières uses temperature-controlled fermentation and a long maceration, and his Cuvée Spéciale gets some wood-ageing. Rosé and a small amount of white wine are also made. *Open: By appointment only.*

Château Gibalaux
Laure-Minervois, 11800 Trebes. Vineyards owned: 60ha. 60,000 bottles. VP-R
Plantings of Mourvèdre and Syrah have improved the quality and style of the wine since M Bonnet took over in 1969. He makes Minervois red from Carignan and Grenache with 20 percent Syrah; rosé has 50 percent Carignan and 50 percent Mourvèdre. Vin de Pays des Coteaux de Peyriac red and white are also made (the white has 50 percent Chardonnay). The use of stainless steel produces very clean wines. *Open: By appointment only.*

Château de Gourgazaud
La Livinière, 34210 Olonzac. Vineyards owned: 68ha. 500,000 bottles. VP-R
This is the showplace vineyard of the giant Chantovent organiz-ation, which acts as a major *négociant* in Languedoc and Roussillon. The vineyard is planted with a considerable proportion of Syrah, which is blended with Carignan, Merlot and Cabernet Sauvignon to produce a highly drinkable red, good when young but able to age. Minervois Blanc, from Sauvignon, Maccabeo and Marsanne, is well made but much less interesting. New plantings of Cabernet

Sauvignon, Syrah and Chardonnay are proposed. *Open: Mon–Sat 9am–noon; 3–6pm.*

Cave Coopérative des Coteaux du Haut-Minervois
34120 La Livinière. Vineyards owned: 650ha. 300,000 bottles. Coop (180 members)
A variety of vinification techniques are used at this cooperative which was established in 1924. It uses carbonic maceration, heating of the must, and de-stalking before fermentation. The best wine – Cuvée Jacques de la Jugie AC Minervois – is made by carbonic maceration, and then given some ageing in wood. No white wines are made, but about a third of production is of *vin de pays* and *vin de table. Open: By appointment only.*

Domaine de l'Herbe Sainte
Mirepeisset, 11120 Ginestas. Vineyards owned: 40ha. 60,000 bottles. VP-R
Guy Rancoule has owned this vineyard since 1965 and has installed stainless steel and planted some Cabernet Sauvignon, Cot and Merlot to add to his Minervois and Vin de Pays du Val de Cesse. He uses organic methods both in the vineyard and the winery, vinifying in stainless steel but cutting the use of sulphur to a minimum. Although only a small production is bottled at the domaine at present, M Rancoule is planning to bring the figure up to 400,000 bottles soon. *Open: June–Sept 9am–noon; 3–7pm. Otherwise by appointment only.*

Paul Herpe et Fils (Château de Vergel)
11120 Ginestas. Vineyards owned: 22ha. 220,000 bottles. VP-R
Red Minervois is produced here, with 30 percent Syrah giving it attractive, firm fruit. Techniques are traditional, with wood maturation. The estate also makes a *vin de pays.* The firm of Paul Herpe also owns vineyards in Corbières and Coteaux du Languedoc-La Clape. *Open: Appointments preferred.*

Paul Mandeville
Domaine de Vaissière, Azille, 11700 Capendu. VP-R
Cabernet Sauvignon, Merlot and, most unusually, Bleu Portugais

(a red grape associated with Austria and Germany) are planted here. In addition to Minervois, they make Vin de Pays de l'Aude and Vin de Pays d'Oc.

Domaine Jacques Maris
34210 La Livinière. Vineyards owned: 52ha. 190,000 bottles. VP-R
Red, rosé and white Minervois are the main production at this large estate in the heart of the Minervois AC, northwest of Olonzac. While wine is still sold in bulk, the proportion of bottled wine has gone up in the past five years. Some carbonic maceration is used for the Carignan which forms 70 percent of the red and 50 percent of the rosé. Syrah is used in the Cuvée Spéciale, giving a distinct perfume to the wine. Whites are made from 100 percent Maccabeo. *Open: By appointment only.*

Jacques Meyzonnier
Pouzols-Minervois, 11120 Ginestas. Vineyards owned: 10ha. 65,000 bottles. VP-R
M Meyzonnier produces only one wine at this small estate. His red Minervois is made by carbonic maceration and contains 50 percent Carignan, 25 percent Cinsault, ten percent Syrah and 15 percent Grenache. A special Cuvée du Vigneron is sometimes produced. *Open: By appointment only.*

Château de Paraza
Paraza, 11200 Lézignan. Vineyards owned: 130ha. VP-R
Two styles of Minervois are made on this large private estate: a Rouge Tradition, which is vinified traditionally; and a Cuvée Spéciale, made with carbonic maceration, and containing some Syrah. The Cuvée Spéciale is a more attractive style – with a deep colour and intense, concentrated fruit and a perfumed taste. Mme de Girard also makes a rosé, which is designed for drinking young. *Open: By appointment only.*

Domaine du Pech d'André
Azillanet, 34210 Olonzac. Vineyards owned: 19ha. 80,000 bottles. VP-R
The estate, at the base of the hill of the town of Minerve, produces

two red Minervois: one based on 50 percent Mourvèdre with Carignan and Grenache, the other replacing the Mourvèdre with Syrah. Both are excellent examples of the quality that Minervois can now produce, the Syrah wine perfumed and peppery, the Mourvèdre softer, warmer and ready to drink younger. Smaller amounts of rosé and white are also made. *Open: Mon–Sun 8am–8pm.*

Cave Coopérative de la Région de Peyriac-Minervois
11160 Peyriac-Minervois. Vineyards owned: 320ha. 50,000 bottles. Coop (250 members)
Only a small amount of Minervois is bottled at this cooperative, the rest being sold in bulk. The wines are dominated by the traditional Carignan, but carbonic maceration gives freshness and colour. Tour Saint-Martin is the cooperative's top Minervois *cuvée*, which has 50 percent Carignan, and the remaining 50 percent is made up of a blend of Syrah, Grenache and Mourvèdre. Vin de Pays des Coteaux de Peyriac is also made by the cooperative. Much of the wine sold in bulk goes to the big *négociant* firm of Chantovent. *Open: By appointment only.*

Jean de Thelin
Château de Blomac, Blomac, 11700 Capendu. Vineyards owned: 102ha. VP-R
A well-established estate which makes Minervois (using ten percent Syrah in the blend), and Vin de Pays d'Oc and *vin de table*, using 'foreign' varieties – Cabernet Sauvignon, Merlot and Tempranillo (the Spanish red variety from Rioja).

Les Vignerons du Haut-Minervois
34210 Azillanet. Vineyards owned: 301ha. 35,000 bottles. Coop (250 members)
The members at this long-established cooperative have vineyards in Azillanet, Cesseras and Minerve, producing mainly Carignan, but with a smaller amount of Syrah, Grenache, Cinsault and Terret Noir. Most of the production here is of Vin de Pays des Côtes du Brian and Vin de Pays de l'Hérault, much of which is sold in bulk. Winemaking is modern, with temperature control and carbonic maceration. *Open: By appointment only.*

Château de Villerambert
11160 Caunes-Minervois. Vineyards owned: 80ha. 240,000 bottles. VP-R

There are two Minervois estates owned by the Moureau family: the Château de Villerambert and the Château Villegly. The Villegly wines have more character and depth, but both are well made. They also make red and rosé Vin de Pays des Coteaux de Peyriac and a Cabernet Sauvignon/Syrah *vin de pays*, Domaine Moureau. *Open: Mon–Fri 8–11am; 2–7pm.*

Château de Villerambert-Julien
11160 Caunes-Minervois. Vineyards owned: 60ha. 120,000 bottles. VP-R

At this château (founded in Roman times) Marcel Julien uses both traditional vinification and carbonic maceration to make his red Minervois. His top *cuvée*, Cuvée Tradition, has 50 percent Carignan, 25 percent Syrah and 25 percent Grenache and Mourvèdre, giving a wine with plenty of raspberry fruit which should be drunk within three years. The other red is Cuvée Liberté (named to commemorate the centenary of the Statue of Liberty). M Julien also makes a rosé. *Open: By appointment only.*

Saint-Chinian AC

Château Coujan
34490 Murviel lès Béziers. Vineyards owned: 104ha. 170,000 bottles. VP-R

François Guy and his sister Solange Peyre run this model estate producing one of the best Saint-Chinian reds from Syrah, Grenache and Cinsault. For this top wine they use the name Cuvée Marquise de Spinola, who bought wine from this estate in the 18th century. An elegant wine, it is aged for a while in 200-litre barrels, adding a layer of complexity to the wine. Another *cuvée* is Cuvée du Prieur, based on 60 percent Mourvèdre. The estate also produces red and white wine sold as Vin de Pays des Coteaux de Murviel. *Open: By appointment only.*

Pierre et Henri Petit
Villepassans, 34360 St-Chinian. Vineyards owned: 21·5ha.
15,000 bottles. VP-R
Red and rosé Saint-Chinian are produced on this small family
estate, mainly from Carignan and Cinsault, but with a little
Mourvèdre, Syrah and Merlot. Carbonic maceration is used for the
reds. *Open: By appointment only.*

Cave Coopérative du Rieu-Berlou
343 Avenue des Vignerons, Berlou, 34360 St-Chinian. Vine-
yards owned: 530ha. 280,000 bottles. Coop (102 members)
Saint-Chinian AC Berlou Prestige, the top red wine from this
cooperative, is made from Carignan, Grenache and Syrah, using
carbonic maceration, and needing three years in bottle before
drinking. The cooperative also makes a standard red Saint-Chinian
and rosé and white wine. 70 percent of the production here is of *vin
de pays* and *vin de table* which is sold in bulk. New plantings of
Mourvèdre and Syrah should improve quality. *Open: Mon–Fri
10am–noon; 2–6pm.*

Vin Doux Naturel

Coopérative du Muscat de Frontignan
14 Avenue du Muscat, 34110 Frontignan. Vineyards
owned: 670ha. 2·2 million bottles. Coop (350 members)
This is by far the biggest producer of the sweet Muscat de
Frontignan, the only wine it makes. It operates traditionally, with
some ageing of the wine in wood, and the result is a good
commercial wine which preserves the grapey taste of Muscat and
adds a touch of honeyed sweetness. *Open: By appointment only.*

Cave de Rabelais
BP 14, 34840 Mireval. Vineyards owned: 150ha. 300,000
bottles. Coop (80 members)
Muscat de Mireval is the product from this appropriately named
cooperative. Vinification is in stainless steel, but the rest of the
production is traditional. Mireval is one of the smaller, less
publicized Muscat areas, but its production is just as good as that of

the better-known *appellations. Open: Mon–Fri 8am–noon; 2–6pm. Closed March.*

Aude Producers

Corbières AC

Château de la Baronne – Domaine des Lanes
11700 Fontcouverte. Vineyards owned: 40ha. 150,000 bottles. VP-R
Temperature-controlled carbonic maceration is used for reds at both these estates. The Château de la Baronne also produces a rosé, while Domaine des Lanes (Vin de Pays d'Hauterive) makes a white. *Open: Appointments preferred.*

Château de Caraguilhes
11220 St-Laurent-de-la-Cabrerisse. Vineyards owned: 60ha. 108,000 bottles. VP-R
A soft red is made here, using carbonic maceration. The vineyard is run organically.

Cave Coopérative Embres et Castelmaure
11360 Durban Corbières. Vineyards owned: 276ha. 410,000 bottles. Coop (123 members)
Most of the production here is of Corbières, although there is also Vin de Pays de l'Aude. This is one of the better cooperatives of the many in the Corbières region: its production of white wines is especially good. The château of Castelmaure was the home of the Pompadour family.

Domaine de la Fontsainte
11200 Boutenac. Vineyards owned: 41ha. 123,000 bottles. VP-R
Rosé is made here as well as red. Wood-ageing is used along with carbonic maceration to produce powerful, well-balanced wines.

Château de Lastours
11490 Portel des Corbières. Vineyards owned: 99ha.

450,000 bottles. VP-R

Red, *gris de gris* rosé and white Corbières are made on this estate. The red is the best of the three, with the top *cuvée*, Simone Descamps, an interesting blend of Carignan, Grenache and Cinsault, with a little Syrah and Merlot thrown in. This particular wine needs around five years before it is ready but a new *cuvée*, Arnaud de Berre, is made to be drunk young. The *gris de gris* is 100 percent Grenache, the white 100 percent Malvoisie – a very attractive wine. *Open: Mon–Fri 8am–4pm.*

Château de Mandourelle
11360 Villesque. Vineyards owned: 69ha. 138,000 bottles. VP-R

Red and rosé Corbières are made here; carbonic maceration is used for the reds. This château also produces a top Cuvée: Henri de Monfroid, named after the present owner's grandfather.

Château les Ollieux
Montséret, 11200 Lézignan. Vineyards owned: 45ha. 200,000 bottles. VP-R

Mme Surbézy-Cartier, who owns this vineyard, makes wine the modern way. She has modernized part of the vineyard as well, introducing Syrah and Grenache where previously there was only Cinsault and Carignan. Red and rosé are made under the name of the château and under the Domaine Surbézy-Cartier name. The château itself is old: a Cistercian monastery from mediaeval times, it came into the family in 1855. The estate also makes Merlot de Françoise, a Vin de Pays des Coteaux de la Cabrerisse. *Open: By appointment only.*

Château les Palais
St-Laurent-de-la-Cabrerisse, 11220 Lagrasse. Vineyards owned: 100ha. 162,000 bottles. VP-R

This estate made a name for itself when it pioneered the use of carbonic maceration for red wines in Corbières back in the 1960s. It continues to make soft, fresh, fruity wines, which have made it one of the most familiar Corbières names.

Domaine du Révérend
Cucugnan, 11350 Tuchan. VP-R and N

Now owned by Peter Sichel, the Bordeaux *négociant* and château owner, it was set up with ambitious intentions by the Français family. M Sichel aims to show that it is possible to use Bordeaux techniques such as the use of new wood in the maturing of Corbières wines. Early results are very promising.

Château de la Voulte-Gasparets
Boutenac, 11200 Lézignan-Corbières. Vineyards owned: 50ha. 250,000 bottles. VP-R

Two *cuvées* of red Corbières are the main production from this family-owned estate. The vines are old, with a low yield and consequent high quality. The standard *cuvée* comes from Carignan, Grenache, Cinsault and Syrah. For the Cuvée Réserve, the proportion of Syrah is increased and there is no Cinsault: the wine is deeper, more perfumed and one to keep. A rosé is also made. This is one of the few estates in the area where exports are more important than local sales. *Open: Mon–Sun during working hours.*

Fitou AC

Paul Colomer
11350 Tuchan. Vineyards owned: 19ha. 40,000 bottles. VP-R

This small property produces both Fitou and Rivesaltes Vin Doux Naturel. The Fitou is made in stainless steel, using some carbonic maceration, giving a powerful wine which is better drunk within three years of the vintage. The sweet Rivesaltes Rouge is 100 percent Grenache. M Colomer, whose family have owned the estate for generations, also produces a white, honeyed Muscat de Rivesaltes. *Open: By appointment only.*

Cave Coopérative de Fitou
11510 Fitou. Vineyards owned: 444ha. 300,000 bottles. Coop (185 members)

Fitou is the main production here, made using carbonic maceration and stainless steel. Their Fitou Terre Natale is an attractively spicy wine, benefiting from a dash of Mourvèdre and Syrah. Other wines produced are Rivesaltes Rouge Vin Doux Naturel, much of which is sold in bulk, and a good example of a Muscat de Rivesaltes. They also produce Corbières red, white and rosé. *Open: Mon–Fri 8am–noon; 2–7pm.*

Les Producteurs du Mont Tauch
11350 Tuchan. Vineyards owned: 1,015ha. 3·5 million bottles. Coop (550 members)
The largest cooperative in the Fitou region, producing Fitou, Corbières and Rivesaltes wines. It is a highly mechanized operation, with controlled-temperature fermentation and carbonic maceration. Various brands are produced, d'Aguilar and Don Neuve being the best known. The cooperative has been developed over the past few years so that now 80 percent of its production is bottled. Vin de Pays du Torgan and *vin de table* are also produced. *Open: Mon–Fri 8am–noon; 2–6pm.*

Château de Nouvelles
11350 Tuchan. Vineyards owned: 88ha. 150,000 bottles. VP-R
One of the few private producers in the Fitou area, the property has been in the family since 1834. The wines are made in stainless steel without any wood-ageing and are intended for drinking young – none the worse for that. Apart from the Fitou, they make a range of Corbières wines and Rivesaltes (including an aged Royal Rancio, which is an attractive aperitif). Plantings include the Mourvèdre grape, which is added to the *cépages* of the Fitou. *Open: Mon–Sat 8am–noon; 2–5pm.*

Cave Coopérative des Viticulteurs de Paziols
11530 Paziols. Vineyards owned: 750ha. 600,000 bottles. Coop (215 members)
Fitou and Corbières are the main production at this cooperative, which takes in virtually all the producers in the commune of Paziols. Some carbonic maceration is practised, but methods are traditional. An interesting touch with the Fitou is the use of ten percent white Maccabeo to lighten the wine. Red and Muscat Rivesaltes are also made. *Open: By appointment only.*

Cabardès VDQS

Château Rivals
11600 Villemoustaussou. Vineyards owned: 19·4ha. 30,000 bottles. VP–R
Red and rosé Cabardès are made from Grenache, Merlot and Cabernet Sauvignon (for the red) and Grenache and Carignan (for the rosé). Despite the blend, the red is made to be drunk young. White *vin de pays* is made from 100 percent Maccabeo. An interesting estate, whose owner, Madame Charlotte Troncin-Capdevila, is experimenting with Bordeaux-style wines. *Open: By appointment only.*

Pyrénées–Orientales Producers
Banyuls/Collioure AC

Groupement Interproducteurs du Cru Banyuls
Route de Mas Reig, 66650 Banyuls-sur-Mer. Vineyards owned: 4,305ha. 3·9 million bottles. N and Coop (1,200 members)
This is a large-scale operation, a grouping of three cooperatives which also acts as a *négociant*. It dominates the Collioure and Banyuls AC areas (with 2,600 hectares in Banyuls). There has been considerable investment in equipment and the general quality is good. Brand names used include Templers and Cellier des Templiers. The group makes considerable quantities of Rivesaltes red, muscat (under the name Aphrodis) and Côtes du Roussillon. *Open: Mon–Fri 9:30am–noon; 2–6pm. All day in summer.*

Cave Coopérative Les Dominicains
66190 Collioure. Vineyards owned: 2,800ha. 26,660 bottles. Coop (287 members)
Despite the address, most of the land belonging to this cooperative produces Banyuls, with 400 hectares making Collioure. Most of the wine is sold to *négociants*, but some is bottled under the Le Dominicain name, and there is an attractive Collioure Cuvée Matisse. *Open: By appointment only.*

Société Coopérative Agricole l'Etoile
26 Avenue du Puig del Mas, 66650 Banyuls-sur-Mer. Vine-
yards owned: 170ha. 290,000 bottles. Coop (70 members)
Virtually all the production here is of Banyuls Vin Doux Naturel,
made principally from Grenache Noir and Carignan. They make a
range of these wines: Grand Cru Select Vieux, Grande Réserve,
Doux Paille, Extra Vieux, a Muscat-based Tuile and drier styles.
They also produce a small amount of Collioure, which is made in
stainless steel. *Open: By appointment only.*

Domaine du Mas Blanc
9 Avenue Général de Gaulle, 66650 Banyuls-sur-Mer.
Vineyards owned: 13ha. 38,000 bottles. VP-R
Production from this 17th-century estate is split evenly between
Banyuls Vin Doux Naturel and red Collioure, which rejoice in
some particularly lurid labels. The Banyuls is made with the usual
cépages of Grenache Noir, Mourvèdre and Carignan with the
addition of some Syrah. The Collioure is made with 40 percent
Mourvèdre, 40 percent Syrah and 20 percent Grenache: a wine that
can take considerable ageing. *Open: By appointment only.*

Côtes du Roussillon AC

Société Coopérative Vinicole de Bélesta
66720 Bélesta. Vineyards owned: 350ha. 50,000 bottles.
Coop (140 members)
This old-established cooperative, founded in 1925, makes both
Côtes du Roussillon and the superior Côtes du Roussillon Villages
Bélesta. The Villages wine is made using carbonic maceration. The
cooperative also makes a small amount of Vin Doux Naturel, some
based on Muscat. *Open: Mon–Sat 8am–noon; 2–6pm.*

Domaine de Canterrane
66300 Trouillas. Vineyards owned: Domaine de
Canterrane 102ha; Domaine du Clos St-Georges 48ha.
920,000 bottles. VP-R
These two estates have adapted modern techniques to traditional
methods, with the use of stainless steel and temperature-controlled

fermentation. Both make a range of Roussillon wines, including Côtes du Roussillon, Rivesaltes red Vin Doux Naturel and Muscat de Rivesaltes. Large-scale production does not seem to harm quality. *Open: Mon, Wed–Sat 8am–noon; 2–6pm.*

Cazes Frères
4 Rue Francisco Ferrer, 66600 Rivesaltes. Vineyards owned: 85ha. 400,000 bottles. VP-R
One of the most go-ahead private firms in the area, producing a whole range of wines – 15 in all – from Côtes du Roussillon and Côtes du Roussillon Villages, through Vins Doux Naturels to Vin de Pays Catalan. Quality on the whole is good, and most of the production is now bottled on the premises. *Open: Mon–Fri 8am–noon; 2–6pm.*

Château de Corneilla
66200 Corneilla-del-Vercol. Vineyards owned: 60ha. 381,000 bottles. VP-R
Red Côtes du Roussillon is the most important wine to come from this ancient estate (the château dates from the 15th century). Philippe Jonquères d'Oriola, the owner, makes a top *cuvée* of the red which he ages in wood – a full-bodied wine with a touch of spice. He also makes white and rosé Côtes du Roussillon. Other wines from the estate include Rivesaltes Vin Doux Naturel, Muscat de Rivesaltes and a red *vin de pays* called Domaine de la Chapelle du Paradis, made from Syrah, Merlot, Cabernet Sauvignon and Grenache: a surprisingly sophisticated wine from the French deep south. *Open: June–Sept, Mon–Sat 4–7pm.*

Château de l'Esparrou
Canet-Plage, St-Nazaire, 66140 Canet. Vineyards owned: 99ha. 18,000 bottles. VP-R
Côtes du Roussillon, made using a high percentage of Mourvèdre and Syrah and some carbonic maceration, is the top wine from this estate. It receives some barrel maturation which adds to the complexity. Other wines made here are Rivesaltes, Muscat de Rivesaltes and *vin de pays.*

Château de Jau
**Cases de Pène, 66600 Rivesaltes. Vineyards owned: 202ha.
VP-R**
Art and wine go together here, with exhibitions of modern art being held regularly in the cellars. The Côtes du Roussillon has a high – and improving – reputation, as do Muscat de Rivesaltes and some white wines made using Malvoisie and Maccabeo.

Société Coopérative Vinicole Lesquerde
**66220 St Paul de Fenouillet. Vineyards owned: 434ha.
275,000 bottles. Coop (70 members)**
A well-run cooperative producing Côtes du Roussillon red, white and rosé and Côtes du Roussillon Villages. Most of the production is now bottled at the cooperative. The wines are sound and break few viticultural records. Vins Doux Naturels – both red and Muscat-based – are also made.

The Mediterranean wine region of Roussillon

Mas Rancoure
**Laroque-des-Albères, 66740 St-Genis-des-Fontaines.
Vineyards owned: 8ha. VP-R**
A small estate that produces a splendid red, Cuvée Vincent, a wine that ages well.

Chais de l'Oratoire
Domaine de Montcalm, 66300 Thuirs. N
A large *négociant* firm that buys wine from all over the Languedoc-

Roussillon region. It sells Côtes du Roussillon, Corbières, Coteaux du Languedoc, Minervois, Saint-Chinian, Fitou and Costières de Nîmes under different château names. *Open: By appointment only.*

Sarda-Malet
134 Avenue Victor d'Albiez, 66000 Perpignan. Vineyards owned: 33ha. 120,000 bottles
The bulk of this estate produces Côtes du Roussillon and Rivesaltes Vin Doux Naturel. There is a cold-fermentation Côtes du Roussillon white from 100 percent Grenache Blanc, and a range of red Côtes du Roussillon including a wood-aged Carte Noire which requires ageing for four or five years. The Vins Doux Naturels include red Rivesaltes and Muscat de Rivesaltes. The estate also produces Vin de Pays Catalan. *Open: By appointment only.*

Cave Coopérative Vinicole Les Vignerons de Maury
128 Avenue Jean Jaurès, 66460 Maury. Vineyards owned: 1,800ha. 1 million bottles. Coop (350 members)
The Vin Doux Naturel of Maury in all its forms is what matters at this cooperative. It makes aged Rancio as well as the younger styles and wines like Maury Vieille Réserve. It also makes a small amount of Muscat de Rivesaltes, plus Côtes du Roussillon Villages and Côtes du Roussillon white. *Open: By appointment only.*

Vin Doux Naturel

Mas Pechot
66600 Rivesaltes. Vineyards owned: 139ha. 199,500 bottles. VP-R
The Muscat de Rivesaltes made on this estate is produced from the higher quality Muscat à Petits Grains (as opposed to Muscat d'Alexandria) and has a deservedly high reputation. The estate also makes a red Côtes du Roussillon.

Rhône

The red wines of the Rhône were traditionally regarded as some of the finest in France. Hermitage had pride of place long before Bordeaux achieved its present eminence. Today, the best wines from the Rhône can achieve the same quality as bordeaux, and certainly provide much greater reliability than burgundy.

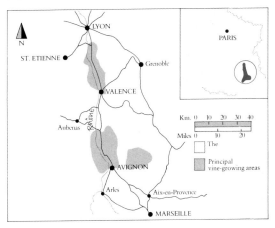

The Rhône vineyards are currently the most exciting source of red wine in France. Exciting, because we – the consumers – are rediscovering the greatness of Hermitage and Côte-Rôtie and Cornas; and exciting because the vast sprawl of Côtes du Rhône vineyards has come to life with wines that display a rare combination – quality and value. Even white wines – not normally considered an important part of the Rhône Valley wine output – have improved with the arrival of new equipment. The two small areas of Condrieu and Château Grillet command, with their rarity value, extravagantly high prices.

Conventionally, the Rhône vineyards are divided into two areas: the northern Rhône and the southern Rhône. The northern Rhône starts south of Lyon at the ancient Roman city of Vienne, which faces the first vineyards of the northern Côtes du Rhône and Côte-Rôtie.

In this first stretch of Rhône vineyards, the valley is narrow, with the eastern edge of the Massif Central cut in two by the fast-flowing river. Vineyards are steeply terraced, expensive to work and spectacular to look at.

The red wine Côte-Rôtie vineyards, facing east and southeast, run into the small AC white areas of Condrieu and the tiny plot of Château Grillet. Immediately after this white interlude, the northern end of the Saint-Joseph AC is reached, while before long – on the opposite bank – the vineyards of Crozes-Hermitage begin.

The vineyards of Crozes-Hermitage lap around the edge of the huge dome-shaped hill of Hermitage which marks the end of the steep slopes on the eastern bank of the river. On the western bank, the town of Tournon faces Tain l'Hermitage. Behind Tournon are the terraced vineyards which produce the best Saint-Joseph; only a short gap divides them from Cornas and then Saint-Péray. Here the northern Rhône stops.

Nothing happens in the way of vineyards around the nougat town of Montélimar, except a small area of Côtes du Rhône around Brezème. Perhaps the smell of all that sweet sticky stuff does not agree with the vines. South of Montélimar the valley opens out in both directions – east towards the foothills of the Alps and west to the Cévennes. Coteaux du Tricastin is on the east bank. Next, the vast Mistral-swept plain of the Côtes du Rhône begins, the boundary of the ancient Roman Provincia (Provence) is passed – and you are in the Mediterranean world.

On the eastern edge of the Côtes du Rhône, where the Alps begin, are the prime hillside vineyard sites of many of the Côtes du Rhône Villages and Gigondas. The new AC of Côtes du Ventoux runs along the southern edge of Mont Ventoux. Facing Mont Ventoux and hard on the eastern bank of the Rhône is the outcrop of rolling hills which marks Châteauneuf-du-Pape, facing, on the western bank, Tavel and Lirac. By the time the city of Avignon has been reached, the Côtes du Rhône has run its course. The only vineyards left are the outlying Côtes du Lubéron and the Coteaux de Pierrevert away to the east. The latter are hardly separated from Aix-en-Provence, and are grouped with the wines of Provence, which they more closely resemble.

In the past the division between north and south has not only been a question of convenience, but one of styles of wine. The northern Rhône vineyards were dominated by the Syrah grape; the southern by a mélange of grape varieties, of which Grenache and Cinsault were perhaps the most important.

Today the differences are becoming a little more blurred. The change has come from the movement of grape varieties – in particular the Syrah. The Syrah fulfils the same role in the Rhône as the Cabernet Sauvignon does elsewhere. It has become what the French call a *cépage améliorateur* – a noble grape variety which is used to lift the quality of a local wine. The increasing use of the Syrah in southern Rhône vineyards is one of the chief reasons for the improvement in quality of Côtes du Rhône.

Another has been the development of new techniques of winemaking. Some producers are now blending together wine made from free-run juice with wine that is the result of a long maceration of the grapes, stalks and all. The maceration brings out the colour and fruit (with the stalks adding some tannin) while the free-run juice gives elegance and freshness.

The other reasons are standard. There has been considerable investment in new equipment, the cellars tend to be cleaner than they used to be, and many of the younger generation of wine producers have been to colleges and universities to study their craft. The Rhône Valley has also been given its very own Université du Vin. Housed in a spectacular château in the village of Suze-la-Rousse, in the middle of the Côtes du Rhône vineyards, this runs courses particularly for local producers but also for producers from other parts of France. It has a fine library and tasting rooms. For any visitors to the area, a tour round the château is a must (telephone (75) 04 86 09).

While the Côtes du Rhône is the heart of the southern Rhône vineyards, there has also been a development of vineyards in the surrounding areas. New ACs and VDQS have been created – Ventoux, Tricastin, Lubéron, Vivarais – which have brought recognition and an improvement in quality to areas that were previously comparatively unknown.

The southern Rhône has the potential for a range of quality wines at affordable prices. A very different situation applies in the north, where demand regularly outstrips supply. Here the vineyard area is long-established and in some areas the best-quality hillside vineyards have already been planted, leaving little room for expansion without a diminution of quality. Prices for the northern Rhône wines, especially Hermitage and Côte-Rôtie, represented superb value a few years ago, but have recently rocketed. Much of the running has been made by a few of the *négociant* firms who dominate this area, and who argue that they are simply charging the prices the vines are worth. They have forced the individual growers along in their wake. But in the less popular ACs – Saint-Joseph, Crozes-Hermitage and, to a lesser extent, Cornas – the wines are still affordable.

The Appellations

Côtes du Rhône AC

The huge area of the Côtes du Rhône AC stretches from vineyards behind the slope of the Côte-Rôtie in the north to Avignon in the south. In all, there are 41,000 hectares of vines in six *départements*: Rhône, Loire, Ardèche, Drôme, Vaucluse and Gard. The bulk of the vineyards are on the wide plain east of Orange and north of Avignon, but areas of good quality are also found on the edges of the Crozes-Hermitage AC area in the north and around the edges of Tavel and Lirac in the south. Red, rosé and white wines are made under this general AC. The reds and rosés must have at least 70 percent of the noble grape varieties: Cinsault, Grenache, Mourvèdre and Syrah, with Carignan allowed up to 30 percent and Camarèse, Counoise, Muscardin, Vaccarèse and Terret Noir also permitted. Whites are made from Bourboulenc, Clairette, Grenache Blanc, Marsanne, Roussanne and Ugni Blanc. The reds are best drunk comparatively young – probably within three years of the vintage – although in great years some wines will age very well. Vintages: '85, '86, '88, '89, '90. For producers *see* Southern Rhône.

Northern Rhône AC

Château Grillet The smallest AC in France, and one of only two that are entirely owned by one producer (the other is Coulée de Serrant in the Loire). Here white wine is produced from the rare Viognier grape from a 2·6-hectare vineyard arranged in a semi-circle high above the Rhône, south of the town of Condrieu. Some years (such as 1978) may produce only about 4,000 bottles; others (such as 1980) may yield as many as 16,500. The taste of the wine is like an intense version of Condrieu – apricots, honey and ripe fruits are often cited, but the wine is dry. It is bottled in brown flute bottles – the only wine on the Rhône to use this shape and colour. It can live for up to ten years in good vintages, sometimes even longer. Vintages: '85, '86, '88, '89, '90.

Condrieu A slightly larger area than Château Grillet with 200 hectares available for planting, although only a little over 20 are actually in use. The vineyard has declined not least because of the notoriously low yield and unreliability of the Viognier grape. Unlike Château Grillet, there are two styles of Condrieu – a sweet and a dry. The dry, although somewhat more obvious than Château Grillet, has similar attractions, with its intense spicy fruit and apricots and honey bouquet. The wine does not keep for as long as Château Grillet: it reaches maturity after three to four years and rarely goes beyond ten. Vintages: '86, '88, '89, '90.

Cornas 100 percent Syrah wine from the steep hillside on the western bank of the Rhône, south of Tournon and Tain l'Hermitage. The vineyard area was once 25 percent larger, but now has only 60 hectares planted on the slope above the village of Cornas. New housing, low prices and the sheer physical difficulty of working the land were the main reasons for the decline. A rise in price after the '83 and '85 vintages put this situation into reverse. The wine is fuller than a Côte-Rôtie, very closed up and tannic when young, but in good years the fruit of the Syrah breaks through with intense earthy, spicy, violet flavours; often the equal of

Hermitage. Some lighter wines are made lower down the slope on sandy soil. Top wines are not ready for drinking for ten years; lighter wines are maturing after four to five. Vintages: '76, '78, '79, '81, '83, '85, '86, '88.

Côte-Rôtie The success story vineyard of the northern Rhône, Côte-Rôtie has been taken up in the past six years with great enthusiasm and a consequent rise in prices. The vineyards start just south of Vienne on the west bank on steep hillsides, facing south and southeast, and have ideal exposure – hence the name of 'roasted slope'. The core of the vineyard level with the village of Ampuis is divided into the Côte Brune (on clay soil) and the lighter soil (and hence lighter wine) of the Côte Blonde. Some wines are labelled as a blend of the two vineyards, but most Côte-Rôtie is a blend of more than just these two. A small amount of white Viognier is normally blended with the Syrah to lighten its tannic intensity, and about five percent of the vineyard has the white vine. Recent plantings on the plateau above the hill have brought the total area under vine to 130 hectares. Most tasters, however, agree that the plateau does not produce the right style of wine and the best growers have nothing to do with these new plantings. The wine is rich, very smooth when mature, with the characteristic spicy fruit of the Syrah toned down by the Viognier. Vintages: '76, '78, '80, '82, '83, '85, '86, '88.

Coteaux du Lyonnais Not strictly in the northern Rhône orbit – it comes from the Gamay rather than the Syrah – the Coteaux du Lyonnais is more an outlying district of the Beaujolais. The vineyards cover an area south of Villefranche-sur-Saône and around Lyon. Reds are from the Gamay, white from Chardonnay, Aligoté and Melon de Bourgogne. Cheap, cheerful and mainly consumed in Lyon.

Crozes-Hermitage Long regarded as the poor relation of Hermitage, this large vineyard area is now coming into its own following the price rise in Hermitage and an improvement of quality in Crozes. The village of Crozes-

Hermitage itself lies behind the Hermitage hill, but the vineyards stretch along the Rhône's eastern bank, around the base of the hill and out into the plain as far as Roch-de-Glun and Pont d'Isère to the south. The total area is now over 800 hectares. Red is from the Syrah, while the small proportion of white comes from the Marsanne and Roussanne grapes. Some producers are now bottling single-estate wines, although in the past most Crozes-Hermitage has been bought in by the *négociants*. Quality of the top estates is very good, approaching that of Hermitage, but there is still some indifferent wine under anonymous labels. Good wines have a spicy aroma, with the presence of blackcurrant fruit when young. They develop quite fast – within three to four years – and age up to six and eight years for better wines. Vintages: '85, '86, '88, '89, '90.

Hermitage The superb position of the vineyards on the hill of the Hermitage, which receives the sun virtually the whole day, guarantees the high quality of this AC. The Hermitage is a small chapel at the top of the hill once occupied by a crusading knight and now a magnificent viewing point. The band of Hermitage vineyards stretches around the hill from the top almost into the town of Tain l'Hermitage. They are divided into a number of smaller sections, which sometimes appear on the labels: Chante-Alouette, la Chapelle, les Bessards, les Greffieux and le Méal are among the best known. The total AC Hermitage area is small – 125 hectares – and almost completely planted. While nearly all the granitic soil of the vineyard is planted with Syrah, a small amount of Marsanne and Roussanne are grown which can be added to the red (up to 15 percent) or used to make a white Hermitage. All attention, though, is focused on the reds with their superb keeping powers, their intense blackcurrant fruit when young and their chocolaty richness when mature. Along with fine Côte-Rôtie, and the occasional Cornas, Hermitage is the finest wine on the Rhône. Wines from good years seem capable of surviving almost for ever and should not be touched before ten years. Vintages: '73, '75, '76, '78, '80, '83, '85, '86, '88.

Saint-Joseph This vineyard runs parallel to Crozes-Hermitage
on the opposite (western) bank of the river, stretching
much further north to the southern edge of Condrieu and a
little further south almost to Cornas – a distance in total of
nearly 70 kilometres. The original area was the southern
end, around the town of Tournon and into the side valleys
a little to the south. But changes in the AC legislation in
1972 extended the area from the previous 240 hectares to
around 600 hectares today. Sadly, as with Côte-Rôtie, the
new plantings do not produce such good wine as the
original, and the best wines still come from the southern
communes of Tournon, Mauves and Saint-Jean de Muzols.
The style of Saint-Joseph – even the best – is much lighter
than Crozes-Hermitage, deriving its character from the
sand and gravel which are mixed in with the granite base of
the vineyard soil. The style brings out the fruit of the Syrah
rather than the intense flavours, and makes Saint-Joseph a
wine to enjoy younger than some other wines from the
area. After three years it is certainly mature, and very few
Saint-Joseph wines last beyond ten or 11 years. Vintages:
'78, '82, '83, '85, '86, '88.

Saint-Péray The end of the northern Rhône vineyards is
marked with the appearance of a 60-hectare white wine
AC. This is made in a still and sparkling style (*see below*).
The still wine is from Marsanne and Roussanne grapes, and
is dry with a high natural acidity, a pale gold colour and a
relatively short life (two to three years).

Saint-Péray Mousseux The more interesting version of Saint-
Péray. The sparkling wine comes from the sandy, clay soil
around the small town of Saint-Péray and the surrounding
villages which stretch into the side valley towards Lamastre.
It is made by the *méthode champenoise* and is generally a
blended non-vintage wine, although a few growers do
make vintage wines. Full and fruity, the wine is popular in
France but rarely seen outside.

Southern Rhône AC

Châteauneuf-du-Pape The vineyards of Châteauneuf-du-Pape
– with their characteristic gnarled vines and huge heat-
reflecting stones – mainly produce red wine although a
small amount of white is also made. The vineyards are
large, covering 3,000 hectares in five communes. There
are 13 grape varieties permitted for the red (in order
of importance): Grenache (Noir and Blanc), Syrah,
Mourvèdre, Cinsault, Clairette (white), Bourboulenc
(white), Roussanne (white), Picpoul (white), Counoise,
Terret Noir, Vaccarèse, Muscardin and Picardan (white).
Very few growers actually use more than five, although
two of the best – Domaine de Mont-Redon and Château de
Beaucastel – use all 13. Châteauneuf-du-Pape is a highly
alcoholic wine, but the richness and smoothness of the fruit
should compensate for this. White Châteauneuf comes from
Grenache Blanc, Clairette, Bourboulenc and Roussanne. It
tends to be flowery but on the full side. Domaine-bottled
wines now come in bottles bearing the Papal coat-of-arms;
négociant-bottled wines do not. Vintages (reds): '78, '81, '83,
'85, '86, '88.

Châtillon-en-Diois East of the main Rhône vineyards are two
small ACs in the heart of Alpine scenery, of which this is
one, centred on the little town of Châtillon-en-Diois in the
valley of the Bez. Red, white and rosé wines are made. Red
comes from Gamay, Syrah and Pinot Noir; whites from
Chardonnay and Aligoté. The occasional Chardonnay can
be attractive, but on the whole they are not exciting.

Clairette de Die Still wines from the same area as the
Mousseux (*see below*). Not often seen outside Die – and
really best as a base for the sparkling wines.

Clairette de Die Mousseux Another small area only a few
miles from Châtillon, back in the valley of the Drôme, but
still in spectacular mountain scenery. Dry and medium-
sweet sparkling wines are made from Clairette and Muscat

à Petits Grains. The dry sometimes uses the *méthode champenoise*, while the medium-sweet adopts a local *méthode dioise*, using the sugar left over from an arrested first fermentation to start the second fermentation. The medium-sweet Clairette de Die is similar to, if a little drier than, Asti Spumante, and quite as delicious.

Coteaux du Tricastin Red, rosé and dry white wines from a large (2,000-hectare) area south of Montélimar and at the northern end of the big Côtes du Rhône plain around Orange. The soil is clay with large stones. Reds and rosés come from Grenache, Syrah, with a little Carignan, Cinsault and Mourvèdre. Whites come from Marsanne and Bourboulenc. Little distinguishes these wines from their Côtes du Rhône neighbours, especially with the increasing use of Syrah, and their quality, like those of the Côtes du Rhône, is getting better all the time. Best drunk within two to three years of the vintage, when their full fruit and peppery flavour are at their best. Vintages: '86, '88, '89, '90.

Côtes du Lubéron Red, rosé and dry white wines from the southern slopes of the Montagne de Lubéron in the Durance Valley east of Avignon. The reds and rosés come from Grenache, Syrah, Mourvèdre, Cinsault, with some Gamay. The whites are from Grenache Blanc, Clairette, Bourboulenc, Marsanne and some Ugni Blanc, with some Chardonnay and Sauvignon being planted. The quality from the better producers is good and improving.

Côtes du Rhône Villages Superior (in alcohol and, generally, quality) Côtes du Rhône which can either be simply AC Côtes du Rhône Villages (if it is a blend from a number of different, specified, communes) or can come from a specific one of 17 communes – in which case the name of the commune will appear on the label. Red, rosé and dry white wines are made. Reds and rosés come from Grenache (maximum 65 percent), Carignan (maximum ten percent) and at least five percent in total of Syrah, Mourvèdre and Cinsault. Whites are made from Bourboulenc, Clairette and

Roussanne. The 17 Villages communes are mainly on the eastern edges of the Côtes du Rhône plain: Rousset-les-Vignes, Saint-Pantaléon-les-Vignes, Valréas, Visan, Vinsobres, Saint-Maurice-sur-Eygues, Roaix, Cairanne, Rochegude, Rasteau, Séguret, Sablet, Vacqueyras and Beaumes-de-Venise. Three communes (Saint-Gervais, Chusclan and Laudun) are on the west side of the Rhône, opposite Orange. The red wines last a little longer than ordinary Côtes du Rhône – up to eight to nine years for good vintages. Vintages (red): '81, '83, '85, '86, '88, '89.

Côtes du Ventoux Along the southern slopes of Mont Ventoux are the 6,400 hectares of Côtes du Ventoux vineyard. Red, rosé and dry white are made on sedimentary soil. The red and rosé are made from Grenache, Syrah, Mourvèdre, Cinsault, with smaller amounts of Camarèse, Counoise, Muscardin, Terret Noir and Vaccarèse. Whites come from Bourboulenc, Clairette, Grenache Blanc, Marsanne and Roussanne. The reds are lighter in style than Côtes du Rhône and are best drunk two or three years after the vintage. The whites can be very fresh if made with modern equipment. Vintages (reds): '88, '89, '90.

Gigondas Lies between the two Côtes du Rhône Villages of Sablet and Vacqueyras and shares many of the characteristics of each (it was a Villages wine until 1971). Only red and rosé wines are made on the 1,200 hectares. Grapes are: Grenache (maximum 80 percent), Syrah, Mourvèdre and Cinsault. Clay soil produces very rich reds, with spicy fruit and often a vegetal farmyard smell. Wines can last seemingly for ever, and are not really drinkable for four to five years. Vintages: '78, '81, '83, '85, '86, '88.

Lirac Mainly red and rosé wines (and a tiny amount of white) from a small area (650 hectares) northwest of Avignon on the west side of the Rhône, adjacent to Tavel (*see below*). The red and rosé come from Grenache (minimum 40 percent), Syrah, Mourvèdre and Cinsault; the whites come from Bourboulenc, Clairette, Picpoul, Calitor and

Maccabeo. The reds are a sort of lighter version of Châteauneuf-du-Pape, more long-lasting than Côtes du Rhône, and worth keeping for five years. At the moment they are some of the best-value red Rhônes around. The rosés are a little heavy. The whites are also very good, fresher and more acidic than many Rhône whites. Altogether, an AC producing wines that are worth looking out for. Vintages (reds): '83, '85, '86, '88, '89.

Tavel The most famous rosé AC in France, with vines planted on nearly 750 hectares of clay soil west of Avignon. The wines are made from Grenache and Cinsault, Syrah and Mourvèdre with the permitted addition of the white grapes of Bourboulenc, Picpoul and Clairette. The wine is invariably very dry, with little fruit, more tannin, a characteristic onion-skin colour from wood, and comparatively low acidity. More modern techniques are enhancing the fruit and acidity and decreasing the use of wood. They age for around four years, but are at their best after two to three years.

Southern Rhone VDQS

Côtes du Vivarais Red, rosé and dry white wines from the west bank of the Rhône between Pont Saint-Esprit and Montélimar. Red and rosé come from the standard Côtes du Rhône grapes with the addition of Gamay. Whites (of which the production is very small) also come from Côtes du Rhône varieties. Three communes are allowed to add their name to the basic *appellation*: Orgnac, Saint-Montan and Saint-Remèze. Reds are lighter than Côtes du Rhône and delicious slightly chilled.

Vins de Pays

Regional Vins de Pays

Vin de Pays des Comtes Rhodaniens A large region covering eight *départements* (Ain, Ardèche, Drôme, Isère, Loire, Rhône, Savoie and Haute-Savoie). Most of the *vin de pays* wines produced within its boundaries are actually entitled to the zonal *vin de pays* classification, and therefore in practice this wine is rarely seen.

Vin de Pays de la Drôme Wine production mainly from the south of the *département* of Drôme, east of Montélimar. Most of the production (92 percent) is of red wine from the normal varieties of Carignan, Cinsault and Syrah, supplemented by Gamay, Cabernet Sauvignon and Merlot.

Other regional *vins de pays*: Vin de Pays de l'Ardèche, Vin de Pays du Puy-de-Dôme.

Zonal Vins de Pays

Vin de Pays des Collines Rhodaniennes Situated in the heart of the Rhône Valley, among the Côtes du Rhône vineyards, this *vin de pays* takes in mainly outlying non-AC areas. Production is of mainly red wines, from Gamay and Syrah grapes, and a little Merlot.

Vin de Pays du Comté de Grignan East of Montélimar, this area, producing almost entirely red wines, includes peripheral Côtes du Rhône vineyards, using the same mix of grapes.

Vin de Pays des Coteaux de l'Ardèche In the southern half of the Ardèche *département*, to the west of the Côtes du Rhône AC area, this zone has built a reputation for the production of 100 percent varietal *vins de pays*, most notably Chardonnay and Gamay, but also including a selection of grapes from Burgundy, Bordeaux and the south of France. The arrival of Burgundian *négociants* in the area has given impetus to the development of these wines.

Vin de Pays des Coteaux des Baronnies In the southeast of the Drôme *département*, to the east of Nyons, this zone brings together Rhône grapes plus Merlot and Cabernet Sauvignon. For the small production of whites, Chardonnay is used in the blend.

Vin de Pays de la Principauté d'Orange Around Orange, just east of the Châteauneuf-du-Pape vineyards, this is an

area of predominantly red wines from local grape varieties.
There is a tiny production of rosé, and an even smaller
amount of white.

Other zonal *vins de pays* are: Vin de Pays des Balmes Dauphinoises
and Vin de Pays des Coteaux du Grésivaudan.

Vins Doux Naturels

Two communes in the Côtes du Rhône Villages also produce
fortified sweet Vins Doux Naturels for which they have separate
ACs.

Muscat de Beaumes-de-Venise A Muscat-based sweet white
  VDN, made from the Muscat de Frontignan, which has
  achieved greater worldwide popularity than any other
  VDN from the south of France. It has the grapey, honeyed,
  smooth taste characteristic of all these wines.

Rasteau A VDN made from the Grenache, which can be either
  red or pale tawny (made by removing the skins early in the
  fermentation). There is also a version called Rasteau Rancio
  which results from leaving the wine in cask.

Northern Rhône Producers

Château Grillet AC

Neyret-Gachet (Château Grillet)
42410 Verin. Vineyards owned: 3ha. 12,000 bottles. VP-R
The one and only producer of Château Grillet from the smallest AC
in France, M Neyret-Gachet actually lives in Lyon, where he is a
businessman during the week. At weekends, however, he is down
on his farm, where *maître de chai* A Canet is in charge. The wines,
considered by some overpriced because of their rarity value, are
never to be forgotten once tasted. Almost luscious, yet dry, they
have the taste of ripe peaches or apricots with a hint of sweet spice.
The figure of 12,000 bottles per year is at the top end of the scale – in
1978 only 3,800 bottles were made. *Open: By appointment only.*

Condrieu AC

Pierre Dumazet
Limony, 07340 Serrières. Vineyards owned: 0·6ha. 2,000 bottles. VP–R
M Dumazet produces tiny quantities of Condrieu from a vineyard on the terraces above the river. Much of the wine goes to top restaurants in France, but a little does get exported. He uses a mix of wood and stainless steel and blends together wine made by both methods. All the apricot flavours of ripe Condrieu are the result. These are very fine wines. *Open: By appointment only.*

Domaine du Château du Rozay
Le Rozay, 69420 Condrieu. Vineyards owned: Condrieu 2·3ha; Côtes du Rhône 1ha. 10,000 bottles. VP–R
The Multier family make two styles of Condrieu. One, from old vines, they call Château du Rozay; the second is a straight Condrieu from younger vines. The wine is fermented in a mixture of stainless steel and wood. Those who admire the style of the Condrieu will be delighted to know that more land has just been planted. The family also own a small plot of Syrah wines from which they produce Côtes du Rhône. *Open: By appointment only.*

Georges Vernay
1 Rue Nationale, 69420 Condrieu. Vineyards owned: Condrieu 6ha; Côte-Rôtie 2ha; St-Joseph 1ha. 52,000 bottles. VP–R
Traditional methods and modern equipment are sensibly combined here to give wines of considerable style. M Vernay is certainly the big man of Condrieu, of which he makes about 30,000 bottles in a good year. He uses ten percent new wood each vintage for both red and white wines. *Open: By appointment only.*

Cornas AC

Guy de Berjac
07130 Cornas
Very traditional winemaking is the order of the day here. There is

no fining or filtration, which means the wines throw a sediment in the bottle. Old vines – the average age is 50 years – help the concentration of the wines, giving a deep, dark colour. They mature over a ten-year period, and then seem to hold that level for a long time.

Auguste Clape
07130 Cornas. Vineyards owned: Cornas 4ha; Côtes du Rhône 1ha. 17,000 bottles. VP-R
Superb wines are produced by M Clape in his small cellar on the main road of Cornas. His vineyards are high on the hill above. Although impenetrable wines when young, they nevertheless start life full of fruit lurking in the inky-black colour. With age – at least ten years – they produce a rich, earthy, spicy wine, perfumed and surprisingly elegant. *Open: By appointment only.*

Marcel Juge
Place de la Salle des Fêtes, 07130 Cornas. Vineyards owned: Cornas 3ha. 15,000 bottles. VP-R
'My style never changes,' writes M Juge. And he is right. Heavy and tannic wine when young, his Cornas develops into rich, soupy wine full of herby fruit, with immense ageing ability. Not for the faint-hearted. *Open: By appointment only.*

Robert Michel
Grande Rue, 07130 Cornas. Vineyards owned: 5ha. 17,000 bottles. VP-R
M Michel makes three styles of Cornas. The lightest comes from vineyards at the foot of the hill. The second in quality and depth comes from the hillside itself, while the third comes from old vines on the hill: this *cuvée* is called La Geynale. The wine is bottled unfined, giving a very rich, earthy taste. Old-fashioned style. *Open: By appointment only.*

Noel Verset
07130 Cornas
M Verset produces what is certainly one of the longest-lived Cornas – and one of the best. It comes from vineyards which have an ideal exposure on the steep slopes of Cornas, and his yields are the lowest

in the *appellation*. The results are aged in a bewildering mix of barrels, fined with egg white and then bottled unfiltered.

Alain Voge
07130 Cornas. Vineyards owned: Cornas 6ha; St-Péray 3ha. 25,000 bottles. VP-R
M Voge must be one of the few producers of Cornas who uses stainless steel in his cellar. This softens the tannin that can sometimes cover the fruit in Cornas, and his wines mature comparatively quickly. His Saint-Péray is made with Marsanne (98 percent) and Roussanne. *Open: By appointment only.*

Côte-Rôtie AC

Bernard Burgaud
69420 Ampuis
A relatively young vineyard, mainly situated at the top of the Côte-Rôtie slopes, with a portion on the flat plateau above. The wine is fermented at a high temperature to extract colour and concentration, and then aged in small barrels, some of which are new. Bernard Burgaud is in his thirties, and is seen as a rising star in the *appellation*.

Emile Champet
69420 Ampuis
The main part of M Champet's vineyard is on the Côte Brune, and he owns a portion of the named vineyard of La Viaillère. Wines contain five percent Viognier, and are matured in a wide range of old barrels, from small to large. The style is slightly rustic, and the wines are not the weightiest of the *appellation*, but have quantities of fragrant fruit flavours.

Albert Dervieux-Thaize
Ampuis, 69420 Condrieu. Vineyards owned: 3·1ha. 15,000 bottles. VP-R
President of the local Syndicat des Vignerons, Albert Dervieux vinifies separately the grapes from the three parcels, in the Côte Blonde and Côte Brune and in the Viaillère vineyard, that make up

his small estate. Although he says his wine can take 15 or more years to reach maturity, others have found his three wines tend to be on the lighter side. *Open: By appointment only.*

E Guigal
Ampuis, 69420 Condrieu. Vineyards owned: 12ha. 120,000 bottles. VP-R and N

The major force in Côte-Rôtie, now that it owns Vidal-Fleury (*qv*). Happily, its size does not adversely affect quality, which has a justifiably high reputation. Vinification takes place in stainless steel. Three styles of Côte-Rôtie are produced: a traditional blended Côte Brune and Côte Blonde; a lighter Côte Blonde La Mouline which has 12 percent white Viognier; and La Landonne, which is 100 percent Syrah, deep, well-structured and seemingly able to live for ever. Guigal make wines from many other Rhône *appellations*, including a very superior Côtes du Rhône and Gigondas. *Open: By appointment only.*

Joseph Jamet
69420 Ampuis

Very big, very concentrated wines, sometimes almost black in colour, come from vineyards scattered about the hillside of Côte-Rôtie. Wines mature after 15–20 years.

Robert Jasmin
Ampuis, 69420 Condrieu. Vineyards owned: 3·5ha. 12,000 bottles. VP-R

One of the top producers in Côte-Rôtie, M Jasmin's tiny cellars in the centre of Ampuis are a delight to visit. He makes a blend of wines from the Côte Brune and Côte Blonde for his Chevalière d'Ampuis, pressing and then leaving the must to macerate for around ten days. Everything is done in wood. The result, though, is surprisingly soft wines which are full of fruit even when young. He expects them to reach maturity after ten years. *Open: By appointment only.*

René Rostaing
69420 Ampuis

René Rostaing, whose father-in-law is Albert Dervieux (*qv*), runs this small vineyard on a part-time basis, but manages to make high-quality wines. He makes a Côte Brune, a Côte Blonde and wine from the La Landonne vineyard. Unlike many other growers (but like Guigal), he uses a percentage of new wood for maturing.

Domaine de Vallouit
Avenue Désiré Valette, 26240 St-Vallier. Vineyards owned: 13ha. 500,000 bottles. VP-R and N
While the bulk of this firm's business is as a *négociant* for all the northern Rhône area, their principal vineyard holdings are in Côte-Rôtie, where they have ten hectares. They also own land in Crozes-Hermitage and Hermitage. As *négociants* they produce Saint-Joseph and a Côtes du Rhône. Their whites are a Saint-Joseph, a Hermitage and a Crozes-Hermitage. *Open: By appointment only.*

Vidal-Fleury
BP 12, Ampuis, 69420 Condrieu. Vineyards owned: 8ha. 32,000 bottles. VP-R and N
Now owned by Guigal (*qv*), Vidal-Fleury makes Côte-Rôtie from Côte Brune and Côte Blonde, both separately and together, using vineyard names like La Chatillonne, Le Clos, La Turque, La Pommière and Pavillon-Rouge. The firm is the oldest in the area, having been founded in 1781, and its reputation has remained high for much of that time. They still remain firmly committed to traditional ways. *Open: By appointment only.*

Crozes-Hermitage AC

Cave des Clairmonts
Beaumont-Monteux, 26600 Tain l'Hermitage. Vineyards owned: 79ha. 100,000 bottles. Coop (12 members)
Red and a small amount of white Crozes-Hermitage are made in this modern cooperative, using autovinification and temperature control. These techniques produce a modern, fresh white and a soft, young-maturing red with plenty of colour and simple fruit. The red is more attractive than the white. *Open: During working hours.*

Domaine Pradelle
26600 Chanos-Curson
Both a red and a white are produced on this estate on the east side of the Hermitage hill. The red is better than the white, ageing in wood for one year, with a full, if slightly rustic, character.

Raymond Roure
26600 Gervans
Very low yields from vineyards on the hilly slopes by the Rhône in the north of the *appellation* produce highly concentrated wines that spend up to two years in wood. They are sold under the name of Les Picaudières.

Charles-Jean Tardy et Mme Bernard Ange
GAEC de la Syrah, Chanos-Curson, 26600 Tain l'Hermitage. Vineyards owned: Crozes-Hermitage 15ha. 65,000 bottles. VP-R
Red and white Crozes-Hermitage are made, using traditional methods and ageing the wine in wood, with a proportion of new oak. The quality of their wines is very high indeed: a 1983 Domaine des Entrefaux tasted in 1986 was quite the best Crozes-Hermitage I have ever drunk. Other names (after portions of the estate) used include Domaine des Pierrelles and Domaine de la Beaume. *Open: Mon–Sat 9am–noon; 3–7pm.*

Hermitage AC

M Chapoutier
18 Rue du Dr Paul Durand, 26600 Tain l'Hermitage. Vineyards owned: Hermitage 30ha; Crozes-Hermitage 5ha; St-Joseph 6ha; Côte-Rôtie 3ha; Châteauneuf-du-Pape 27ha. 1 million bottles. VP-R and N
One of the largest firms in Hermitage, the family-owned Chapoutier remains true to tradition, even down to pressing most of the grapes by foot-treading. They make the full range of northern Rhône wines, and have a major holding on the hill of Hermitage itself – from where they boldly display their name on the terrace walls. In some respects, their whites are more

remarkable than their reds – especially the Hermitage Chante-Alouette which ages for a considerable time. They blend vintages to produce top quality non-vintage wines under the name Cuvée Numerauté. As a *négociant* firm, they also make wine from Côtes du Ventoux, Coteaux du Tricastin, Tavel, Cornas and Gigondas. *Open: By appointment only.*

Domaine Jean-Louis Chave
Mauves, 07300 Tournon. Vineyards owned: 12ha. 30,000 bottles. VP-R

One of the great names in Hermitage, Gérard Chave produces thoroughly traditional red and white wines which – certainly for the red – seem to live forever. His Hermitage is made from 100 percent Syrah – unlike some other Hermitage producers – and he carries out all the winemaking in wood. The family has recently celebrated 500 years of winemaking from the same vineyard on the hill of Hermitage.

Delas Frères
07300 Tournon. Vineyards owned: Hermitage 25ha; Cornas 12ha; Côte-Rôtie 6ha; Condrieu 5ha. VP-R and N

An old established firm of *négociants* who own vineyards in the main northern Rhône ACs, while buying in wine from the southern Rhône. They have maintained traditional standards while expanding their business. Now owned by the champagne firm of Deutz. *Open: By appointment only.*

Desmeure Père et Fils
26600 Tain l'Hermitage. Vineyards owned: 17ha. 33,000 bottles. VP-R

A limited production of Hermitage and Crozes-Hermitage made traditionally and sold in bulk. *Open: By appointment only.*

Domaine Fayolle et Fils
Les Gamets, 26600 Gervans. Vineyards owned: Hermitage 1·5ha; Crozes-Hermitage 8ha. 45,000 bottles. VP-R

Fermentation of reds is in wood at this traditional family firm. They vinify the crop from each parcel of land separately: Le Dionnières for Hermitage; Le Pontaix and Les Voussères for red Crozes-

Hermitage (Les Blancs for white). Of the Crozes-Hermitage wines, Le Pontaix is probably the best. Vinification takes place in a mixture of wood and cement tanks and the whole process is very traditional. *Open: By appointment only.*

Paul Jaboulet Aîné
BP 46, 76600 Tain l'Hermitage. Vineyards owned: Hermitage 25ha; Crozes-Hermitage 36ha. 1·5 million bottles. VP-R and N
The most successful and most go-ahead firm in the northern Rhône, which has pioneered new, lighter styles of wines and has made the running in the increased reputation for the wines of the area. Their Hermitage La Chapelle is the most famous wine they produce, but they also make a full range from other areas of the Rhône. Their Crozes-Hermitage Domaine de Thalabert is generally considered one of the best wines of that AC. *Négociant* wines take in Châteauneuf-du-Pape, Côtes du Rhône (including the well-known Parallèle 45), Côtes du Ventoux, Saint-Joseph and Côte-Rôtie. A brand new plant outside Tain l'Hermitage is the outward symbol of their success. *Open: By appointment only.*

Marc Sorrel
Avenue Jean-Jaurès, 26600 Tain l'Hermitage. Vineyards owned: Hermitage 3ha. 12,000 bottles. VP-R
Old vines are behind the quality from this small vineyard, where traditional methods reign. M Sorrel has vineyards exclusively in Hermitage: Le Méal, Les Bessards, Les Greffieux and Les Rocoules. He makes a red Hermitage, Le Gréal, and a white (100 percent Marsanne), Les Rocoules. *Open: By appointment only.*

Cave Coopérative de Tain l'Hermitage
22 Route de Larnage, 26600 Tain l'Hermitage. Vineyards owned: 650ha. 500,000 bottles. Coop (500 members)
Besides having members with vineyards in Crozes-Hermitage, Saint-Péray, Saint-Joseph and Cornas, this cooperative controls two-thirds of the Hermitage AC. Standards are good, if old-fashioned, and quality is on the whole sustained. Their wines tend not to have the infinite ageing ability of the private Hermitage producers, but are attractive after nine or ten years. Whites are

made in a modern style and are fresh and crisp. *Open: During working hours.*

Saint-Joseph AC

Pierre Coursodon
Place du Marché, Mauves, 07300 Tournon. Vineyards owned: 8ha. 35,000 bottles. VP-R
Le Paradis, Saint-Pierre, L'Olivaie are some of the names that M Coursodon uses for his red and white produced from vineyards in the southern part of the Saint-Joseph AC. The red is from 100 percent Syrah grapes – fermentation takes place in wood; the white is from 100 percent Marsanne and made in lined tanks. *Open: By appointment only.*

Emile Florentin
Route Nationale, Mauves, 07300 Tournon. Vineyards owned: St-Joseph 4ha. 16,000 bottles. VP-R
M Florentin produces red and white Saint-Joseph on his small estate, called Clos de l'Arbalestrier. His vines are old and yields are low, resulting in complex wines. The red is perhaps a little too tannic for the fruit, but the white, from Roussanne, is very good indeed. *Open: By appointment only.*

Bernard Gripa
Mauves, 07300 Tournon. Vineyards owned: St-Joseph 4ha; St-Péray 1ha. 25,000 bottles. VP-R
Wood fermentation is still the only way they make wine *chez* Gripa, and the resultant quality makes him probably the best producer of Saint-Joseph. His vineyards are actually in the heart of the AC, in the area known as Saint-Joseph. The red has the soft richness typical of the AC; the white, from Marsanne, is perhaps less exciting. M Gripa's still Saint-Péray (he does not make a sparkling wine) is from a blend of 90 percent Marsanne and 10 percent Roussanne. *Open: By appointment only.*

Jean-Louis Grippat
La Sauva, 07300 Tournon. Vineyards owned: St-Joseph

4·5ha; Hermitage 2·6ha. 24,000 bottles. VP-R
A small yield from the terraces of Saint-Joseph gives M Grippat an intense wine, but one whose fruit and life bring it round comparatively quickly – after five years. Part of his holding is in the area of Saint-Joseph. His white Hermitage (which, like the red Hermitage, is from Les Murets vineyard) is very highly regarded, and can age well for five or six years. M Grippat and M Gripa (*see entry above*) are cousins. *Open: By appointment only.*

Raymond Trollat
St-Jean-de-Muzols
M Trollat's vineyard in St-Jean-de-Muzols is in the southern part of the *appellation*, with the hillside sites. His reds are firmly fruity and can age anything up to ten years; his whites are similarly fruity, with a lovely peachy flavour.

Saint-Péray AC

Jean-François Chaboud
07130 St-Péray
M Chaboud makes mainly sparkling Saint-Péray, with a smaller proportion of still wines as well. The sparkling wine, which is better, is made from 100 percent Marsanne, while the still wine blends in 20 percent Roussanne.

Southern Rhône Producers

Châteauneuf-du-Pape AC

Château de Beaucastel
Société Fermière des Vignobles Pierre Perrin, 84350
Courthézon. Vineyards owned: Châteauneuf 76ha; Côtes
du Rhône 25ha. 350,000 bottles. VP-R
This large family estate has pioneered organic methods, cutting out artificial fertilizers in the vineyard and adopting heat treatment of the grapes in the cellar before fermentation to give greater extract and avoid the need for sulphur. The vineyard has many old vines

and yields are low, but the extra efforts are well rewarded by one of the top two or three Châteauneuf available. They age superbly, full of rich vegetal fruit. In addition to the Château de Beaucastel which is Châteauneuf AC (and uses all 13 permitted grape varieties), they also produce a white Châteauneuf and an equally fine Côtes du Rhône Cru du Coudoulet (qv) on part of the estate which is outside the Châteauneuf AC. *Open: By appointment only.*

Domaine de Beaurenard
84230 Châteauneuf-du-Pape. Vineyards owned: Châteauneuf 30ha; Côtes du Rhône Rasteau 45ha. 420,000 bottles. VP-R

Domaine de Beaurenard is the name for both the Châteauneuf and the Côtes du Rhône wine produced here. It is one of the oldest concerns in the area, started in 1695, and Paul Coulon is the seventh generation. He uses a mixture of carbonic maceration and juice from pressed grapes to give a rich, fruity wine, low in tannin. The Côtes du Rhône Rasteau is a good, quick-maturing wine, which again is full of fruit. *Open: By appointment only.*

Domaine Berthet-Rayne
Route de Roquemaure, 84350 Courthézon. Vineyards owned: 6·7ha. 15,000 bottles. VP-R

This small estate produces Châteauneuf and Côtes du Rhône, using thermovinification at controlled temperatures. They also make a small amount of Châteauneuf white. *Open: By appointment only.*

Le Bosquet des Papes
84230 Châteauneuf-du-Pape. Vineyards owned: 22ha

Going up the lane to the ruins of the papal castle, you pass the medium-sized vineyard of Les Bosquets des Papes, run by the Boiron family. Both white and red Châteauneuf are made. The red is a blend of 70 percent Grenache, plus Syrah, Mourvèdre and Cinsault. The wines are concentrated and age well.

Domaine de Cabrières-les-Silex
84230 Châteauneuf-du-Pape. Vineyards owned: 60ha. 150,000 bottles. VP-R

One of the top estates of Châteauneuf, both because it is at the highest point of the AC area and because of the quality of the wine. The 'soil' here consists almost completely of the large round stones so often seen in pictures of the Châteauneuf vineyards. Traditional methods are used, fermenting and ageing in wood for the herby, meaty, spicy red. The white is also full and traditional in style. *Open: By appointment only.*

Domaine Les Cailloux (André Brunel)
84230 Châteauneuf-du-Pape
Two separate vineyards make up this estate: one in the northwest corner, and one on the flatter land in the southeast. There is as much as 70 percent Grenache in the blend, but this is being reduced in favour of Syrah and Mourvèdre. Vinification is a mixture of traditional long maceration after crushing, and the newer method of vinifying using whole berries. The wines age up to 12 years, and can last longer. A quick-maturing white is also made.

Domaine Chante-Cigale
84230 Châteauneuf-du-Pape. Vineyards owned: 40ha.
80,000 bottles. VP-R
Everything is done traditionally in wood here, and the intense colour of the wine is achieved by macerating the grapes for nearly three weeks. They use only Grenache, Cinsault, Mourvèdre and Syrah in the blend and the wine is kept for 18 months in wood. A white is now also made. *Open: Mon–Fri 8am–noon; 2–6pm.*

Domaine les Clefs d'Or
84230 Châteauneuf-du-Pape
Very traditional wines, with great power and richness, come from an estate divided in two. The cellars are on the edge of the town of Châteauneuf. Both a red and a white are made. Vinification for the red is a mixture of traditional and whole berry maceration.

Georges Pierre Coulon (Domaine de la Pinède)
84230 Châteauneuf-du-Pape. Vineyards owned: 10ha.
38,000 bottles. VP-R
Red and white Châteauneuf are made at this small estate, as well as a little attractive rosé *vin de table* called Réserve de la Pinède, and red Côtes du Rhône. *Open: Appointments preferred.*

Diffonty et Fils (Cuvée du Vatican)
BP 33, 84230 Châteauneuf-du-Pape. Vineyards owned: Châteauneuf 16ha; Côtes du Rhône 6ha; Vin de Pays 16·5ha. 15,000 bottles. VP-R

The sure-fire name Cuvée du Vatican is used both for the Châteauneuf and the Côtes du Rhône produced by this firm. The Châteauneuf has a long fermentation on the skins, giving it a very deep colour. Diffonty also makes Vin de Pays du Gard in rosé and white, which are sold under the name Mas de Brès. *Open: Mon–Sat 8am–noon; 2–6pm.*

Domaine Durieu
84230 Châteauneuf-du-Pape

The underground cellars of Paul Durieu are in the middle of the village of Châteauneuf. Here he keeps wines that are in an elegant, not too heavy style that mature well for up to ten years. The proportion of Syrah and Mourvèdre grapes in his vineyards is being increased.

Château de la Font du Loup
Route du Châteauneuf-du-Pape, 84350 Courthézon. Vineyards owned: Châteauneuf 15ha. 80,000 bottles. VP-R

While fermentation has changed in recent years to stainless steel, ageing remains in wood. The red is elegant, less tannic than some Châteauneuf. The white is produced in small quantities, using a microvinification technique which gives considerable fruit and freshness and cuts down the tannin. *Open: By appointment only.*

Château Fortia
84230 Châteauneuf-du-Pape. Vineyards owned: 28ha. 75,000 bottles. VP-R

A traditional red and a modern-style white Châteauneuf are made at what is generally regarded as one of the top Châteauneuf estates. The family of Le Roy de Boisaumarié, the owners, are proud of the fact that their ancestor mapped out the best land in Châteauneuf and instigated what became the first AC area in France in 1923. *Open: Appointments preferred.*

Château de la Gardine
84230 Châteauneuf-du-Pape. Vineyards owned:
Châteauneuf 53ha; Côtes du Rhône Villages 48ha. 450,000
bottles. VP-R

The Brunel family have been *vignerons* since 1670, working on land to the west of Châteauneuf. They have recently increased the quantity of Syrah on the estate to 20 percent and cut down the amount of Grenache. This gives the wine greater ageing ability than some other Châteauneuf wines. The Côtes du Rhône Villages comes from near Rasteau and Roaix, and again Syrah is an important element in the wine. *Open: Mon–Fri 8:30am–noon; 1–5:30pm.*

Robert Girard (Cuvée de Belvedere)
84230 Châteauneuf-du-Pape

Small production of a finely charged wine, with an excellent, if old-fashioned, style. An unusual element in the vineyard is 15 percent of Counoise, which can impart a fatness to the wine.

Domaine du Grand Tinel
84230 Châteauneuf-du-Pape. Vineyards owned: 72ha

Very powerful wines are made here by Elie Jeune. The vineyards are in the eastern part of the *appellation*, around Courthézon, with some more centrally placed near the village of Châteauneuf. There is also a second label, Les Caves St-Paul.

Lançon Père et Fils (Domaine de la Solitude)
84230 Châteauneuf-du-Pape. Vineyards owned:
Châteauneuf 40ha; Côtes du Rhône 40ha. 300,000 bottles.
VP-R

A combination of traditional and modern techniques including carbonic maceration for the red wines. Interestingly, the Château-neuf has a high (20 percent) proportion of Mourvèdre, which gives some power as well as an attractive perfume. M Lançon makes white wines in both AC areas. The estate has been in the family since the 16th century. *Open: During working hours.*

Domaine Mathieu
Route de Courthézon, 84230 Châteauneuf-du-Pape.

Vineyards owned: 15ha. 70,000 bottles. VP-R
Full-bodied, aromatic Châteauneuf, made principally from Grenache in a traditional way. A white wine is also made from vines planted in 1985. Part of the production goes to *négociants*. *Open: By appointment only.*

Clos du Mont-Olivet
15 Avenue St-Joseph, 84230 Châteauneuf-du-Pape.
Vineyards owned: Châteauneuf 24ha; Côtes du Rhône 8ha.
180,000 bottles. VP-R
Traditional Châteauneuf style, big, robust reds, with plenty of herby, spicy flavour. A small amount of white wine is also made, plus Côtes du Rhône red from vineyards to the east of Châteauneuf at Bollène. *Open: Mon–Wed 8am–noon; Thur-Fri 2–6pm; Sat 8am–noon.*

Domaine de Mont-Redon
84230 Châteauneuf-du-Pape. Vineyards owned:
Châteauneuf 95ha; Côtes du Rhône 35ha. 500,000 bottles.
VP-R
One of the largest Châteauneuf estates – and also one of the best. The Châteauneuf vineyard is on the high plateau to the west of the AC area, looking north to Orange. They grow all 13 varieties of vines permitted under the AC rules, and also have small plantings of some which have virtually disappeared. Each variety is vinified separately and then blended. The Abeille family is highly serious in producing aromatic, very fruity wines, using some carbonic maceration. They also own a Côtes du Rhône vineyard at Roquemaure to the southwest. *Open: By appointment only.*

Louis Mousset (Château des Fines Roches)
84230 Châteauneuf-du-Pape. Vineyards owned:
Châteauneuf 200ha; Côtes du Rhône 100ha. 10 million
bottles. VP-R and N
A huge *négociant* firm centred on the mock-Gothic Château des Fines Roches (now a first-class restaurant), producing wines from all over the Rhône Valley, including *vin de pays*. Their own estates produce Château des Fines Roches Châteauneuf and Côtes du Rhône La Patrasse and Château du Prieuré. The *négociant* wines

reach an acceptable standard, the Châteauneuf is much better.
Open: (Château) By appointment only; (Restaurant) Reservations only.

Domaine de Nalys
Route de Courthézon, 84230 Châteauneuf-du-Pape.
Vineyards owned: 52ha. 240,000 bottles. VP-R
All 13 grape varieties of Châteauneuf are planted in this large estate
on the eastern side of the AC area, which has been in existence since
1778. They age the wine for 12 months in wood, producing a
quick-maturing wine with a floral, perfumed bouquet and a soft
texture. Smaller quantities of white are also made. *Open: Mon–Fri
9am–noon; 2–6pm.*

Château la Nerthe
84230 Châteauneuf-du-Pape. Vineyards owned: 63ha.
200,000 bottles. VP-R
Now part of Burgundy *négociants* Richard and David Foillard, this
estate has a great tradition of Châteauneuf. The wine is matured in
wood, some of which is new. They make a white wine, Clos de
Beauvenir, and also two reds, Cuvée des Cadettes and the superior
Château la Nerthe. *Open: By appointment only.*

Nicolet Frères (GAEC Chante Perdrix)
84230 Châteauneuf-du-Pape. Vineyards owned: 20ha.
60,000 bottles. VP-R
Big, old-style wines are made on this estate on the western edge of
the Châteauneuf AC area. They make only a red wine. *Open: By
appointment only.*

Clos de l'Oratoire des Papes
**Rue St-Joseph, 84230 Châteauneuf-du-Pape. Vineyards
owned: 40ha. 140,000 bottles. VP-R**
Red and white Châteauneuf are produced from a vineyard whose
centrepiece is an 18th-century altar which probably has little to do
with Popes and more to do with an insurance policy by a *vigneron*.
Today the owner, Mme Amouroux, runs the estate traditionally,
making classic wines. *Open: Mon–Fri 8am–noon; 2–6pm.*

Traditional Châteauneuf vineyards at Clos des Papes

Clos des Papes
84230 Châteauneuf-du-Pape. Vineyards owned: 37ha.
110,000 bottles. VP-R
Paul Avril, whose family has been making wine in the area for 300 years, produces traditional Châteauneuf using a long maceration and wood-ageing for up to 18 months. His wines are well structured, if tannic, and need a long time in bottle before drinking. 90 percent of production is red, with the remainder white. *Open: By appointment only.*

Père Anselme
BP 1, 84230 Châteauneuf-du-Pape. Vineyards owned:
None. 1 million bottles. N
Père Anselme, owned by J-P Brotte, president of the local Syndicat, is one of the biggest firms in the area, acting as *négociants* for wine from all over the Rhône especially in Côtes du Rhône, Côtes du Rhône Villages, Coteaux du Tricastin, Côtes du Ventoux and Gigondas as well as Châteauneuf. A fascinating museum at their cellars in Châteauneuf is well worth a visit. *Open: Mon–Fri 8am–noon; 2–6pm.*

Domaine Pierre Quiot
Château Maucoil, 84100 Orange. Vineyards owned:
Châteauneuf 30ha; Gigondas 14ha; Côtes du Rhône 14ha.
150,000 bottles. VP-R
Four brand names are used at this estate: Château Maucoil and

Quiot Saint-Pierre for Châteauneuf; Pradets for Gigondas and Patriciens for Côtes du Rhône. The Châteauneuf vineyard is probably the oldest named land in the area and records date back to the 16th century. The style is traditional in all three estates. *Open: Appointments preferred.*

Château Rayas
84230 Châteauneuf-du-Pape. Vineyards owned: Châteauneuf 13ha; Côtes du Rhône 12ha. VP–R

A small estate in Châteauneuf terms, but one which is highly regarded for the quality of its traditionally made red Châteauneuf, which, unusually, is made from 100 percent Grenache, with low yields even for Châteauneuf, and aged in wood for up to three years. They also make Côte du Rhône red and white from the estate of Château Fonsalette. *Open: By appointment only.*

Domaine du Vieux Télégraphe
84370 Bedarrides. Vineyards owned: Châteauneuf 50ha. 70,000 bottles. VP–R

A very traditional estate, producing concentrated firm wines which need many years for maturity. The Brunier family vineyard is planted with 80 percent Grenache and also Cinsault, Mourvèdre and Syrah. The yields are low and grape bunches are fermented whole to give tannic wines. *Open: By appointment only.*

Clairette de Die AC

Albert Andrieux
26340 Saillans. Vineyards owned: Clairette de Die 11ha. 50,000 bottles. VP–R

This estate produces a range of Clairette wines – from the still, dry Domaine du Plot to the dry *méthode champenoise* and semi-dry *méthode dioise* sparkling wines. *Open: Mon–Fri 8am–noon; 2–6pm.*

Buffardel Frères
Boulevard de Cagnard, 26150 Die. Vineyards owned: None. 300,000 bottles. N

Sweet and dry Clairette de Die are the only wines produced by this firm of *négociants*. Both are made by the *méthode champenoise*, and sold under a number of different brand names: Buffardel Frères, Albert Reymond, Leblanc Père et Fils, J & R Leblanc and Jacques Leblanc. The dry wine is probably their best. *Open: By appointment only.*

Union Producteurs du Diois
Cave Coopérative de la Clairette, Avenue de la Clairette, 26150 Die. Vineyards owned: 800ha. 3·2 million bottles. Coop (530 members).
This cooperative controls 80 percent of Clairette de Die production, an attractive muscat wine made by the *méthode dioise*. A dry *méthode champenoise*, Voconces Brut, is also made, as is still Clairette de Die and Châtillon-en-Diois. *Open: During working hours.*

Domaine de Magord
Barsac, 26150 Die. Vineyards owned: 9ha. 40,000 bottles. VP-R
This small firm produces sweet Clairette de Die using the *méthode dioise*, and a *brut* version using the *méthode champenoise*. *Open: Appointments preferred.*

Coteaux du Tricastin AC

Domaine de la Tour d'Elyssas
26290 Les Granges-Gontardes
By far the most interesting estate in this *appellation*. There are a number of wines made: two single-vineyard wines, called Le Devoy and Les Echirousses; and a 100 percent Syrah *cuvée*. The quality is high, while the prices are low.

Côtes du Lubéron AC

Château de Canorgue
84480 Bonnieux. Vineyards owned: 15ha. 60,000 bottles. VP-R
Red, rosé and white Côtes du Lubéron in a fresh style for the white

and rosé wines and with some ageing in wood for the red version. The style is attractive and easy to drink. *Open: Mon–Fri 9am–noon; 3–7pm.*

Cellier de Marrenon
Quartier Notre-Dame, 84240 La Tour d'Aigues. Vineyards owned: Côtes du Lubéron 11,000ha; Côtes du Ventoux 3,000ha. 9·9 million bottles. Coop (5,000 members)
This huge cooperative dominates the Côtes du Lubéron, and has done much to bring the quality of the wines from the area up to an acceptable level. Red, rosé and white Côtes du Lubéron and Côtes du Ventoux are made; the red made for drinking young by carbonic maceration. They also produce Vin de Pays de Vaucluse, a little Côtes du Rhône and Châteauneuf-du-Pape and *vin de table*. *Open: By appointment only.*

Château de Mille
84400 Apt
Highly praised Côtes du Lubéron is produced by Conrad Pinatel. Both red and rosé are made, and, unusually for most Côtes du Lubéron, the reds have ageing ability.

Château Val-Joanis
84120 Pertuis. Vineyards owned: 170ha. 500,000 bottles. VP-R
This brand new model estate produced its first wine in 1982, and has set new standards for the whole of the Côtes du Lubéron. The Chancel family have invested a fortune in top-class equipment for the vineyard and the winery. The wines themselves are improving year by year: they have planted Chardonnay and Sauvignon as well as Ugni Blanc for whites. Reds are made from Cinsault, Grenache and up to 60 percent Syrah. Gamay is used for rosés. *Open: During working hours.*

Côtes du Rhône AC

For producers making Côtes du Rhône Villages from a specific village, *see under* Southern Rhône producers.

Vignerons Ardechois
Quartier Chaussy, 07120 Ruoms. Vineyards owned:
6,363ha. 6 million bottles. Coop (a grouping of 21
cooperatives with 4,228 members)
The largest single production unit in the Rhône, this Union des
Coopératives brings together smaller cooperatives in Côtes du
Rhône, Coteaux du Tricastin and Côtes du Vivarais. While the vast
production of 4·2 million bottles of Vin de Pays des Coteaux de
l'Ardèche (much of it as varietal wines such as Syrah, Merlot,
Gamay, Chardonnay – some of which goes to Louis Latour in
Burgundy) dominates the operation, they also make considerable
amounts of the AC wines. The Côtes du Rhône is basic, sound
wine, and there is a smaller amount of Côtes du Rhône Villages
made from 80 percent Grenache and 20 percent Syrah. *Open: Mon–
Sat 8am–noon; 2–6pm.*

Domaine de la Berthete
Route de Jonquières, 84150 Camaret sur Aigues. Vineyards
owned: 50ha. 250,000 bottles. VP-R
Traditional and modern techniques mix in this producer's cellars,
which have been owned by the same family for 200 years. They use
a combination of stainless steel and lined cement tanks for
vinification. Quality is good, especially for a fresh white Côtes du
Rhône, made from Grenache, Bourboulenc and Clairette. They
also make white Vin de Pays de la Principauté d'Orange and red
Vin de Pays de Vaucluse. *Open: Mon–Sat 9am–noon; 2–7pm.*

Domaine du Cabanon
5 Place de la Fontaine, Saze, 30650 Rochefort-du-Gard.
Vineyards owned: 20ha. 30,000 bottles. VP-R
M Payan uses some carbonic maceration for his red Côtes du
Rhône, which is the only wine he makes. The blend includes ten
percent Syrah which gives a deep long-lasting colour to the wine;
not designed for ageing. *Open: Mon–Sat 9am–noon; 2–6pm.*

Coopérative Vinicole Le Cellier des Templiers
84600 Richerenches. Vineyards owned: 750ha. 65,000
bottles. Coop (150 members)
While much of the wine here goes for bottling elsewhere, a small

amount of Côtes du Rhône and Coteaux du Tricastin is bottled on site. The wine is generally on the light side, and should be drunk young. *Open: Mon–Fri 8am–noon; 2–6pm.*

Chambovet Père et Fils
Rue St–Jean Prolongée, 84100 Orange. Vineyards owned: 82ha. 300,000 bottles. VP-R
The vineyards belonging to this company are near the village of Suze-la-Rousse. They come from three estates: Château d'Estagnol, La Serre du Prieur and Domaine Sainte-Marie. All three estates produce excellent wines – although my preference goes to La Serre du Prieur, which is dominated by the Syrah. In addition to reds, they also make white Côtes du Rhône, including an unusual 100 percent Bourboulenc with apricot flavours and good fresh acidity. *Open: By appointment only.*

Emile Charavin
84110 Rasteau. Vineyards owned: 30ha. 30,000 bottles. VP-R
Domaine Wilfried produces Côtes du Rhône Villages from Rasteau and Cairanne. Most of the production is of red wine, with a small amount of rosé and some red Vin Doux Naturel from Grenache. Wood is used extensively in the traditional cellars. *Open: Appointments preferred.*

Domaine de la Chartreuse de Valbonne
St–Paulet de Caisson, 30130 Pont St–Esprit. Vineyards owned: 6ha. 30,000 bottles. VP-R
This beautiful Carthusian monastery founded in 1203 is now a medical centre which owns the surrounding vineyard. The red Côtes du Rhône is of good quality though limited production. It has 60 percent Grenache and 30 percent Syrah although the flavours of the Syrah dominate. *Open: Mon–Fri 9–11:30am; 2–6pm. Mon–Sun in summer.*

Cru du Coudoulet
Château de Beaucastel, 84350 Courthezon
This is the Côtes du Rhône vineyard directly next door to the Châteauneuf-du-Pape vineyard of Château de Beaucastel (*qv*).

Both are owned by the Perrin family, and the soil of the Coudoulet vineyard is virtually identical to the stony pebbles of Châteauneuf. The quality is high, one of the best of any Côtes du Rhône, and the wines are made using the same organic methods as Château de Beaucastel. Syrah, Cinsault, Mourvèdre and Grenache are used in the blend.

Château de Domazon
Modern vinification techniques produce a richly fruity Côtes du Rhône based on Grenache, Syrah and Cinsault. The wines are not for keeping, but are immensely enjoyable when drunk young.

Château de Fonsalette
84230 Châteauneuf-du-Pape
Owned by Jacques Reynaud of the Châteauneuf estate of Château Rayas (*see entry*), this is a highly regarded Côtes du Rhône estate. Two *cuvées* of Côtes du Rhône are made, with 50 percent Grenache, 30 percent Cinsault and 20 percent Syrah, a traditional blending but one which, through low yields and careful selection, produces rich, concentrated, powerful wines. There is also a 100 percent Syrah wine, which has been compared to the wines of Hermitage. Wine that is not considered good enough for Château Rayas has also been used in the blend, increasing its quality still further. A white Côtes du Rhône is also made.

Domaine de Grand-Cyprès
470 Avenue du Maréchal Foch, 84100 Orange. Vineyards owned: 12ha. 70,000 bottles. VP-R
M Lindeperg runs this small vineyard at Sormelongue near Orange, using traditional techniques and ageing the wine in wood. He makes only a red (70 percent Grenache and 30 percent Syrah) which is designed for ageing. His label – with a row of cypresses – is particularly attractive.

Château du Grand Moulas
Mornas, 84420 Piolenc. Vineyards owned: 29ha. 96,000 bottles. VP-R
M Ryckwaert's cellars are close to the Rhône surrounded by fruit trees which are an important part of his estate. His vineyards are on

higher ground near Uchaux, where he makes Côtes du Rhône and Côtes du Rhône Villages. He does not make wines for keeping, but they are immediately attractive with perfumed violet flavours that spring out of the glass. He presses 20 percent of the crop and leaves the rest to ferment as whole fruit, giving very good colour and also softening out the tannins. *Open: By appointment only.*

A Gras et Fils (Domaine de Saint-Chétin)
84600 Valreas. Vineyards owned: 25ha. 130,000 bottles. VP-R
Red and white Côtes du Rhône are made here. The red comes in two styles, Domaine des Hauts de Saint Pierre, a blend of Grenache, Mourvèdre, Cinsault and Syrah, and Le Trésor de Saint-Chétin, which adds some Carignan. A white, La Gloire de Saint-André, is also made and has a tiny amount of Viognier in the blend. The wine is bottled for the owners by the local cooperative. *Open: By appointment only.*

Edmond Latour et Fils (Domaine de l'Espigouette)
84150 Violes. Vineyards owned: 21ha. 50,000 bottles. VP-R
Two vineyards form this estate. One, the Domaine de l'Espigouette, produces a Côtes du Rhône, predominantly of Grenache with 10 percent Syrah and other varieties. The other, Plan de Dieu, makes Côtes du Rhône Villages, with 80 percent Grenache and 20 percent Syrah, Cinsault and Mourvèdre. Fermentation at controlled temperatures gives good colour and depth to both wines. Small amounts of white and rosé are also made. *Open: Mon–Fri 8am–noon; 2–7pm.*

Nadine Latour (Domaine de Cabasse)
84000 Séguret. Vineyards owned: 24ha. 96,000 bottles. VP-R
Côtes du Rhône and Côtes du Rhône Villages Séguret are the wines produced on this estate. The Côtes du Rhône is an easy-to-drink wine, while the Villages wine is more serious and takes some bottle-age. *Open: By appointment only.*

Jean-Marie Lombard (Brézème)
Quartier Piquet, 26250 Liuron. Vineyards owned: 2ha.

12,000 bottles. VP-R

This small vineyard is one of the only ones to be found in the gap between the northern and southern Rhône. It is planted entirely with Syrah. The wine is aged for up to two years in wood, giving considerable depth, rich tannic fruit when young, maturing into spicy, vanilla roundness after four or five years. It is good to see the vineyard being expanded. *Open: By appointment only.*

Domaine Martin de Grangeneuve
84150 Jonquières. Vineyards owned: 50ha. 75,000 bottles.
VP-R

Red, rosé and white Côtes du Rhône are produced here. The red is particularly attractive – youthful and peppery, it can age well. The white is one-third each Grenache Blanc, Bourboulenc and Clairette. The estate also produces a Vin de Pays de la Principauté d'Orange, a blend of Grenache and Syrah with ten percent Cabernet Sauvignon. *Open: During working hours.*

Domaine Mousset
84230 Châteauneuf-du-Pape. Vineyards owned: 105ha

The *négociant* firm of Louis Mousset in Châteauneuf (*qv*) makes an acceptable range of single-vineyard Côtes du Rhône, of which the best is probably Château du Bois de la Garde, although Château du Prieuré is also attractive.

Domaine de la Réméjeanne
Cadignac, 30200 Sabran. Vineyards owned: 50ha. 25,000
bottles. VP-R

A high proportion of Syrah (35 percent) in the blend of the red Côtes du Rhône from this estate gives considerable depth and good ageing ability. The white Côtes du Rhône, which ferments for one month at a low temperature, is from Clairette, Bourboulenc and Ugni Blanc. Quality is good for both wines. Much of the wine from the estate is sold in bulk. *Open: Appointments preferred.*

Domaine de la Renjarde
84830 Sérignan du Comtat. Vineyards owned: 52ha.
250,000 bottles. VP-R

This estate was one of the first to harvest entirely by machine. This does not seem to spoil the quality of the deep, peppery Côtes du Rhône Cuvée Henri Fabre, which has 60 percent Syrah. There is also a Côtes du Rhône Villages, Domaine de la Renjarde, which is 80 percent Grenache plus Syrah and Mourvèdre. Domaine de la Renjarde is in a more traditional style, for drinking younger. *Open: By appointment only.*

Domaine du Roure
St-Marcel d'Ardèche, 07700 Bourg St-Andeol. Vineyards owned: 11ha. 12,000 bottles. VP-R
Vines more than 50 years old produce superb wine, full, rich and slow to mature. The Grenache dominates, with smaller amounts of Syrah, Cinsault and Carignan. While not all the wine is estate-bottled, there are plans to increase the amount up to around 80,000 bottles. *Open: Mon–Fri 8am–noon.*

Château de Ruth
84190 Gigondas
Owned by the Meffre family, whose most famous wine is Gigondas from Château Raspail. Characteristically, wine from this large estate is good, commercial but enjoyably fruity, and should be drunk young.

Domaine Saint-Apollinaire
84110 Puymeras
A 100 percent organic vineyard, owned by Frédéric Dumas, near the small village of Puymeras, not far from Rasteau. In addition to a blended Côtes du Rhône, there is also a wine made from 100 percent Syrah grapes. The wines have considerable intensity and depth of flavour, a result of the fact that they are only lightly filtered before bottling.

Château Saint-Estève d'Uchaux
Route de Sérignan, Uchaux, 84100 Orange. Vineyards owned: 55ha. 300,000 bottles. VP-R
An excellent estate on a sandy ridge north of Orange, giving a light style of wine. A full range of Côtes du Rhône wines is produced by the Français family, including a rare 100 percent Viognier Blanc de Cépage and a *méthode champenoise* Blanc de Blancs. Wines have both

the Côtes du Rhône AC and the Villages AC – the Villages wine has 40 percent Syrah. There is a very fine Grande Réserve red, containing 50 percent Syrah. Other brand names include La Cuvée Friande, La Couloubrière and Cuvée des Deux Perdreaux. *Open: Mon–Fri 8am–noon; 2–6pm. Sat 8am–noon.*

Coopérative Vinicole La Suzienne
26790 Suze-la-Rousse. Vineyards owned: 1,000ha. 1 million bottles. Coop (937 members)
A huge cooperative in the heart of the Côtes du Rhône plain, under the shadow of the Université du Vin. They make Côtes du Rhône, Côtes du Rhône Villages and Coteaux du Tricastin under the name of La Suzienne. Quality is variable but getting better. All the bottling is done by the Union des Vignerons at Tulette. *Open: By appointment only.*

La Vieille Ferme
Route de Jonquières, 84100 Orange. N
The *négociant* business, owned by the Perrin family of Château de Beaucastel in Châteauneuf-du-Pape. They produce both red and white Côtes du Rhônes, of a good, consistent quality, from purchased grapes. They also make red and white Côtes du Ventoux which again is of a high standard.

Domaine du Vieux Chêne
Rue Buisseron, 8450 Camaret
Two wines are made here by the Bouche brothers. Cuvée des Capucines is in the forward, fruity style of Côtes du Rhône. Cuvée de la Haie aux Grives, with a greater proportion of Syrah in the blend, is more complex, and should be given time to mature. Both are excellent examples of good value Côtes du Rhône.

André Vignal (Domaine de Saint-Georges)
Vénéjean, 30200 Bagnols-sur-Cèze. Vineyards owned: 30ha. 100,000 bottles. VP-R
Red and white Côtes du Rhône are made on this estate, where the house dates back to the 12th century. The red Château de Saint-Georges is produced using carbonic maceration and matures quickly, with plenty of attractive fruit. There is a superior Cuvée

Syrah, a rosé Côtes du Rhône Villages and a Cotes du Rhône Primeur. The white is fresh and fragrant, not a wine for ageing. *Open: By appointment only.*

Côtes du Rhône Villages AC

Domaine de Boissan
84110 Sabelt
Under the owner Hubert Bonfils, this estate makes a deeply coloured Côtes du Rhône Villages Sablet that has ten percent Syrah and two percent Mourvèdre in the blend.

Romain Bouchard
Val des Rois, 84600 Valréas. Vineyards owned: Valréas 15ha. 50,000 bottles. VP-R
The Bouchard family have been at this estate since 1681, and have commemorated the fact with a Cuvée de la 8ième Génération, a blend of Grenache and Gamay. Their Côtes du Rhône Villages Valréas 'Signature' is 75 percent Grenache and 20 percent Syrah, and can age well – up to ten years. They also make Cuvée des Rois Côtes du Rhône red and rosé. *Open: Mon–Fri 9:30am–noon; 2:30–7pm.*

Domaine Brusset
84290 Cairanne
Half this estate produces Côtes du Rhône Villages Cairanne, while the other half comes under the generic Côtes du Rhône *appellation.* The Cairanne is made in rosé, white, and a red which ages well.

Domaine de la Cantharide
84820 Visan
Good, if uncomplicated red is made at this estate. The style is said to be for ageing, and the colour of the wines and the amount of tannin suggest this is true.

Clos des Cazaux
84190 Vacqueyras
This vineyard produces both reasonable quantities of Côtes du

Rhône Vacqueyras and smaller quantities of Gigondas. They make two *cuvées* of Côtes du Rhône: Cuvée des Templiers and Cuvée Saint-Roch. The former is almost 100 percent Syrah, the latter has 75 percent Syrah and is lighter in style.

Daniel et Jean Couston
Route de St-Roman, 26790 Tulette. Vineyards owned: Visan 50ha; Valréas 40ha. 500,000 bottles. VP-R
There are two estates belonging to this company. The Visan estate is Domaine du Garrigon, where red Villages and white and rosé Côtes du Rhône are made. The Valréas estate is Domaine de la Grande Bellane, producing red and rosé. They also make a Côtes du Rhône Primeur. They prefer to use organic methods in the vineyards and stabilize the wine in the cellar with modern equipment rather than chemicals. *Open: By appointment only.*

Union des Vignerons l'Enclave des Papes
84600 Valréas. Vineyards owned: 2,000ha. 3 million bottles. Coop (800 members)
This huge cooperative produces quick-maturing wine, the bulk of which is Côtes du Rhône, with some Coteaux du Tricastin. There is also some Côtes du Rhône Villages Valréas. The members have increased their plantings of Grenache and Syrah and reduced the amount of Carignan in their vineyards. The Enclave of the Popes is a small area of land which remained Papal territory until the time of the Revolution and is now an enclave of the Vaucluse *département* in the middle of the Drôme. *Open: Mon–Fri 8am–noon; 2–6pm.*

Domaine de la Fourmone
Vacqueyras, 84190 Beaumes-de-Venise. Vineyard owned: Gigondas 9ha; Côtes du Rhône Vacqueyras 12ha; Côtes du Rhône 8ha. 38,000 bottles. VP-R
A traditional producer, M Combe makes a Vacqueyras full of deep fruit which sees at least eight months in wood. He also makes Gigondas under the brand name L'Oustau Fauquet, a big wine, but elegant, which needs seven years to begin to mature. *Open: Appointments preferred.*

Domaine de Grangeneuve
84110 Rasteau
A Côtes du Rhône Villages Rasteau estate, making full-bodied wines which offer excellent value for money.

Caves C N Jaume
26490 Vinsobres
Both red and rosé are made on this Côtes du Rhône Vinsobres estate, of which the red is the better wine. For a Côtes du Rhône it is particularly rich and powerful, probably because of the high percentage of Syrah in the blend. It also ages well.

Domaine des Lambertins
Vacqueyras, 84190 Beaumes–de–Venise. Vineyards owned: Vacqueyras 24ha. 70,000 bottles. VP-R
A traditional family firm run by the Lambert brothers, producing Côtes du Rhône Villages Vacqueyras and Côtes du Rhône, both in red only. *Open: By appointment only.*

Domaine Martin
Plan de Dieu, 84150 Travaillan. Vineyards owned: 48ha. 100,000 bottles. VP-R
Traditional techniques and stainless steel are used at this medium-sized estate. Reds are aged in wood, as is the Rasteau red Vin Doux Naturel made from 100 percent Grenache. Other wines produced are red, white and rosé Côtes du Rhône and red Côtes du Rhône Villages. *Open: Mon–Fri 8am–7pm.*

Domaine du Moulin
26110 Vinsobres. Vineyards owned: Vinsobres 20ha. 40,000 bottles. VP-R
A traditional producer, making only a Côtes du Rhône Villages Vinsobres – a very good one. The red is cherry-fresh, attractive when young, but with the ability to age for three or four years. A white and rosé are also made. *Open: Mon–Fri 8am–noon; 2–7pm.*

GAEC Pelaquié
St-Victor la Coste, 30290 Laudun. Vineyards owned: 14ha. 20,000 bottles. VP-R

Red and white Côtes du Rhône Villages Laudun are produced at this small estate. Stainless steel is used for vinification, which gives a fruity, fresh red for drinking young. There is also a white Côtes du Rhône and some red Lirac. The wines are attractive and well made. *Open: Mon–Sat 8am–noon; 2–6pm.*

Domaine Rabasse-Charavin
Coteaux St-Martin, 84290 Cairanne. Vineyards owned:
21ha. 80,000 bottles. VP-R
A high-quality producer of Côtes du Rhône Villages from Cairanne and generic Côtes du Rhône red and white. The estate also makes a 100 percent Syrah Côtes du Rhône, called Cuvée d'Estevenas, aged in wood, which is very good. The vineyards have a high proportion of 80-year-old vines. *Open: Mon–Fri 8–11:30am; 3–6pm.*

Cave des Vignerons de Rasteau
84110 Rasteau. Vineyards owned: 750ha. 2·2 million
bottles. Coop (180 members)
One of the best cooperatives in the Rhône Valley, producing Côtes du Rhône and Côtes du Rhône Villages Rasteau, including a Cuvée Prestige which is matured in wood and a Côtes du Rhône Primeur. The cooperative is also the biggest producer of sweet Rasteau Vin Doux Naturel, from 100 percent Grenache. One of the reasons for its success is that it pays members on the quality of the grapes, not the potential alcoholic content. Would that more cooperatives did the same. *Open: Mon–Fri 8am–noon; 2–6pm.*

Pierre Rosati
La Verrière, Route de Pegue, 84600 Valréas. Vineyards
owned: Valréas 18ha; St-Pantaléon-les-Vignes 2ha. 26,000
bottles. VP-R
Stainless steel vinification and then wood-ageing for the reds produces some smooth, clean-tasting Côtes du Rhône, both generic and Villages from Valréas. M Rosati also makes white and rosé Côtes du Rhône. All the wines are sold under the name Ferme La Verrière. *Open: Mon–Sun 8am–7pm.*

Château Saint-Maurice l'Ardoise
30290 Laudun. Vineyards owned: 96ha. 450,000 bottles. VP-R
Most of the production at this estate is of Côtes du Rhône Villages or Côtes du Rhône, which is sold under a number of different names: Château Saint-Maurice l'Ardoise, Château Saint-Maurice, Domaine du Mont-Jupiter (there are ruins of an ancient temple on the site) and Clos de Rossignac. M Valat also makes a small amount of Lirac from vineyards in Saint-Laurent-les-Arbres, and Vin de Pays du Gard. *Open: During working hours.*

Cave Coopérative Saint-Pantaléon-les-Vignes
26770 St-Pantaléon-les-Vignes. Vineyards owned: Côtes du Rhône 635ha; Coteaux du Tricastin 56ha; Côtes du Rhône Villages 13ha; Côtes du Rhône Villages St-Pantaléon 47ha; Côtes du Rhône Villages Rousset 35ha. 180,000 bottles. Coop (220 members)
While half of the wine is sold in bulk to *négociants*, 20 percent is bottled for the cooperative at Tulette. The main wines bottled are Côtes du Rhône Villages Saint-Pantaléon and Rousset and some Villages Saint-Pantaléon which is aged in wood. *Open: Appointments preferred.*

Domaine Sainte-Anne
30200 St-Gervais
A wide range of red wines is made at this fine estate in Saint-Gervais. Cuvée Notre Dame des Cellettes has a high percentage of Syrah, while Cuvée Saint-Gervais also has a considerable amount of Mourvèdre (40 percent). The owner, Guy Steinmaier, also makes a Côtes du Rhône Villages blend, and, most unusually, a 100 percent-Viognier white wine, which has been compared to Condrieu (at a much lower price).

Domaine le Sang des Cailloux
Route de Vacqueyras, 84260 Sarrians. Vineyards owned: Vacqueyras 18ha. 85,000 bottles. VP-R
M Jean Ricard makes a Côtes du Rhône Villages Vacqueyras, which he ferments and matures in wood. The quality is high, with herby, spicy fruit and touches of wood tannin which suggest good ageing

ability. *Open: Mon–Fri 8am–noon; 1–6pm.*

Domaine la Soumade
Rasteau, 84110 Vaison la Romaine. Vineyards owned: Rasteau 20ha. 40,000 bottles. VP-R
Côtes du Rhône Villages Rasteau and Rasteau Vin Doux Naturel are the estate's top AC wines. André Roméro also makes generic Côtes du Rhône and an interesting Vin de Pays de Vaucluse from a blend of Cabernet Sauvignon and Merlot. *Open: Mon–Sat 8am–noon; 2–8pm.*

Château de Trignon
84190 Gigondas
A number of Côtes du Rhône wines are made on this large estate; the best is seen as the Côtes du Rhône Villages Sablet. There is also a Gigondas. André Roux, the owner, uses carbonic maceration to achieve freshness in his wines, rather than longevity. There is an increasing proportion of Mourvèdre and Syrah being grown in the vineyard.

Domaine de Verquière
84110 Sablet. Vineyards owned: 50ha. 100,000 bottles. VP-R
M Chamfort is a traditional producer, who uses wood for maturing and is not afraid to leave the wine in cask for some time. He makes red Côtes du Rhône Villages from Sablet, Vacqueyras and generic red and rosé Côtes du Rhône. There is also a high-quality Rasteau Vin Doux Naturel. *Open: Appointments preferred.*

Cave Zanti-Cumino (Domaine du Banvin)
84290 Cairanne. Vineyards owned: Cairanne 18ha. 80,000 bottles. VP-R
Some carbonic maceration is used at this estate. It makes Côtes du Rhône red, white and rosé, plus Côtes du Rhône Villages Cairanne using a blend of Grenache, Syrah and Mourvèdre. The wines are all best drunk young. *Open: By appointment only.*

Côtes du Ventoux AC

Domaine des Anges
84750 Mormoiron. Vineyards owned: 8ha. 25,000 bottles.
VP-R
A small estate owned by an Englishman, Malcolm Swann, who has planted Grenache, Syrah, Cinsault and Carignan to make a full, fresh, easy-drinking Côtes du Ventoux which brings out all the attraction of this AC area. *Open: By appointment only.*

Gigondas AC

Pierre Amadieu
84190 Gigondas. Vineyards owned: Gigondas 120ha; Côtes du Ventoux 35ha. 990,000 bottles. VP-R and N
A traditional firm, with spectacular old cellars dug into the hillside of Gigondas. Style is traditional as well, and none the worse for that. The principal wines are Gigondas and Côtes du Ventoux from the firm's own estates, but Châteauneuf-du-Pape and Côtes du Rhône are also made. *Open: During working hours.*

Edmond Burle
La Beaumette, 84190 Gigondas. Vineyards owned:
Gigondas 1·6ha; Vacqueyras 1ha; Côtes du Rhône 8ha; *vin*
***de table* 5ha. 30,000 bottles. VP-R**
This is a small traditional firm which matures wine in wood, and whose pride and joy is their Gigondas Les Pallierondas, a rich and powerful wine. But M Burle also makes generic Côtes du Rhône, Vacqueyras and *vin de table. Open: During working hours.*

Domaine du Cayron
84190 Gigondas VP-R
High proportions of Syrah and Cinsault produce wines which not only have great intensity and power, but which also age well. M Faraud adopts traditional techniques, including long ageing in large wooden barrels, and minimum fining and filtering.

Cave des Vignerons de Gigondas

84190 Gigondas. Vineyards owned: 250ha. 500,000 bottles. Coop (120 members)
This cooperative uses carbonic maceration to soften the tannins and increase the fruit in its Gigondas. As a result it is soft and quite quick to mature. The brand name used is Cuvée du Président. More traditionally made wines are sold under the names Signature and Tête de Cuvée. A smaller amount of Côtes du Rhône is also made. *Open: By appointment only.*

Domaine les Goubert (Jean-Pierre Cartier)
84190 Gigondas
This is a comparatively new estate, founded in 1973, now producing red Côtes du Rhône Villages (from Beaumes-de-Venise) and white Côtes du Rhône Villages (from Sablet) as well as the more significant Gigondas. The style is elegant rather than too powerful, and the wines age well. A top *cuvée*, Cuvée Florence, aged in new wood, is made in small quantities in good years.

Domaine de Longue-Toque
84190 Gigondas
Carbonic maceration is used for half the vinification of the Chapalain family's Gigondas. The wines therefore have predominant soft fruit, and are ready to drink quickly. There is 20 percent Syrah and five percent Mourvèdre in the blend.

Domaine du Grand Montmirail
Gigondas, 84109 Beaumes-de-Venise. Vineyards owned: 30ha. 66,000 bottles. VP-R
This estate, now owned by the merchant house of Pascal, is being revived by the energetic owner Denis Cheron. He has increased the proportion of Syrah in the blend, and restricted yields to produce concentrated wines with considerable ageing ability. Names used are Domaine du Roucas de Saint-Pierre, Domaine de Saint-Gens and Domaine du Pradas. *Open: By appointment only.*

Les Fils de Hilarion Roux (Domaine de Pallières)
84190 Gigondas. Vineyards owned: Gigondas 25ha. 80,000 bottles. VP-R
A long-established (founded 1765) vineyard still in the original

family. There is a traditional approach to winemaking, with long fermentation and ageing for up to three years in wood. The result is a red Gigondas of immense power, considerable tannin and a very long life. The estate also produces a rosé. *Open: By appointment only.*

Le Mas des Collines
84190 Gigondas. Vineyards owned: Gigondas 15ha; Côtes du Rhône 38ha. 60,000 bottles. VP-R
Mas des Collines is the name M Detaxis uses for his Gigondas. He calls his Côtes du Rhône La Bruissière. Both are traditionally made wines, with good tannin and firm fruit. Much of the Gigondas vineyard is planted with old vines. *Open: Appointments preferred.*

Gabriel Meffre
84190 Gigondas. Vineyards owned: Gigondas 92ha; Châteauneuf-du-Pape 88ha; Côtes du Rhône 500ha; Côtes du Provence 60ha. 2·5 million bottles. VP-R and N
The largest private producer of Gigondas, Gabriel Meffre has maintained good quality and has done much to help the reputation of the AC area. Modern, large-scale techniques are used, with stainless steel much in evidence. Many famous names come under the Meffre banner: Château de Ruth in Sainte-Cecile-les-Vignes; Château Raspail in Gigondas; and Château de Vaudieu in Châteauneuf. New plantations are currently under way to produce white Côtes du Rhône. *Open: By appointment only.*

Château de Montmirail
84190 Vacqueyras
Both Côtes du Rhône Vacqueyras and Gigondas are made at this estate in Montmirail. The style is light and quick-maturing, with a high proportion of Grenache in the blend.

Domaine Raspail-Ay
Gigondas, 84190 Beaumes-de-Venise. Vineyards owned: Gigondas 18ha. 30,000 bottles. VP-R
Red and rosé Gigondas are made by Dominique Ay in a traditional style, using wood for fermentation and maturation. A blend of Grenache, Mourvèdre and Syrah gives a big, complex, long-lasting wine. *Open: By appointment only.*

Domaine Saint-Gayan
84190 Gigondas. Vineyards owned: Gigondas 14ha; Côtes du Rhône Villages 16ha. 70,000 bottles. VP-R
Roger Meffre produces firm, rich wines from his three estates. The Gigondas is powerfully tannic, a Côtes du Rhône Rasteau has a delightful perfumed flavour from the high (35 percent) proportion of Mourvèdre. Generic Côtes du Rhône from vineyards in Sablet comes in red, rosé and white. The estate has been in the family since 1400. *Open: Mon–Sat 9–11:45am; 2–7pm.*

Lirac AC

Château de Clary
30126 Lirac
Roman remains have been found on this estate, with the suggestion that wines have been made here since then. The current wine is red, powerful and strongly ripe.

Domaine de Castel-Oualou
30150 Roquemaure. Vineyards owned: Lirac 52ha. 250,000 bottles. VP-R
Red Lirac is the principal wine made by the Pons-Mure family. The approach is traditional, with long fermentation to produce a floral, violet-flavoured wine. The estate also produces small amounts of white and rosé Lirac. *Open: During working hours.*

Domaine de Devoy
St-Laurent-des-Arbres, 30126 Tavel. Vineyards owned: Lirac 40ha. 200,000 bottles. VP-R
Traditional and modern techniques mix, with stainless steel being used for fermentation and no wood-ageing. The Lombardo brothers make red, rosé and white Lirac. *Open: Mon–Fri 8am–noon; 2–6pm.*

Château de Ségriès
30126 Lirac. Vineyards owned: Lirac 20ha. 20,000 bottles. VP-R
The Comte de Régis, one of the pioneers of the Lirac AC, makes

traditional, quite tannic reds and rosés and a softer white at this estate, whose château dates from the 17th and 18th century. *Open: By appointment only.*

Domaines Verda (Château Saint-Roch)
30150 Roquemaure. Vineyards owned: Lirac and Côtes du Rhône 60ha. 250,000 bottles. VP-R
There are two Lirac estates owned by the Verda family. The original is Château Saint-Roch which produces red, rosé and white Lirac. The reds include a special *cuvée* which has two years in wood and two in bottle before sale. The other estate is Domaine Cantegril-Verda, acquired in 1983, where they make a lighter style of wine for more immediate drinking, and where they also make Côtes du Rhône. All their wines reach a high standard. *Open: Mon–Fri 8am–noon; 2–6:30pm.*

Tavel AC

Château d'Aquéria
31026 Tavel. Vineyards owned: Tavel and Lirac 55ha. 300,000 bottles. VP-R
The 17th-century property has been owned by the Olivier family since 1920. The bulk of production here is of Tavel rosé, with smaller quantities of red Lirac. They combine traditional and modern techniques to produce a classic Tavel, full of raspberry fruit and with a good balance of acidity and fruit. The vineyard is being expanded. *Open: Mon–Fri 8am–noon; 2–6pm.*

Domaine de la Genestière
30126 Tavel. Vineyards owned: Tavel 30ha; Lirac 11ha. 200,000 bottles. VP-R
The owners of this estate, the Bernard family, produce mainly Tavel rosé, but they also make some Lirac red and white. They use traditional methods. *Open: Appointments preferred.*

Domaine Jean-Pierre Lafond
Route des Vignobles, 30126 Tavel. Vineyards owned:

Tavel 30ha; Lirac 10ha; Côtes du Rhône 10ha. 150,000 bottles. VP–R

This old-established family estate works with modern methods to make a deliciously fruity, fresh Tavel. M Lafond also makes red Lirac and Côtes du Rhône. Brand names include Roc-Amande and Cuvée Lafond as well as Domaine Pierre Lafond. *Open: Mon–Fri 9am–noon; 2–6pm.*

Domaine Maby
BP 8, 30126 Tavel. Vineyards owned: Tavel 40ha; Lirac 30ha; Côtes du Rhône 30ha. 500,000 bottles. VP–R

The Maby family has owned vineyards for several generations. They use stainless steel for the Tavel and for a white Lirac, while wood is preferred for the red Lirac and Côtes du Rhône. The styles reflect the vinification, with fresh rosés and whites, and reds which need at least four years in bottle. *Open: Appointments preferred.*

Les Vignerons de Tavel
BP 3, 30126 Tavel. Vineyards owned: Tavel 400ha.
1 million bottles. Association of VP–R (130 members)

Modern techniques such as cold fermentation and centrifugation are employed by this group of producers along with the traditional cold maceration on the skins. This avoids the problem of tannin which can affect some Tavel rosés. The wine is designed to be drunk young and fresh. This is not a cooperative but more of a marketing organization. *Open: Mon–Sun 9am–noon; 2–6pm.*

Château de Trinquevedel
30126 Tavel. Vineyards owned: Tavel 26ha. 100,000 bottles. VP–R

Carbonic maceration for 72 hours is used to make this Tavel quite a deep rosé colour. It is fresh, attractively fruity and one of the most refreshing Tavels around. *Open: By appointment only.*

Le Vieux Moulin
30126 Tavel

The Tavel Rosé is made in a modern, fresh style, to be drunk young. Grape varieties are Grenache and Cinsault.

Côtes du Vivarais VDQS

Domaine de Belvezet
07700 St-Remèze
There is a little Cabernet Sauvignon and Merlot in this vineyard, as well as the more usual southern Rhône varieties. The wine style is fruity but powerful, and it can be drunk young.

Union des Producteurs
07150 Orgnac l'Aven. Vineyards owned: 450ha. 350,000 bottles. Coop (83 members)
This cooperative dominates the VDQS of Côtes du Vivarais, producing red, rosé and white. The red has 30 percent Syrah and 40 percent Grenache, the white 50/50 Clairette and Grenache Blanc. The brand name is Vins d'Orgnac. *Open: By appointment only.*

Domaine de Vigier
Lagorce, 07150 Vallon Pont d'Arc. Vineyards owned: 35ha. 70,000 bottles. VP-R
Côtes du Vivarais is made from 100 percent Syrah. The estate also produces varietal Merlot and Chardonnay Vin de Pays des Coteaux de l'Ardèche. *Open: Mon–Fri 8am–noon; 2–6pm.*

The Southwest

Producers in the Southwest are probably pretty tired of being described as 'forgotten' or of being told that their wines are being 'rediscovered'. Yet there is something about the wines of this secret countryside in the hinterland of Bordeaux and in the foothills of the Pyrenees that sets it apart from the rest of French wine.

The Southwest's vineyards, wedged between the great expanses of Bordeaux and the Midi, are tiny by comparison with most. Not so long ago they were still struggling to survive the effects of phylloxera, which almost wiped out the whole area. What was left was disappearing through indifference. Yet, gradually, the Southwest has been rejuvenated through the efforts of cooperatives, which have performed a vital role in bringing together tiny plots of land to make commercial sense. The determination of a few private estates, some newly established, some ancient, has also helped, by providing a quality standard to emulate. And we must not forget the contribution made by travellers who went on wine-buying trips to the Southwest and came back with tales – and samples – of the wines.

There are two distinct wine traditions here. Historically, the northern vineyards of the region, Bergerac, Côtes du Marmandais, Côtes de Duras and Cahors, were closely linked to Bordeaux. At one time their wine was more famous than the wines of Bordeaux itself, later they were used to beef up insipid wine from the vineyards of the Gironde. Some of these areas today make Bordeaux look-alikes sold at lesser prices, while Cahors, for example, has moved along a distinct path of its own. But even now, they all have a recognizable link with Bordeaux.

That is not true of the wines from further south. Here we get into strange territory indeed. Grape varieties from a dim, almost mythical past, with difficult Basque names, yield wine with a range of tastes that is found nowhere else. There are sweet whites and impenetrable reds, sparkling wines made by methods unique to the area, and increasingly there are some excellent dry white wines.

In this 'secret countryside' there are quiet valleys, deep rivers, miles of woods, and small, ancient towns and villages perched on hilltops or clinging to river valleys. The part of the Southwest called Gascony is home of one of the richest gastronomic traditions in France – home, too, to armagnac brandy.

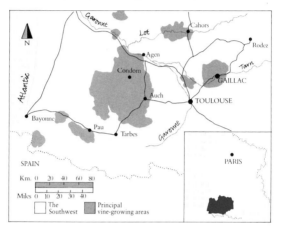

The region enjoys an Atlantic rather than a Mediterranean climate, but one protected from the ocean storms by the vast pine forests of the Landes, which stretch from the edge of the Bordeaux vineyards to the Pyrenees. The summers are cooler than in Languedoc and Roussillon, the rainfall higher too and the winters often harsh. The consequence for the wines is immediately apparent: they are lower in alcohol than the wines of the Midi, and tend to have more complex, varied flavours. The whites, while full-bodied, often also have good acidity; the reds, when deep and tannic, can age well, while lighter reds, made sometimes to be drunk chilled, can be as fresh as Loire reds. Vintages: most dry whites and rosés should be drunk young, as should many reds.

The Appellations

Appellations Contrôlées

Béarn Red, rosé and dry white wines from a large area of the *département* of the Pyrénées-Atlantiques. The Béarn AC surrounds the smaller, superior ACs of Madiran and

Pacherenc du Vic-Bilh as well as Irouléguy and Jurançon.
Reds and rosés are made from up to 60 percent Tannat,
Courbu Noir, Fer, Manseng Noir, Pinenc and Cabernet
Sauvignon and Cabernet Franc. Whites are a similar mix of
local and Bordeaux grapes: Gros Manseng, Petit Manseng,
Courbu, Baroque, Lauzat, plus Sémillon and Sauvignon.

Béarn Bellocq A new, small *appellation* within the Béarn AC;
the same grape varieties are planted. It covers the
communes of Orthez and Sallies-de-Béarn.

Bergerac The area-wide AC for the Bergerac region. Red and
rosé are made from Cabernet Sauvignon, Cabernet Franc,
Merlot, Malbec and the local Fer. Light wines, which
should be drunk young. Vintages: '85, '86, '88, '89, '90.

Bergerac Sec The white equivalent of Bergerac. Wines can be
made from Sémillon, Sauvignon, Muscadelle, Chenin Blanc
and the local Ondenc. A number of new-style wines, made
with Sauvignon, are of high quality.

Buzet Vineyards on the left bank of the Garonne, between
Agen and Aiguillon, producing red, rosé and dry white
wines. Reds come from Cabernet Franc, Cabernet
Sauvignon, Merlot and Malbec. The small amount of white
made comes from Sémillon, Sauvignon and Muscadelle.
Most of the wine is produced by the cooperative, which has
high standards. Vintages: '83, '85, '86, '88, '89, '90.

Cahors Red wine only from vineyards on the slopes and the
valley floor of the Lot river between Puy l'Evêque and
Cahors, established before the Roman times, and highly
regarded by Avignon Popes and Russian Tsars. Grapes are
Malbec (known locally as Auxerrois) up to 70 percent, then
Merlot, Tannat and Jurançon Noir. The wine at its best is
deep-coloured, with high tannins, but also has good fruit
that needs a good four years before softening out. Lighter
wines of lesser quality are also made. Production is now 10
million bottles a year. Vintages: '83, '85, '86, '88, '89.

Côtes de Bergerac Red wine from the Bergerac region with a
higher alcoholic content than straight Bergerac. Around 2
million bottles are produced. Grapes are the same as for
Bergerac: Cabernet Franc, Cabernet Sauvignon, Merlot,
Malbec, Fer. Vintages: *see* Bergerac.

Côtes de Bergerac Moelleux Sweet white wine from the
general Bergerac AC, made from Sémillon, Sauvignon and
Muscadelle. Soft, at best clean and fruity.

Côtes de Duras Dry and sweet white and some red wine from
an area immediately adjacent to the Bordeaux Entre-Deux-
Mers AC area. Whites are from Sémillon, Sauvignon,
Muscadelle, Mauzac and Ondenc, plus Ugni Blanc. Dry
whites are better than sweet, which tend to be sulphured.
Reds are from Cabernet Franc, Cabernet Sauvignon,
Merlot and Malbec, and have attractive fruit and depth.

Côtes du Frontonnais Red and rosé wines from a small area
north of Toulouse on the east bank of the River Garonne.
The grapes are up to 70 percent Négrette, plus Cabernet
Sauvignon, Cabernet Franc, Cinsault, Malbec, Merlot,
Syrah and Gamay. Excellent wines at good prices, with
fresh, soft fruit. The commune of Villaudric is allowed to
add its name to the AC. Vintages: '86, '88, '89, '90.

Côtes du Marmandais Soft, attractive reds and less interesting
whites from vineyards adjoining the Bordeaux region, on
both sides of the Garonne. The grapes include Bordeaux
varieties – Cabernet Franc, Cabernet Sauvignon and Merlot
– with local varieties, Fer, Abouriou, Malbec, and one from
the south of France, Syrah, and Gamay. The small
production of white comes from Sémillon, Ugni Blanc and
Sauvignon. An *appellation* created in 1990.

Côtes de Montravel Small amounts of sweet white wine from
within the general Bergerac area. Certain hillside slopes in
certain communes are allowed to use the Côtes de
Montravel AC, whose wines are generally of higher quality

than simple Montravel (*qv*). Sémillon, Sauvignon and Muscadelle are the permitted grape varieties.

Gaillac A range of white, medium white, red, rosé and sparkling wines from the valley of Tarn, betwen Albi and Rabastens. Over half the production is white, from Mauzac Blanc and Loin de l'Oeil, with Ondenc, Sauvignon, Sémillon and Muscadelle. Much is dull, especially the slightly sparkling Perlé. Reds come from a variety of grapes: Fer, Duras, Gamay, Négrette and up to 60 percent Syrah, with smaller amounts of Cabernet Sauvignon, Cabernet Franc, Jurançon Noir, Merlot, Portugais Bleu (the German Blauer Portugieser), and the white Mauzac. Occasional reds can be superb. Vintages: (red) '85, '86, '88, '89, '90.

Gaillac Doux Sweet white wines from Mauzac Blanc, Loin de l'Oeil, Ondenc, Sauvignon, Sémillon and Muscadelle.

Gaillac Mousseux Sparkling Gaillac made by the *méthode gaillaçoise* (involving a second fermentation in the bottle, but, unlike champagne, without added sugar or yeast). Some of it can be very good. Other sparklers are made by the classic *méthode champenoise*. Grapes used are the usual Gaillac selection: Mauzac Blanc, Loin de l'Oeil, Ondenc, Sauvignon, Sémillon and Muscadelle.

Gaillac Premières Côtes Rare dry and medium-sweet white wine, higher in alcohol than simple Gaillac.

Haut Montravel Sweet white wines from the Montravel region of Bergerac. The rules are similiar to Côtes de Montravel (*qv*). Grapes used: Sauvignon, Sémillon, Muscadelle.

Irouléguy Red, rosé and white wines from the foothills of the Pyrenees in the valley of the Nive. Most of the production is of rosé, and both rosés and reds are made from Tannat, Fer, Cabernet Sauvignon and Cabernet Franc. The small amount of white comes from Gros Manseng, Petit Manseng, Courbu, Lauzat, Baroque, Sauvignon and Sémillon.

Jurançon Sweet wines from an area southwest of the town of Pau. Grapes are Gros Manseng, the better quality Petit Manseng and Courbu. For this increasingly rare but outstanding sweet wine, grapes are picked as raisins, with concentrated sugars, giving a spicy wine with a lemony tang and golden colour. Examples, when found, can be a revelation. Vintages: (sweet) '83, '86, '88, '89, '90.

Jurançon Sec A dry, and much duller, version of Jurançon, from the same grapes: Gros Manseng, Petit Manseng, Courbu.

Madiran Red wine from the southern edge of the Armagnac region. The principal grape is the Tannat, which makes a hard, tough, tannic wine when young, that has to spend 20 months in bottle. It needs at least five years before it begins to open out, with some elegance but more rough power. Other grapes used are Cabernet Sauvignon, Cabernet Franc and Fer. The more Cabernets are used, the more sophisticated (but less typical) the wine becomes. The white wine of the area is called Pacherenc du Vic-Bilh (*qv*). Vintages: '78, '82, '83, '85, '86, '88.

Marcillac Sound, simple red and rosé wines from just north of Rodez in the Aveyron *département*. Grape varieties include both Cabernets, Gamay, Jurançon Noir and Merlot, with at least 80 percent of Fer. An *appellation* created in 1990.

Monbazillac A famous name in sweet wines, but one which has fallen on bad times. The wine can be as good as Sauternes, but almost never is because it is sulphured and not enough attention is paid to the degree of botrytis in the grapes. The few producers who do it well make wines that are even richer than Sauternes, developing faster and fading more quickly. Grapes used are Sémillon, Sauvignon and Muscadelle. Vintages: '83, '86, '88, '89, '90.

Montravel A range of white wines from dry to sweet made at the western edge of the Bergerac region, along the lower slopes bordering the road to St-Emilion. Wines are made from Sémillon, Sauvignon, Muscadelle, Ugni Blanc, Chenin Blanc and Ondenc.

Pacherenc du Vic-Bilh White wine from the same area as Madiran (*qv*). It can be dry or slightly sweet, but always has intense fruit and a luscious smell, sometimes likened to ripe pears. Grapes are Ruffiac (or Pacherenc), Gros Manseng, Petit Manseng, Courbu, plus Sauvignon and Sémillon. Production is small, almost all consumed locally.

Pécharmant The best red wines of Bergerac come from a small area on the right bank of the Dordogne river, east of the town of Bergerac. Grape varieties are Cabernet Sauvignon, Cabernet Franc, Malbec and Merlot. The wines, higher in alcohol than simple Bergerac, are also aged longer in wood and mature well for five or six years. Better quality than any simple Bordeaux AC. Vintages: '78, '79, '82, '83.

Rosette Medium-sweet wine from the slopes north of the town of Bergerac. Production is small, most of the white in the area going as Bergerac Sec. Grapes used are Sauvignon, Sémillon and Muscadelle.

Saussignac A rare white wine, normally dry, made around the village of Saussignac, west of Monbazillac. The wines need an alcohol level of 12·5 percent, making them richer and fuller than ordinary Bergerac Sec. Grapes are Sémillon, Sauvignon, Muscadelle, Ondenc and Chenin Blanc.

VDQS

Côtes du Brulhois Vineyard area just south of Buzet, on both sides of the Garonne river. Red and rosé only, made from Cabernet Sauvignon, Cabernet Franc, Merlot, Tannat and Malbec. Elevated to VDQS status from *vin de pays* in 1984.

Côtes de Saint-Mont Red, rosé and white wines from the southwestern corner of the Armagnac region. Reds come from Tannat, with both Cabernets and Merlot, and are attractive, simple and slightly rough. Whites are from Meslier, Jurançon, Picpoul and Sauvignon. The main producer is the local Madiran cooperative.

Tursan Red, rosé and dry white wines from the eastern Landes, bordering the AC area of Madiran and Pacherenc du Vic-Bilh. The style is like a minor version of these wines. Reds and rosés are from Tannat, Cabernet Franc, Cabernet Sauvignon and Fer; white from the local Baroque.

Vin d'Entraygues et du Fel Red, rosé and dry whites from the southern slopes of the Massif Central. Tiny production. Reds and rosés from a range of grapes: both Cabernets, Jurançon Noir, Fer, Gamay, Merlot, Négrette, Pinot Noir. Whites from Chenin Blanc and Mauzac.

Vin d'Estaing Another tiny area producing no more than 1,000 bottles or so a year, from the same area and grape varieties as the Vin d'Entraygues et du Fel.

Vin de Lavilledieu Almost exclusively red wines from another small area on the Garonne river to the north of the Côtes du Frontonnais. Virtually every local grape variety seems to be thrown into the vat, but the principal ones are Négrette, with Fer, Gamay, Jurançon Noir, Mauzac Noir and Picpoul.

Vins de Pays

Regional Vin de Pays

Vin de Pays du Comté Tolosan Covering the whole of the Southwest region, from the southern borders of the Gironde department of Bordeaux to the Pyrenees, and east to Toulouse. Like many of the regional *vins de pays*, its production is small, and most wines are classified by smaller zones. Reds are made from Duras, Fer-Servadou, Tannat and the Bordeaux grapes and Syrah and Gamay. Only three percent of production is white.

Departmental Vins de Pays

Vin de Pays de la Dordogne A *vin de pays* covering much the same area as the Bergerac AC. The tiny production, made from Bordeaux grapes (60 percent of which is white) comes from areas which are not covered by the AC regulations.

Vin de Pays de la Haute-Garonne South of Toulouse, this is a *vin de pays* surrounding the AC vineyards of Fronton. The grapes are typical of the Southwest: Tannat, Jurançon Noir and Négrette, plus the Bordeaux grapes Syrah and Gamay. Production is 90 percent red.

Vin de Pays du Tarn-et-Garonne Most of the tiny production is from west of Montauban, and is principally of red wines, with some rosé. A melange of Southwestern grapes is employed. Whites are made from Mauzac.

Other departmental *vins de pays* are: Vin de Pays des Landes, Vin de Pays du Lot-et-Garonne, Vin de Pays de l'Aveyron, Vin de Pays du Gers, Vin de Pays du Lot and Vin de Pays des Pyrénées-Atlantiques.

Zonal Vins de Pays

Vin de Pays de l'Agenais Between Agen, of crystallized prune fame, and Marmande. These wines are mainly red, with some white, and made from local grape varieties (Abouriou, Fer-Servadou for red, Gros Manseng for white) and also Bordeaux *cépages nobles.*

Vin de Pays des Charentais This *vin de pays* uses the surplus grapes produced initially for cognac production. Unsurprisingly therefore, the wines are mainly white (with Chardonnay and Chenin Blanc mingling with Bordeaux grapes, and also Ugni Blanc – the cognac grape). The smaller amount of red wine is made from Bordeaux grapes and from Gamay.

Vin de Pays des Coteaux du Quercy South of Cahors, this is a zone producing mostly red wines, from the local Cahors grapes (Auxerrois or Cot) and Tannat and the Bordeaux varieties.

Vin de Pays des Côtes de Gascogne One of the most familiar *vin de pays* areas, due largely to the fact that it fulfils a huge demand for white wines. Covering much of the armagnac production zone, the white wines (84 percent of production) are made from local grapes: Colombard, Ugni Blanc and Gros Manseng.

Vin de Pays des Côtes du Tarn From the region of Gaillac, around Albi, this area produces large quantities of both red and white wines, and also a small amount of rosé. Red wines are made from Bordeaux *cépages nobles* and also Gamay and local grapes; white wines are made from Loin de L'Oeil, Muscadelle and Mauzac. The latter are especially important on the export market.

Vin de Pays des Terroirs Landais A small quantity of wine, produced from vineyards among the forests of the Landes. There are four different areas: in the sand dunes along the Atlantic coast; the Coteaux du Chalosse in the south of the *département*; the Côtes de l'Adour, along the valley of that river; and Les Sables Fauves, part of the Armagnac area. These are mostly white wines.

Vin de Pays de Saint-Sardos A tiny production, mainly of red wines, from vineyards southwest of Montauban.

Other zonal *vins de pays* are: Vin de Pays de Thézac-Pérricard, Vin de Pays de Bigorre, Vin de Pays des Coteaux de Glanes, Vin de Pays des Coteaux et Terrasses de Montauban, Vin de Pays des Côtes de Montestruc, Vin de Pays des Côtes du Condomois, Vin de Pays des Gorges et Côtes de Millau.

Producers
Béarn AC

Les Vignerons de Bellocq
64270 Bellocq. Vineyards owned: 120ha. 600,000 bottles.
Coop (50 members)
The most important source of Béarn wine, this cooperative makes a range of rosé (the vast majority), red and white wines, using controlled-temperature techniques and eschewing any use of wood. Reds include a 100 percent Cabernet Franc and Cabernet

Sauvignon wine, and two top red *cuvées*, Cuvée des Vignerons and Cuvée Henri de Navarre. *Open: By appointment only.*

Bergerac AC

Domaine de l'Ancienne Curé
Colombier, 24560 Issigeac. Vineyards owned: 20ha. 35,000 bottles. VP-R
M Christian Roche makes a range of Bergerac wines: Monbazillac, Bergerac Sec (100 percent Sauvignon), a Côtes de Bergerac Moelleux and red and rosé Bergerac. Temperature-controlled fermentation is used for the whites, but reds are vinified in wood. *Open: By appointment only.*

GAEC du Bloy (Guillermier Frères)
Bonneville, 24230 Vélines. Vineyards owned: 33ha. 70,000 bottles. VP-R
Red Côtes de Bergerac is this company's mainstay, using Merlot, Cabernet Franc, Cabernet Sauvignon and a little Malbec. The Guillermier brothers also make rosé Bergerac, dry white Montravel and Bergerac as well as some sweet Côtes de Bergerac. *Open: Mon–Fri 8:30am–1pm; 2:30–5:30pm.*

Château la Borderie
24240 Monbazillac. Vineyards owned: 63ha. 400,000 bottles. VP-R
Two estates make up the family property of Château la Borderie. On the larger estate, which bears the château name, the Vidal family makes Monbazillac, red Côtes de Bergerac, dry white Bergerac (from 100 percent Sauvignon) and Bergerac rosé. The smaller, ten-hectare Château Treuil de Nailhac estate produces the Monbazillac, the red and the dry white. *Open: Mon–Fri 8:30am–noon; 2–6:30pm.*

Comte de Bosredon (Château de Belingard)
24240 Pomport, Sigoulès. Vineyards owned: 85ha. 500,000 bottles. VP-R
This ancient family estate is home to some Celtic remains as well as

the Bosredon family. However, their wine production has moved with the times and some carbonic maceration is used on the red Côtes de Bergerac so that it can be drunk young. Some of the sweeter Monbazillac and Côtes de Bergerac is matured for a time in wood. A modern-style Bergerac Sec is attractive. *Open: Appointments preferred.*

Michel Brouilleaud
24240 Monestier. Vineyards owned: 8ha. 15,000 bottles.
VP-R
M Brouilleaud's main production is of a full, rich red Bergerac, made from 60 percent Cabernet Sauvignon and 40 percent Merlot. He makes much smaller quantities of Bergerac rosé and sweet and dry Bergerac white. He uses the brand name Clos de la Croix Blanche. *Open: Mon–Sat 8am–noon; 2–7pm.*

Château Champerel
Pécharmant, 24100 Bergerac. Vineyards owned: 6·6ha.
26,000 bottles. VP-R
A very fine, intense red Pécharmant, made from 50 percent each Merlot and Cabernet Sauvignon, is the only wine from this small vineyard. It is fermented in stainless steel, and aged for at least a year in new *barriques*. *Open: By appointment only.*

Château Corbiac
Pécharmant, 24100 Bergerac. Vineyards owned: 11ha.
120,000 bottles. VP-R
This château and its estate has belonged to the same family since the Middle Ages. They make full, rounded Pécharmant, normally deeply coloured and full of fruit. *Open: Mon–Sun.*

Château Court-les-Mûts
Razac de Saussignac, 24240 Sigoules. Vineyards owned:
23ha. VP-R
An excellent example of modern winemaking run by a young oenologist, Pierre-Jean Seydoux. He makes red Bergerac that is full of fruit, in stainless steel, and a dry and a sweet white from the Saussignac *appellation*. He also produces a sparkling bottle-fermented *brut*, called Vin de Fête.

Château Le Fagé
24240 Pomport, Sigoulès. Vineyards owned: 40ha. 120,000 bottles. VP-R

A traditional estate, which has been in the Gerardin family for 200 years, making white Bergerac Sec, Monbazillac and a Côtes de Bergerac red, which is matured in cement tanks and normally bottled in the year after the harvest. They also use the name Château de Géraud. *Open: Mon–Sun.*

Domaine du Haut Pécharmant
Pécharmant, 24100 Bergerac. Vineyards owned: 23ha. 300,000 bottles. VP-R

The Pécharmant made on this estate, owned by the Roches family, is a blend of 40 percent Cabernet Sauvignon, 30 percent Merlot, 20 percent Cabernet Franc and ten percent Malbec. The wine is designed for ageing, with deep, tannic fruit initially. Good, if austere. *Open: Mon–Fri 8am–noon; 2–7pm.*

Château de la Jaubertie
Colombier, 24560 Issigeac. Vineyards owned: 46ha. 300,000 bottles. VP-R and N

Modern techniques, inspired by Australian winemakers, have produced a range of wines from this estate which have been a great success in the UK market – helped by the fact that the owner, Henry Ryman, is himself English. His whites, especially a 100 percent Sauvignon, are characterized by excellent fruit and good varietal character. Reds are also well made: the barrel-aged *réserve* is especially good. The approach may not be typical Bergerac, but it works. *Open: Appointment necessary.*

Domaine de Libarde
Nastringues, 24230 Vélines. Vineyards owned: 20ha. 60,000 bottles. VP-R

A traditionally run estate, right at the western end of the Bergerac region, just before it turns into Bordeaux. Bergerac rouge, Montravel dry white and Haut-Montravel sweet white are all produced. The Haut-Montravel is especially worth seeking out. *Open: By appointment only.*

Cave Coopérative de Monbazillac
Monbazillac, 24220 Sigoulès. Vineyards owned: 876ha. 5·5 million bottles. Coop (150 members)
The largest producer of Monbazillac, and owner of the showpiece Château de Monbazillac, a 20-hectare estate surrounding a superb mediaeval castle. They also make red and dry white Bergerac, Pécharmant and *vin de table*. Quality could be better, but the wines are reliable. The cooperative forms part of the giant Unidor group of cooperatives (*qv*). *Open: Mon–Fri 9am–noon; 2–5pm.*

René Monbouché
Gendre Marsalet, 24240 Monbazillac. Vineyards owned: 26ha. 45,000 bottles. VP-R
The domaines of M Monbouché comprise three estates: Gendre Marsalet, which produces Côtes de Bergerac red; Grand Conseil, producing white Bergerac Sec, and Theulet et Marsalet which makes Monbazillac. The reds and the Monbazillac are matured for a time in wood. *Open: Appointments preferred.*

Château Michel de Montaigne
24230 Vélines. Vineyards owned: 15ha. VP-R
This is the country estate of the Mähler-Besse family, part-owners of Château Palmer in the Médoc and major Bordeaux *négociants*. At this former home of the philosopher Montaigne they produce a red Bergerac from Merlot and Cabernets. *Open: By appointment only.*

Château de Panisseau
Thénac, 24240 Sigoulès. Vineyards owned: 50ha. 300,000 bottles. VP-R
This large estate surrounds a very pretty little 13th-century château. The Becker family produces two whites, one from 100 percent Sauvignon the other from 90 percent Sémillon (with only a touch of Sauvignon). They also make a classic Bergerac rouge, and a rosé from 100 percent Cabernet Sauvignon. The Sémillon dry white is particularly worth seeking out. *Open: Mon–Fri 8am–noon; 2–6pm (not the château).*

Clos Peyrelevade
Pécharmant, 24100 Bergerac. Vineyards owned: 10ha.

40,000 bottles. VP-R
Only Pécharmant is produced on this estate – a blend of 55 percent
Merlot, 20 percent Cabernet Sauvignon, 16 percent Cabernet Franc
and nine percent Malbec. They make a wine that, although it is not
matured in wood, needs some time in bottle. Three-quarters of
their production is bottled in half-bottles and magnums. *Open:
Appointments preferred.*

Château la Raye
24230 Vélines. Vineyards owned: 15ha. 60,000 bottles.
VP-R
Itey de Peironnin has a charming château and from here he
produces a very fine red Bergerac (a blend of 50 percent Merlot and
50 percent Cabernets) and a sweet Côtes de Montravel. *Open: By
appointment only.*

Château Thénac
Thénac-le-Bourg, 24240 Sigoulès. Vineyards owned: 15ha.
120,000 bottles. VP-R
Modern techniques are making a red Bergerac using 33 percent
Merlot, 33 percent Cabernet Franc and 33 percent Cabernet
Sauvignon (one percent Malbec), and a clean-tasting Bergerac Sec.
Open: By appointment only.

Château de Tiregand
Creysse, 24100 Bergerac. Vineyards owned: 33ha. 175,000
bottles. VP-R
The Saint-Exupéry family have owned this estate with its 17th-
century château since 1830. It is the largest producer of Pécharmant,
which makes up almost the entire production. It is aged in wood for
anything up to two years. A little white Bergerac Sec is also made.
Open: Mon–Sat 8am–noon; 2–6pm.

UNIDOR
Unions des Coopératives Vinicoles de la Dordogne, 24106
St-Laurent-des-Vignes. Vineyards owned: 4,009ha. 5
million bottles. Coop (8 coops as members)
This is an amalgamation of cooperatives controlling nearly 40
percent of all Bergerac. It also takes in wine from Côtes de Duras

and the eastern edges of the Bordeaux vineyard at Ste-Foy-le-Grande. They mature and bottle the wine and the whole plant is run on very modern lines. Few excitements. Brands include: Monsieur Cyrano, Domaine de la Vaure, L'Océanière, Fort Chevalier, Les Trois Clochers, Séléction Unidor, Château Septy. *Open: By appointment only.*

Buzet AC

Domaine Padère
Ambrus, 47160 Damazan. VP-R
A producer from Beaujolais, M Bloud has crossed France to produce soft, fruity Buzet from a greatly expanded vineyard around a 150-year-old château. Early vintages have seen no wood, but three months' barrel-ageing is now being tried out.

Les Vignerons Réunis des Côtes de Buzet
Buzet-sur-Baïse, 47160 Damazan. Vineyards owned:
1,000ha. 6·6 million bottles. Coop (430 members)
The cooperative controls most of the Buzet AC production, and very well they do it, too. They use a number of different labels, but their best wine is the Cuvée Napoleon, a ripe, rich wine which comes from older vines. The standard generic Buzet is good, too, as an easy-to-drink wine. Other labels they use for red wines are Château de Gueyze, Château du Bouchet and Domaine Roc de Caillou. They also make small amounts of rosé and white. *Open: (Summer) Mon–Fri. Appointments at other times.*

Cahors AC

Domaine de la Caminade
Resses et Fils, 46140 Parnac. Vineyards owned: 19ha.
150,000 bottles. VP-R
Some stainless steel is used for vinification on this family estate, and the grapes are de-stalked before fermentation. The results are wines that are not too austere. They are now ageing some of the wine in new wood. *Open: By appointment only.*

Château de Cayrou
46700 Puy-L'Evêque. Vineyards owned: 40ha. 200,000
bottles. VP-R
M Jouffreau owns two estates: the 16th-century Château de Cayrou
and the smaller ten-hectare Clos de Gamot. He uses organic
methods in his vineyards, while employing stainless steel in the
caves. His wines, austere while young, age well. He uses the brand
names Comte de Guiscard as well as the estate names. The family
has owned the Cayrou estate for 300 years. *Open: Appointments
preferred.*

Château de Chambert
Floressas, 46700 Puy-L'Evêque. Vineyards owned: 55ha.
300,000 bottles. VP-R
This estate was restored in the 1970s by a local *négociant*, Caves
Saint-Antoine, and the first vintage of any size was in 1979.
Vinification takes place in stainless steel, followed by wood-ageing
in *barriques*. With the maturing of the vines, the quality is now
concentrated and impressive, and the estate is one to follow. *Open:
By appointment only.*

Pont Valentré – spanning the river Lot at Cahors

Durou et Fils (Domaine de Gaudou)
Gaudou, Vire-sur-Lot, 46700 Puy-L'Evêque. Vineyards
owned: 20ha. VP-R
A change of generation from father to son may mean a change in

production methods, although stainless steel has already been used here since 1980. What may change is Durou père's dislike of new wood (his wines were always aged for 12 months in old wood). The vineyards are situated in some of the best land in the *appellation*. There is also a small production of white *vin de table*.

Domaine de Garriques
Vire-sur-Lot, 46700 Puy-L'Evêque. Vineyards owned: 17ha. 100,000 bottles. VP-R
M Roger Labruyère makes his Cahors using stainless steel and aiming at a lighter style, with plenty of fruit. Unusually, he has a little Jurançon in the blend which typically is dominated by 70 percent Malbec (Auxerrois). *Open: Mon–Sun.*

Les Côtes d'Olt
Parnac, 46140 Luzech. Vineyards owned: 1,400ha. 100,000 bottles. Coop (500 members)
The largest cooperative in Cahors, using a number of brand names: Côtes d'Olt, Comte André de Monpezat, Marquis d'Olt and the wood-aged Impernal. Standards improved considerably during the 1980s, with the introduction of stainless steel and the use of new wood. This means that more of the production from here is sold in bottle and less in bulk. Much of the wine is sold in bulk to merchants and *négociants*. *Open: By appointment only.*

Domaine de Paillas
Floressas, 46700 Puy-L'Evêque. Vineyards owned: 27ha. 210,000 bottles. VP-R
A young vineyard, producing soft wines using stainless steel for vinification. The Lescombes family bought the estate in 1978 and have replanted on the slopes above the valley floor. Although the wine can be drunk reasonably young, it does repay some ageing in bottle. *Open: Appointments preferred.*

Domaine de la Pineraie
Leygues, 46700 Puy-L'Evêque. Vineyards owned: 25ha. 200,000 bottles. VP-R
Stainless steel vinification and wood maturation are combined to produce wines with good fruit but also some ageing ability. The

blend is simply Auxerrois (Malbec) 85 percent and Merlot 15 percent, and the long maceration of 15 days brings intense colour to the wines. *Open: Mon–Sat 8am–noon; 2–7pm.*

Domaine de Quattre
Bagat-en–Quercy, 46800 Montcuq. Vineyards owned: 53ha. 300,000 bottles. VP-R

The three estates owned by the Heilbronner family include the 19-hectare Domaine de Quattre, the 16-hectare Domaine de Guingal and the 18-hectare Domaine de Treilles. Most of the wines from the three estates are produced to be drunk young, although some *cuvées* from Domaine de Treilles are aged in wood. The Domaine de Guingal wines are 100 percent Malbec (Auxerrois). *Open: Appointments preferred.*

Luc Retnauer
46002 Cahors. Vineyards owned: 11ha. 24,000 bottles. N

A dynamic *négociant* in Cahors, who is president of the local Syndicat d'Initiative. His wines are not designed for long ageing, and he believes they should show fruit rather than tannin. While most of his wine is *négociant* wine, he also has small quantities of an estate wine, Domaine des Vignals.

Rigal et Fils
Parnac, 46140 Luzech. Vineyards owned: 69ha. VP-R, N

The family grew wine long before they became *négociants*, but now it is the latter part of their business which is most important. They distribute the wines of a number of estates: Domaine Eugenie, Le Castelas, Soullaillou, du Park. Their *négociant* blend is called Carte Noire. They also make wine from their own properties: Château St-Didier, Prieure de Cenac, Château de Grezel. There is considerable use of new wood throughout the business.

Clos Triguedina
46700 Puy-L'Evêque. Vineyards owned: 42ha. 300,000 bottles. VP-R

This large and important estate produces two qualities of wine. Clos Triguedina is designed to be drunk young, while Prince Probus, aged in new oak and from 100 percent Malbec (Auxerrois) needs some bottle-age. The Baldès family have owned the estate since 1830, and in the last few years have invested large sums putting in stainless steel for vinification. *Open: Appointments preferred.*

Georges Vigouroux
9 Place de la Republique, 46500 Gramat. Vineyards owned: 67ha. 4 million bottles. VP-R and N
Georges Vigouroux, one of the big names in Cahors, owns the Château de Haute-Serre and the small Château de Mercues (the château is now a four-star hotel). The Haute-Serre wine, produced in a vineyard reclaimed from scrub in the 1970s, is rich in fruit and tannin when young, needing time to become enjoyable; Mercues ages more quickly. *Open: Mon–Sun 10am–noon; 3–6pm.*

Côtes de Duras AC

Domaine des Cours
Ste Colombe, 47120 Duras. Vineyards owned: 10ha. 30,000 bottles. VP-R
The Lusoli family make a white 100 percent Sauvignon and a red which is 50 percent Merlot and 50 percent a blend of the two Cabernets. The white is particularly attractive, made from free-run juice with temperature-controlled fermentation, giving plenty of fruit. The red is more traditional. *Open: Appointments preferred.*

Société Coopérative Agricole les Vignerons des Coteaux de Duras
47120 Duras. Vineyards owned: 315ha. 500,000 bottles. Coop (83 members)
As with so many of these smaller AC areas in the Southwest, it is the local cooperative which takes much of the production and keeps the area ticking over. Production is divided equally between red and white, but interestingly, they make varietal reds – 100 percent Cabernet Sauvignon (designed for a little ageing), 100 percent Merlot (to be drunk young) and a 100 percent white Sauvignon, as well as a more usual blend including Sémillon and Muscadelle as well as Sauvignon. The brand name they use is Berticot. *Open: By appointment only.*

Côtes du Frontonnais AC

Domaine de Baudare
Campas, 82370 Labastide St-Pierre. Vineyards owned: 27ha. 120,000 bottles. VP-R
A typically Frontonnais fruity style is achieved on this estate. Controlled fermentation brings out the colour and flavour of the Négrette in the red and rosé, both of which are bottled under the Domaine de Baudare name. The estate also produces Vin de Pays du Comté Tolosan – red, and sweet and dry white. *Open: By appointment only.*

Château Bellevue la Forêt
D49, 31620 Fronton. Vineyards owned: 105ha. 800,000 bottles. VP-R
A newly developed estate which has revived the area. It has been planted with the traditional varieties – 50 percent Négrette, with Cabernet Franc, Cabernet Sauvignon, plus Gamay and Syrah. The standard wine is called André Daguin, while the wine that goes under the name of the château is red or rosé. Small quantities of Cuvée Spéciale, a red aged in new wood, are produced. *Open: Appointments preferred.*

Domaine de la Colombière
31620 Villaudric. Vineyards owned: 20ha. 170,000 bottles. VP-R
Baron François de Driésen makes a wide range of red and rosé wines on his estate. He uses carbonic maceration for Négrette and Gamay, and the Gamay goes into a rosé *vin gris*. Baron de D Rouge is 50 percent Négrette, 40 percent Cabernets and ten percent Gamay, while the longer-lasting Villaudric Réserve is 60 percent Négrette, 35 percent Cabernets and five percent Gamay. The style is attractively forward and fruity. *Open: Appointments preferred.*

Cave Coopérative Les Côtes du Fronton
31620 Fronton. Coop (586 members)
This is one of the biggest cooperatives in France, mainly due to its huge production (830,000 cases) of *vin de table* and *vin de pays*. It also makes Côtes du Frontonnais to an acceptable standard. Two estates

are made separately: Châteaux Marguerite and de Craussac.

Côtes du Marmandais AC

Cave Coopérative de Cocumont
Cocumont, 47250 Bouglon. Vineyards owned: 1,001ha.
1 million bottles. Coop (340 members)
This modern, well-run cooperative produces Côtes du Marmandais, some Bordeaux AC wines and Vin de Pays de l'Agenais. *Open: Appointments preferred.*

Société Coopérative Vinicole des Côtes du Marmandais
Beaupuy, 47200 Marmande. Vineyards owned: 430ha.
4 million bottles. Coop (623 members)
About half the production from this cooperative is of Côtes du Marmandais, the rest being of Vin de Pays de l'Agenais and *vin de table*. Stainless steel is used and standards have certainly been rising. The wine is very much like a sub-claret, soft and with a good dollop of Merlot. A number of château names are used for the Marmandais wines. This cooperative has linked up with the cooperative at Buzet (*qv*) for sales purposes. *Open: Appointments preferred.*

Gaillac AC

Boissel-Rhodes
81600 Gaillac. Vineyards owned: 30ha. VP-R
The Boissel family owns the Château de Rhodes. They produce a dry sparkling bottle-fermented wine under the name of René Rieux and red wines made from Duras, Syrah, Fer and Gamay. There is also a *primeur*, made exclusively from Gamay.

Domaine des Bouscaillous
81140 Castelnau de Montmirail. Vineyards owned: 18ha.
100,000 bottles. VP-R
Yvon Maurel makes a range of Gaillac wines. In the reds, there is a 100 percent Gamay *primeur* as well as a wine designed for some ageing, in which the Duras grape predominates. There is also a rosé,

a blend of Jurançon and Gamay. Whites include a dry white with 80 percent Loin de l'Oeil and 20 percent Sauvignon, and a sweet white made from Mauzac. Mauzac is also the grape in a delicious low-alcohol Pétillant de Raisin. *Open: Appointments preferred.*

Jean Cros Père et Fils
Mas des Vignes, 81140 Cabuzac-sur-Vère. Vineyards owned: 10ha. 60,000 bottles. VP-R
High quality is everywhere at this small family concern. They own two vineyards: Domaine Jean Cros and Château Larroze, from which they produce a full range, including a white from 100 percent Mauzac, and reds from Duras plus Syrah and Braucol. The reds are very fine. *Open: Mon–Sat 11am–7pm.*

Domaine de Labarthe
Castanet, 81150 Marssac. Vineyards owned: 22ha. 120,000 bottles. VP-R
The Albert family have been making wine at this estate since the 17th century and now produces a full range of Gaillac wines. They make a *primeur* from Gamay, and a soft, warm *vin de garde* from the local Duras and Braucol plus the Bordeaux Cabernets and Merlot. Rosé comes from Gamay and Syrah. Loin de l'Oeil is balanced with Sauvignon in a dry white, while 100 percent Mauzac is used for the sweet white. They also make a bottle-fermented wine from Mauzac and Loin de l'Oeil. *Open: By appointment only.*

Cave de Labastide de Levis
81150 Marssac sur Tarn. Vineyards owned: 1,644ha. 7 million bottles. Coop (521 members)
The cooperative dominates the Gaillac AC area, producing wines that are mostly sold ready for drinking. Their semi-sparkling Gaillac Perlé can be quite attractive, and the Gaillac Primeur red is full of fresh fruit. They also make a sweet, low-alcohol Pétillant de Raisin. *Open: Appointments preferred.*

Domaine de Moussens
81150 Cestayrols. Vineyards owned: 14ha. 15,000 bottles. VP-R
Syrah dominates the wines from this estate – and the more there is

the better they seem to be, as in the 1984 vintage. Duras and Braucol are the other grapes. A rosé is made from Gamay and Syrah, and a Pétillant de Raisin from 100 percent Mauzac. Plans are afoot to make a dry white from Loin de l'Oeil and Sauvignon. *Open: By appointment only.*

Domaine de Pialentou
Brens, 81600 Gaillac. Vineyards owned: 12ha. 25,000 bottles. VP-R
The red is the best wine from this small estate, in good vintages having enough tannin to keep for three or four years in bottle, but with enough fruit to be drunk younger. M Ailloud also makes a dry white and a rosé. *Open: Appointments preferred.*

Mas Pignou
81600 Gaillac. Vineyards owned: 20ha. 80,000 bottles. VP-R
Dry white and red are produced at this estate, owned by Jacques Auque. His red, using Braucol, Duras, Merlot and the two Cabernets, has some wood maturing which gives it good ageing ability without losing fruit. The white is a 50/50 Sauvignon and Loin de l'Oeil blend. *Open: Mon–Sun 8am–noon; 2–6pm.*

Robert Plageoles (Domaine de Très Cantous)
81600 Gaillac. Vineyards owned: 21ha. 50,000 bottles. VP-R
One of the best producers in Gaillac, M Plageoles owns two estates – the ten-hectare Domaine de Très Cantous and the 11-hectare Domaine de Roucou Cantemerle. His wines are sometimes a blend of both estates. His reds are made from the Duras and Gamay grapes. For whites, he makes sparkling Gaillac Mousseux, delicious Sauvignon dry and Mauzac sweet white, still wines, and a rare AC Gaillac Premières Côtes, the sherry-like Vin de Voile, from Mauzac, which stays in cask for six years. He also makes a sweet wine from the Ondenc grape, a style not seen for around a century. *Open: By appointment only.*

Irouléguy AC

Cave Coopérative des Vins d'Irouléguy et du Pays Basque
64430 St-Etienne-de-Baïgorry. Vineyards owned: 80ha.
300,000 bottles. Coop (60 members)
This cooperative virtually controls the whole of Irouléguy
production and has gone some way towards saving the *appellation*
for posterity. The aim is to increase the area under vine to 200
hectares by the turn of the century. They make various qualities of
red and rosé, the top wines being called Cuvée des Maîtres
Vignerons. In good years, they also make a red Cuvée Réserve.
Open: By appointment only.

Jurançon AC

Domaine Cauhapé (Henri Ramonteau)
64360 Monien. VP-R
One of the dynamic figures trying to revitalize the Jurançon area.
Henri Ramonteau is constantly experimenting with barrel-ageing
for sweet wines, and barrel fermentation and the use of skin contact
for dry white wines to give greater intensity of flavour. His
vineyards contain Petit and Gros Manseng and Courbu. For his
sweet wines, he leaves the grapes on the vines to increase their
sweetness and concentration. He also makes Béarn red.

Domaine Guirouilh
Route de Belair, Lasseube, 64290 Gan. Vineyards owned:
8ha. 50,000 bottles. VP-R
An ancient estate, which has been in the Guirouilh family since the
17th century. It specializes in a traditional sweet Jurançon made
from dried grapes and aged in oak. Most of their production is of
the less interesting dry white. *Open: Appointments preferred.*

Caves des Producteurs de Jurançon
63 Avenue Henri-IV, 64290 Gan. Vineyards owned: 400ha.
2 million bottles. Coop (300 members)
Jurançon dry and sweet in different qualities are the only AC wines
from this cooperative. By far the bulk is of dry Jurançon, made

from Gros Manseng, in three styles: Séléction Viguerie Royale, Primeur and Millésime. The same styles apply to the sweet Jurançon. They also sell wine from two small estates: Château les Astous and Domaine Lasserre. *Open: Mon–Sat 9am–noon; 2–6:30pm. Open Sundays during the summer.*

Cru Lamouroux
La Chapelle de Rousse, 64110 Jurançon. Vineyards owned: 6ha. 30,000 bottles. VP-R

Jean Chigé and Richard Ziemek produce only sweet Jurançon Moelleux from their small vineyard which has been in the Chigé family since 1880. The wine, made from 60 percent Petit Manseng and 40 percent Gros Manseng, is vinified in stainless steel and matured in wood for 18 months before bottling. The result is a classic sweet wine with intense flavours of pineapple and honey. *Open: Appointments preferred.*

Clos Uroulat
64360 Monein. Vineyards owned: 5·5ha. 18,000 bottles. VP-R

Charles Hours, the owner of this small property, makes a classic style of sweet Jurançon Moelleux, ageing the wine in *barriques* for 12 months, using 100 percent Petit Manseng. He also makes Jurançon Sec, using stainless steel for vinification and a blend of Gros Manseng and Courbu. The quality of both wines is high. *Open: By appointment only.*

Madiran AC and Pacherenc du Vic-Bilh AC

Château Arricau-Boudes
65700 Madiran. VP-R

This is a newly recreated estate, based around a ruined 12th-century château (associated with d'Artagnan of the *Three Musketeers*). In 1980 new plantings of Tannat, Cabernet Sauvignon and Cabernet Franc were put in. The wine is aged in stainless steel, although there are plans to use some wood maturation in the future. At present the wines tend to lightness, but they improve with every vintage.

Domaine Barréjat
Maumusson, 32400 Riscle. Vineyards owned: Madiran
14ha; Pacherenc 2ha. 90,000 bottles. VP–R
The Capmartin family have owned this estate for three generations.
They make a traditional style of Madiran, using a slow maceration
to get maximum colour, and the finished wine needs some years in
bottle. The blend is 50/50 Tannat and Cabernets. The Pacherenc du
Vic-Bilh is vinified in stainless steel. *Open: Mon–Sat 8am–noon;
2–7pm.*

Alain Brumont
Maumusson, 32400 Riscle. Vineyards owned: Madiran
77ha. 500,000 bottles. VP–R
M Brumont owns three estates, all producing Madiran. Domaine
Bouscassé is the largest with 36 hectares; Château Moutus has 29
hectares; and Domaine Meinjarre has 12 hectares. The Domaine
Bouscassé spends a year in wood, while Château Moutus spends
time in new wood. He also makes Rosé de Béarn and dry and sweet
Pacherenc from a newly bought property. *Open: Mon–Sat
8am–8pm.*

Pierre Leplace
Haute Biste, Aydie, 64330 Garlin. Vineyards owned: 40ha.
300,000 bottles. VP–R
The Madiran from Château d'Aydie, M Leplace's estate, is
dominated by Tannat (up to 60 percent), with 20 percent each of
Cabernet Franc and Cabernet Sauvignon. It is made traditionally
and aged in wood, giving initially quite a tough wine, but one that
mellows with time. A new wine is made from 100 percent Tannat,
aged in new wood. He also makes smaller amounts of white
Pacherenc du Vic-Bilh, using stainless steel, to give a fresh, crisp
wine. *Open: Mon–Fri, in working hours.*

Lucien Oulie (Domaine du Crampilh)
Aurion-Idernes, 64350 Lembeye. Vineyards owned: 20ha.
132,000 bottles. VP–R
Red Madiran and white Pacherenc du Vic-Bilh are both produced
at M Oulie's vineyard. He uses the full range of local grape varieties
in both his wines. The Madiran needs four or five years' ageing; the

white Pacherenc should be drunk young and fresh. *Open: By appointment only.*

Château Peyros
Corbères, 64350 Lembeye. Vineyards owned: 23ha. 140,000 bottles. VP-R
Stainless steel is used for vinification in this carefully run estate which M de Robillard purchased in 1967. He makes only Madiran, using 50 percent Cabernet Franc, 45 percent Tannat and five percent Cabernet Sauvignon. The result is a wine which is lighter and less tannic than some from this AC. More recently, some wood-ageing has been tried. *Open: Appointments preferred.*

Domaine Pichard
Soublecause, 65700 Maubourguet. Vineyards owned: Madiran 12ha; Pacherenc 0·6ha. 84,000 bottles. VP-R
M Vigneau makes what is locally considered a fine Madiran, using 45 percent Tannat, 40 percent Cabernet Franc and 15 percent Cabernet Sauvignon. He ages the wine in wood before bottling. His small production of Pacherenc du Vic-Bilh is bottled young. *Open: Mon–Sun.*

Union de Producteurs Plaimont
32400 St-Mont. Vineyards owned: 1,860ha. 6 million bottles. Coop (1,350 members)
This large cooperative brings together three smaller cooperatives to produce Madiran, Côtes de Saint-Mont and Vin de Pays des Côtes de Gascogne. Their white *vin de pays* has been a runaway success for its clean, perfumed taste, given by the Colombard grape. Some Madiran and Côtes de Saint-Mont (known as the Collection Plaimont) are aged in new wood, while their standard range is known as Plaimont Tradition. *Open: Appointments preferred.*

Domaine de Teston
Maumusson, 32400 Riscle. Vineyards owned: 20ha. 157,000 bottles. VP-R
Madiran, Pacherenc du Vic-Bilh and the VDQS wines of Côtes de Saint-Mont are all made by M Laffitte. He uses stainless steel and modern technology, but then matures the red in new wood. He

says he is particularly proud of his newly acquired Côtes de Saint-Mont vineyard, which is planted with 70 percent Tannat, 20 percent Cabernet Sauvignon and ten percent Fer Servadou. *Open: By appointment only.*

Marcillac AC

Pierre Lacombe
Avenue de Rodez, 12330 Marcillac. Vineyards owned: 3ha. 8,000 bottles. VP-R
M Lacombe makes small quantities of red Marcillac, light, fruity and easy to drink. He uses only Fer Servadou grapes and vinifies in wood.

Laurens–Teulier
Domaine du Cros, 12390 Rignac. Vineyards owned: 5ha. 20,000 bottles. VP-R
M Teulier makes his wine entirely from Fer Servadou (which he sometimes calls Mancoi), avoiding herbicides in the vineyard and fining with white of egg. Many of his vines are over 40 years old and produce a deep, intense wine, aged in wood and with a good life expectancy. His best wine is called Domaine du Cros, which is matured in wood for two years. *Open: Mon–Sun 9am–1pm; 2–7pm.*

Cave des Vignerons du Vallon
Valady, 12330 Marcillac. Vineyards owned: 105ha. 400,000 bottles. Coop (60 members)
Inevitably with such a small VDQS area, the cooperative dominates production and keeps it all going. It makes a Cuvée Réserve and Marcillac Tradition red and rosé, all using 100 percent Fer Servadou. *Open: Mon–Sat 9am–noon; 2–6pm.*

The following is a list of VDQS producers in the Southwest: Henri Avallon; Cave Coopérative du Canton d'Auvillar; Cave Coopérative de Cocumont; Pierre Lacombe; Laurens-Teulier; Société Coopérative Vinicole des Côtes du Marmandais; Les Vignerons de Tursan; Cave des Vignerons du Vallon; Cave Coopérative La Ville Dieu du Temple.

Index

Index

Index

Index

Index